Aces and Kings

Inside Stories and

Million-Dollar

ACES and KINGS

Strategies from Poker's

Greatest Players

Michael Kaplan and Brad Reagan

WENNER BOOKS I NEW YORK

Photo Credits:
Puggy Pearson by Ulvis Alberts © 2005
Amarillo Slim Preston by Ulvis Alberts/www.poker-images.com © 2005
Doyle Brunson by Ulvis Alberts/www.poker-images.com © 2005
Chip Reese © www.pokerpages.com
Stu Ungar by Ulvis Alberts/www.poker-images.com © 2005
Erik Seidel by Bill Burlington/poker-images.com © 2005
Phil Hellmuth by Edis Jurcys Photography
Men "The Master" Nguyen © www.menmaster.com
Howard Lederer by Ulvis Alberts © 2005
David "Devilfish" Ulliott by Martin Le Piriz
Annie Duke by Ulvis Alberts © 2005
Chris "Jesus" Ferguson by Bill Burlington/poker-images.com © 2005
Chris Moneymaker by Bill Burlington/poker-images.com © 2005
Barry Greenstein © www.pokerpages.com
Daniel Negreanu by Matthew Hranke/Art + Commerce Anthology

Library of Congress Cataloging-in-Publication Data

Kaplan, Michael.
   Aces and kings: inside stories and million-dollar strategies from poker's
greatest players / Michael Kaplan and Brad Reagan.
     p. cm.
   Includes bibliographical references.
   ISBN 1-932958-00-2
   1. Poker—Anecdotes. I. Reagan, Brad. II. Title.
GV1253.K36 2005
795.415—dc22

2004026449

Wenner Books are available for special promotions and premiums. For details contact Michael Rentas, Manager, Inventory and Premium Sales, Hyperion, 77 West 66th Street, 11th floor, New York, New York 10023, or call 212-456-0133.

Book design by Richard Oriolo

FIRST EDITION

10   9   8   7   6   5   4   3   2   1

For Ron Kaplan.

—MK

For my parents, who encouraged me to write.

—BR

Contents

Introduction

NEAR MIDNIGHT, ON A COMMERCIAL street lined with discount appliance stores and shuttered fast-food joints, three casually dressed men disappear through the unmarked entrance of an unremarkable building. They walk up a steep flight of stairs to a windowless steel door, where a surveillance camera hanging from the ceiling records their every move. Somewhere on the other side of the door someone is making sure that these visitors are not cops. After an electronic buzz and the soft click of a lock opening, they step inside to the sweet percussion of riffling poker chips and the snap of cards being dealt.

It's a typical Tuesday night at New York City's hottest underground poker club.

The decor is utilitarian—white cinder-block walls, thick black curtains, TV monitors silently playing tonight's ballgames—and the vibe deliciously illicit. At one table, a clean-cut businessman with a necktie stuffed in his shirt pocket stares down a flinty-eyed Hindu woman draped in an orange sari. Across the room, a kid with dreadlocks under a sand-colored Stetson pushes all in with pocket Kings. The guy next to him, a hairy-chested Russian, turns over three 4s. Raking in the pot, he smirks and tells the Reggae Cowboy, "I read you like a simple novel."

In the club's makeshift smoking room, little more than a glassed-in closet, a middle-aged Asian man in green surgical scrubs takes several deep drags before snuffing out his cigarette and heading for the cashier to buy a fresh rack of chips. He offers a nod of recognition as a journeyman poker pro skulks past him. Just emerging from the club's bathroom—freshly shaved and washed, but unable to rejuvenate his bloodshot eyes, raccooned in black—the pro has been involved in a pot-limit Omaha game for close to 36 hours straight. Like any legitimate casino, this place is a 24/7 operation. Its bathroom is outfitted with a shower for those who play through the night, riding a winning streak, or, like the sleep-deprived pro, struggling to turn things around.

The hour hits midnight, and a stocky, bullet-headed man reaches for the remote. He switches channels, diverting all the club's TV monitors from the baseball game to one of ESPN's countless *World Series of Poker* rebroadcasts. On the screen, slender, goateed Daniel Negreanu contemplates a big bet, raises with nothing, and takes the pot. To the diehards here, Negreanu is a star, and they gaze at him the way Little Leaguers watch Derek Jeter or Randy Johnson. But this is poker, so the adoration is cut with self-affirming bravado. They're not thinking, "Someday that could be me." They're thinking, "I'm going to take him down next year." And that's the great thing about poker: Any one of them just might be right.

Across the country, tonight and every night, some 50 million Americans harbor poker dreams of their own. As anyone with cable television and an Internet connection knows, poker has blown up. It's jumped out of the closet, crossed over, and is now competing against the Super Bowl for viewers. From the casinos of Las Vegas, where plush card rooms expand to meet the endless influx of new acolytes; to a finished basement in Atlanta, where an Israeli émigré holds monthly winner-take-all tournaments; to a newly purchased home near Nashville, where 2003 world champion Chris Moneymaker hosts a game in which players routinely win or lose $40,000 per night, poker is hot. In suburban Houston, high school students regularly stage Texas Hold 'Em tournaments modeled after the ones they watch religiously on *World Poker Tour*. Montana's back-of-the-bar card rooms, once sparsely populated, are packed with players who find more adventure there than in the jaw-dropping scenery outside. And in Hollywood, celebs like Tobey Maguire, Leonardo DiCaprio, and Ben Affleck play in casual home games with tens of thousands on the line. Affleck once became so immersed in the competition that he kept a private jet idling on an airport runway—just so he could get in a few more hands.

Each one of those players serves as a point on the upward trajectory of modern-day poker. A living, breathing thing, the game is forever evolving, continually anointing new princes and casting out fresh paupers. In choosing the subjects for this book, we've focused on players who are responsible for shifts or advances in how poker is played. From country boy Puggy Pearson to computer whiz Chris "Jesus" Ferguson, we've uncovered ways in which the game's masters think, traced the steps that got them to the top, and dissected strategies they've developed along the way. By studying their gambling styles—from Doyle Brunson's bulldozer betting to Phil Hellmuth's supertight discipline—players of all skill levels can pick up a slew of valuable tips.

Beyond the challenges of the game itself, poker also offers a romantic, yet hazardous, lifestyle that bears absolutely no resemblance to the nine-to-five world. Like big-game hunters, the top players circle the globe in search of their prey—amateurs with money to burn and tournaments with seven-figure purses. It's an all-cash existence in which boom-and-bust cycles are constant, an inescapable reality made all the more volatile by the 24/7 temptations of the casinos and card rooms where the pros ply their trade. Watching how these players handle their inevitable swings of success and failure can be as instructive as seeing how they deal with small pairs and baby connectors. On the positive side, a disciplined pro like Barry Greenstein lives in a sprawling beachfront home and donates millions to charity. On the other end of the spectrum is Stu Ungar, a poker genius with a wicked cocaine addiction and a massive streak of self destruction. Both have been winners at the table, but only one of them was able to navigate the obstacles inherent in the poker life.

One thing is certain: In the end, luck has little to do with winning.

Take it from Paul Phillips, a dot-com millionaire who now plays poker professionally. "The only reason you could expect to win at poker, in the long run, is because you believe you make better decisions than your opponents," he says. "You can't hope to win because the cards will break better for you than they do for everyone else. It *has* to be because you make better decisions." In these pages we chronicle those decisions, and the gambits, opinions, and confessions that poker's biggest stars occasionally share among themselves, over post-game cocktails and steak dinners, but rarely voice to a public that has become increasingly eager to glean the pros' insights—even if it requires playing against them.

TUESDAY NIGHT AGAIN in Manhattan, 40 blocks uptown and a dozen pages higher on the social register. Several hundred people crowd into Rande Gerber's sleek Stone Rose bar in the city's glossy new Time Warner Center. In stark contrast to the illegal downtown club's subterranean feel, this gathering is so above-ground it comes with a gorgeous view of Central Park. A dozen poker tables, complete with tuxedo-clad dealers, are packed with some of the Big Apple's most bold-faced names, eagerly awaiting their chance to take on poker legends Doyle Brunson, Barry Greenstein, and Howard Lederer.

No cash trades hands here. This is a party celebrating the debut of yet another televised Texas Hold 'Em tournament, and the champagne-sipping socialites risk nothing more than pride in the hope of learning something from poker's demigods. The three veteran rounders, still growing accustomed to their celebrity status, gamely mix with the A-list crowd: Brunson, in a white 10-gallon hat, signs autographs for financier Carl Icahn; Lederer offers Texas Hold 'Em tips to a crowd of fans pressing in around him; and Greenstein smiles wanly as he can't help but outplay amateurs who have the misfortune to sit at his table.

An elegant woman in a sparkly black cocktail dress pops a canapé in her mouth and looks on excitedly. She turns to her silver-haired husband and whispers, "I didn't know what I was missing by not playing poker."

Authors' Note

AS ANYONE WHO HAS EVER sidled up to a poker table is well aware, the game practically has its own language, not to mention Byzantine sets of rules. To neophytes— and even to some veterans—the jargon and unspoken customs that surround the game can be overwhelming. In order to make this book enjoyable for players of all skill levels, we avoided excessive use of poker lingo wherever possible. But it is perhaps unavoidable that there will be occasions when you are puzzled by the terminology or need a refresher on the rules of a particular variety of poker. For those occasions, we've included an extensive glossary and a rules section in the back of the book. Still, there are a few concepts so critical to understanding the action and following along that we've included a quick primer here as well.

First, the stakes: Throughout the book you'll see poker games described by a set of two dollar amounts separated by a slash—for example, $30/$60, or $1,000/$2,000. This is the betting structure of the game. In a $1,000/$2,000 game of limit Texas Hold 'Em, bets and raises can be made only in $1,000 increments for the first two rounds of betting, and in $2,000 increments for the last two rounds.

Second, it's important to understand the distinctions between tournament play and so-called "live games." In a live game—also known as a "cash game"—players buy chips whose total value equals the amount of money they're willing to risk. These games are the lifeblood of the poker economy. If a player buys in for $10,000, he gets $10,000 in chips. He can play as long as he likes, quit at any time, and cash in the chips. He can also buy more chips whenever he feels like it. Hence, in a live game, there is no ceiling on how much a player can win and no floor that prevents him from losing his entire bankroll. In a tournament, by contrast, a player pays an entry fee and receives a set number of tournament chips that cannot be redeemed for cash. The tournament then runs until one player amasses all the chips, and prizes are awarded for the top finishers. So, for example, if the entry fee is $10,000, the most a player can lose in that tournament is $10,000. Because each player starts with a finite number of chips— and can get knocked out of the event with a single, overly aggressive play—there are significant strategic differences between tournaments and live games. The idea of a poker tournament was not hatched until the first World Series of Poker, in 1970, but events with six- and seven-figure payouts are so common now that some professionals can earn a good living by playing only in tournaments. Most pros, however, make their money in live games and look to tournaments for the occasional big score and a little bit of television time.

Third, there's the World Series. Much of the reporting for this book took place at the 2004 World Series. The tournament, held annually for its first 35 years at Binion's Horseshoe in downtown Las Vegas, is the biggest and most prestigious in the world, but its structure is often misunderstood. Like most major tournaments on the circuit, it's actually a series of tournaments featuring different games and buy-ins. On one day, players might vie for the title in Seven-Card Stud with a $5,000 buy-in. The next day, they play again in a $3,500 Hi/Lo event. The day after that it's something else. And so on. In 2004 there were a total of 34 World Series events in a five-week period. Each winner receives a hefty gold bracelet—complete with horseshoe-shaped links—that serves as poker's equivalent of a green jacket from the Masters. The final event, a $10,000 buy-in no-limit Texas Hold 'Em tournament, crowns poker's world champion.

Finally, it's important to note that there are infinite varieties of poker. There are a number of different games, such as Seven-Card Stud and Texas Hold 'Em, and each game's strategy changes significantly depending on whether the betting structure is "limit," in which there are fixed minimum and maximum bets, or "no-limit," in which a player can bet all of his chips at any time. In recent years, partly because of the World Series's popularity, Texas Hold 'Em has become the preferred form of poker. For that reason, Hold 'Em is the primary game featured in this book.

Those are the basics, so let's head to the tables. We hope you enjoy spending time with Puggy, Doyle, Jesus, Stu, and the rest of the gang—and pick up a few tips along the way. We certainly did.

—Michael Kaplan and Brad Reagan

Puggy Pearson, 1977, in Las Vegas

One

PUGGY PEARSON

Raising the Stakes

A fearless country boy muscles into town

and shows the Vegas hustlers what power

poker is all about.

THE BIG-FINNED, BURGUNDY 1960 Cadillac nosed its way across America, on a jagged path from the rowdy pool halls of Nashville to the sawdust-floored casinos of downtown Las Vegas. Behind the wheel, riding low in the Caddie's thick-upholstered leather seat, an elbow poking out the open window, sat Walter Clyde Pearson. He was a professional gambler, known to friends and acquaintances as Puggy or Pug—a nickname that arose from a childhood accident in which he tried to impress a girl by walking on his hands across a two-by-four and fell flat on his already button-shaped nose.

Thirty-three-year-old Pug hit the accelerator, cranked the volume on a Fats Domino song, and puffed from a fat El Producto cigar. Short and thickly built, he favored sharply creased gabardine slacks and candy-colored sport shirts. Thinning brown hair, slicked back with a dab of Top Brass, barely managed to cover Pug's scalp. His eyes radiated cool and welcoming green. It would have been easy to characterize him as little more than an easily excitable hick—especially after you heard the jumpy drawl that overrode his voice and betrayed a Tennessee mountain heritage—but Puggy Pearson was no rube. By the mid-1960s he would become the most fearsome poker stud in the world, a self-proclaimed King Kong dominating Las Vegas's high-limit games and earning enough money in a single day to buy a dozen Cadillacs. He would bring a previously unseen aggression to the casino card tables and reign as an early practitioner of *power poker*—employing a playing style in which he strategically made aggressive bets to scare off opponents and drive pots in his direction. But that loomed in the future.

In 1962, the year he took this trip from his home in Nashville, Pug Pearson was practically broke. Even worse, he had a $500 marker in his pocket, representing a debt he owed to the Fremont Hotel, a high-rise casino on a street full of gambling joints in downtown Vegas. But the debt was no matter to Puggy. He had so much gamble in him that, by his own estimate, he went broke and bounced back 40-odd times over the course of 1962—"like a goddamned yo-yo." And so he sensed a rebound was in the offing—as long as he could find the right sort of sucker to help the situation along. It was more than mere money that sent Puggy off to Vegas, though. In his line of work, one routinely came up against tough, intractable characters who didn't shy away from getting violent. Over the years he had learned when to fight back, and when to skip town for a while. Cronies in Nashville speculated that a run-in with just such a man had preceded Pug's hasty departure west.

The problem began, the story went, one afternoon when Puggy found himself squaring off against a wiry, short-fused bookmaker by the name of Billy Nicholson. Their bets began in a downtown Nashville pool hall, owned by another bookie, Fats Boyd, where Pug and Nicholson played multiple racks of $100-per-game one-pocket (the object was to shoot all your balls into a single pocket). Pug and Nicholson got to wising off at each other, criticizing one another's games, and creating an all-around bad vibe that hung in the air after they left Fats's place. The negativity was still there a couple of days later, when they convened to gamble at Cumberland Golf Course, Nashville's first 18-holer to accommodate black patrons. After Pug accused Nicholson of cheating on an early hole, Nicholson threatened to hit him with a sand-wedge. Puggy popped back: "You grubby little sumbitch. You don't got enough balls to hit me with that thing."

That was all it took. Nicholson swung, caught Puggy's chest, and tore his shirt with the club-head. Puggy retaliated with one of his irons, knocked Nicholson off his feet, and beat him on the skull and face, connecting with enough force and precision that Nicholson began bleeding profusely before losing consciousness. Then, fearing that he might have gone too far, that he might have actually killed the man, Puggy dragged Nicholson to the Cadillac and dropped him off at nearby Vanderbilt Hospital, where doctors discovered a fractured skull. The incident earned a few column inches in the *Nashville Banner*, but no charges were ever filed with the police. Word on the street had it that Nicholson wanted to resolve matters on his own.

Which made Puggy's timing for this particular road trip seem a bit convenient.

Whatever the case, the incident was far behind Puggy as he sang along to the radio and headed toward Las Vegas, driving through the small towns and endless sprawls of farmland that defined the belly of post-Eisenhower America. Upon reaching Kingman, Arizona, Puggy turned off Route 66, drove a straight shot north, and beelined toward the bright lights that shimmered in the distance. Top Vegas casinos back in '62 were places like the Stardust, the Desert Inn, the Hacienda, and the Dunes. Hyped as a "miracle in the desert," the last of these boasted palm trees imported from Southern California and a 90-foot V-shaped pool that ranked as the largest in America. Puggy wasn't impressed by such so-called "carpet joints." He didn't care about their high-gloss floor shows and gourmet dining rooms. Pug was here for the same reason he went everywhere else: to gamble. When it came to winning money, he operated as an equal opportunity exploiter who'd travel to the ends of the earth if the action was good enough to make the trip worthwhile.

Soon after parking his car and checking in at the Fremont, Puggy walked past the craps and blackjack tables—both of which appealed to the gambler in him but were impossible for him, or anyone, to consistently beat and accounted in part for his current round of financial woes. He strolled past a pack of tourists playing slots, and he barely noticed a dozen people heading to the roof, where they could watch mushroom clouds erupting over the nearby Nellis Air Force Base nuclear testing facility. He blocked out everything around him and, with a kind of hyper-aggressive focus, barreled his way straight to the hotel's card room—a utilitarian 30-table affair with dealers wearing white button-down shirts and western-style bow ties. Pug stepped inside and scoped around for his mark, a guy known as Raggedy Ass Phil Halem.

Big bellied, sloppily dressed, Raggedy Ass co-ran the poker room at the Fremont, and he served as a soft touch for Puggy. In poker parlance, he was a *provider*, a player who lost money and literally provided profits for his cagier opponents. A degenerate gambler with a day job in a casino, Raggedy Ass always seemed to be in and out of funds. The trick for a sharp guy like Puggy was to catch him on an upswing and separate him from his cash.

On this particular day, Raggedy Ass was flush. He and Puggy promptly sat down to play heads-up (that is, one-on-one) poker, ranging the games from Seven-Card Stud to Lowball to Razz. The stakes, only $10/$20, sound reasonable by today's standards, but chips had a way of multiplying for Puggy. During a week of nearly nonstop play against Raggedy Ass—as well as several others—he managed to run his winnings up to something in the vicinity of $7,000, a respectable yearly income in 1962. He paid off his marker and headed home with a healthy bankroll.

News of the win beat him to Nashville, but got blown out of proportion along the way. By the time Puggy pulled into town, word was that he had raked in as much as $50,000. Figuring it wouldn't be bad for his rep, he did nothing to correct the exaggeration.

Maybe he should have. Soon after Pug's return, he and his second wife, Andrea, walked in on a trio of burglars who were ransacking their modest home in search of the phantom 50 grand. Initially trying to bully the thieves into leaving, Puggy vowed that they'd wind up dead or in jail. Unimpressed, one of the men aimed a gun at Puggy's face and instructed an accomplice to tie the couple to a pair of wooden chairs. With Puggy and Andrea subdued, the thieves demanded to know where the money was hidden. Bluffing, just as he had against Raggedy Ass Halem, Puggy unwaveringly insisted that all he had was the $2,000 in his pocket; he neglected to mention the $5,000 he had stashed in a hole in the wall. After about 30 minutes, the frustrated thieves believed him—or at least tired of arguing about it. They took the two grand and disappeared into the night.

Once they were alone, Puggy and Andrea wriggled free from the ropes. Puggy took out his new home-movie camera and captured his destroyed house on film. Then he began, for the first time, to seriously consider relocating to Las Vegas. By the fall of 1963, he, Andrea, and son Steve were living there full-time.

THE PEARSONS ORIGINALLY settled into a room at the Chevron Motel, a small, nondescript motor inn located below the Strip, about half a mile from the Sahara Hotel. Puggy would leave Steve and the svelte, long-haired Andrea by the motel pool while he went downtown to the Fremont and the Golden Nugget, twin citadels of low- to medium-stakes poker. Almost immediately, Pug found his rhythm in Las Vegas and went on a rush, running his cash reserve up to $20,000—and this time he held on to his winnings by steering clear of blackjack and craps. He played selectively aggressive, looked like a wild-man, and generated loads of action when he had a strong hand. Through a combination of luck, skill, and style, he couldn't lose.

Puggy's success at the tables did not go unnoticed. Billy Douglas and Joe Nasier, a couple of scuffling hustlers with a decent bit of money between them, saw how much he was winning and offered to back him in the highest game at the Dunes. As far as poker went, in the early '60s, that particular game and venue combined to represent the equivalent of a nightly all-star match at Yankee Stadium. Very quickly, Puggy found himself playing in the big leagues, with an opportunity to make lots of money—fast. But it would not be easy. Stakes at the Dunes were high; the game was tough. Hard-edged big-city players there were unlikely to be impressed or amused by a motor-mouth country boy.

The atmosphere was also a far cry from the grind-it-out joints where Puggy had been accustomed to playing downtown. Set behind the Dunes's luxe showroom, which featured the racy *Vive Les Girls*, was a lavish poker pavilion where hotel bosses Sid Wyman, Charlie "Kewpie" Rich, and Major Riddle squared off against a rogue's gallery of professional gamblers: guys like the dapperly dressed Midwestern underworld figure Joe Bernstein, relentlessly wagering Tommy Abdo, and the notorious card mechanic "Nigger" Nate Raymond, a longstanding suspect in the murder of Arnold Rothstein (famous in his own right for fixing the 1919 World Series).

It was a fast and seedy environment, but Puggy managed to fit himself right in, and proved to be more than just a talented talker. Relying on a combination of youth (he was a good 20 years younger than most of the players in that particular game), single-minded desire (Puggy grew up dirt poor and has said, "I never wanted to have anything other than a Cadillac, my own cue, and money in my pocket"), and a high level of finely tuned people-sense that resided at the core of his poker game (it allowed him to know when to power pots and when to lay off), he thrived at the Dunes. "For some reason, from a very young age, I became a student of the human animal," Puggy says now. "I could never understand how people got themselves into such fixes all the time. So I devoted myself to observing people and figuring out why they did what they did. It got me to the point where I had no fear at the poker table, could read people like they were pictures on a wall, and manipulated them into doing what I wanted."

Beyond all that, his approach to poker was unique at the Dunes. During the 1950s and into the '60s, high-stakes poker in Las Vegas was almost exclusively no-limit—that is, players were able to bet as much money as they had on the table. The game that had been built around Riddle, Rich, and Wyman differed in that it was limit poker—albeit with stakes so high that Puggy wound up logging a number of sessions in which he won upward of $100,000. Puggy had become adept at limit play in Nashville, and he came at the game with a degree of aggression that had not been seen before at the Dunes. He raised with marginal hands—especially against weak players who could be intimidated into folding even when they had superior (but not unbeatable) cards—and pressured people into making bad decisions. Even if he didn't take the pot right then, Puggy's aggressiveness would most likely lead him to control the next round or two of betting.

"Puggy was like a tiger in the jungle," marvels Doyle Brunson, the great poker player who was broken by Puggy in the '60s and did not particularly like him at the time. "He had the instincts to play any game at any stakes." The way some sing with perfect pitch and others can paint portraits, Pug was blessed with an innate ability to read people, analyze situations, and reach quick decisions. He took those skills, sharpened them during years on poker's chitlin' circuit, learned how to manipulate through the power of suggestion, and built a solid playing style that was all about intimidation. His twin barrels of skill and instinct turned Puggy into a player who made it all look very easy. Billy Walters, one of the world's most successful sports bettors, who owns a half-dozen golf courses in Las Vegas, describes Puggy as "the world's greatest *natural* gambler."

Though there were occasional collection problems—Nigger Nate once drew a pistol when Puggy pressed him to make good on a $20,000 debt—for the most part money flowed as free as tap water in Vegas. In fact, the incoming cash—$750,000 in eight months—gushed so hard it caused the Pearsons to suffer a kind of *nouveau riche* whiplash.

Almost overnight the backwoods hustler was transformed into a poker-room dandy, often wearing shoes that perfectly matched his color-coordinated outfits of lavender or lime green or burgundy. The family moved into a generously proportioned, ranch-style house in a fashionable part of town. Pug had a heated pool installed out back and hired landscapers to spruce up the front yard. Son Steve played tennis with Vegas's richest kids when he wasn't attending a charm academy where teachers coached him on how to foxtrot and taught him which forks to use at dinner.

Meanwhile, in the less-than-genteel poker rooms, broke players went to extreme measures in order to have a shot at regaining their money from Puggy. "Early on Dad won property in Winnemucca, Nevada, from a guy named Charlie Shadad," recounts Steve, now 51 years old and a part-time poker player, part-time real estate investor, part-time minder of 75-year-old Puggy. "They were playing high-limit at the Stardust and it was just like the Old West: Charlie ran out of money and threw his deed in the pot to cover a bet. But that was nothing. Dad won cars and lots of jewelry and his first set of golf clubs playing poker. I remember, when I was 10 years old, he came home one day, threw $40,000 on the bed and told me to count it. That was how I learned about money."

Puggy evolved into a Vegas celebrity. Strangers routinely asked for his autograph, local gossip columnists quoted him, paparazzi snapped pictures, and the *Nashville Banner* sent a cub reporter by the name of Al Gore to interview the local boy made good. Puggy and Andrea got comped for shows around town, Steve spent summer afternoons swimming in hotel pools while his mother sat in the Fremont bar and drank straight vodkas with Coca-Cola back.

After dark the Pearsons routinely dined at the Sultan's Table, Vegas's poshest restaurant, which boasted a cadre of roaming violinists and an enormous waterfall near the rear. The restaurant was in the Dunes, and Puggy had a habit of strolling in straight from the golf course, wearing shorts and a polo shirt. "They would tell Dad that a jacket was required," remembers Steve. "So he'd stand there and the maître d' would put a sport coat on over his golf shirt. Everybody thought it was hilarious."

Meanwhile, Puggy enhanced his poker game by shooting all the angles and operating with the belief than if you don't take advantage of a sucker, then *you* are the sucker. Underhandedness was hardly unusual back then, at a time when poker still seemed like an illicit business. In fact, cheating was so common that a notorious card manipulator like Nigger Nate was considered an upstanding member of the poker community. (During one side game in the late 1960s, for example, Nate was spotted with an extra card in his hand, and other players at the table just laughed it off as the elderly Nate croaked,

"Well, a sick old guy like me ought to be able to steal a little.") So Puggy and his subterfuge fit in perfectly. Employing tricks he picked up while gambling in the Deep South, Puggy surreptitiously scooped chips out of pots and shortchanged players when he made his bets. Rather than considering the scams to be cheating, Puggy figured he was taking what was available and rightfully enhancing his bankroll. As the world-class hustler "Amarillo Slim" Preston admiringly puts it, "Puggy stole money out of every pot he played."

One of Puggy's more enduring moves, employed when he had a hand that might not necessarily be the best one, was to call a final bet and push his chips to the pot, but not release his hand from the chips.

Assuming that Puggy was in, the other player would reveal his cards. At that point, if Puggy had a stronger hand, he removed his fingers from the chips, showed his cards, and raked in the pot. If beaten, he pulled the chips back and insisted that he hadn't intended to call the bet, that the other player had misread what Puggy was doing and should have never turned up his cards prematurely. Mayhem routinely ensued, but Puggy was a master at diversion and diffusion, and he insisted (rightfully) that so long as his hand remained on the chips, no bet had been made. Through force of will, he almost always got away with it.

On occasion, though, his scams backfired. Danny Robison, a flashy dresser and a crack Stud player from Dayton, Ohio, had fallen victim to this a couple of times before and was sick of it. So he set a trap that he knew Puggy would fall into.

They were playing Seven-Card Stud, the betting was high, Robison kept raising, and on the last bet Puggy held his hand over the chips before releasing them to the pot. Robison leaned forward, confidently revealed an Ace and seemed poised to show a second one to Puggy. It would have given Robison the winning hand. Anticipating that second Ace, Puggy quickly pulled back his chips. Robison raked in the pot. Then he showed Puggy the rest of his cards: a 2 and a 7, no hand at all. It infuriated Puggy and got huge laughs and a round of applause from others at the table.

But Puggy was no joke, and his cheating played only a modest, albeit consistent, role in his overall success as a player. He was also an astute confidence man and an excellent table-talker. "I've always liked to give people the invisible needle," he says. "Put thoughts into their heads, get them thinking too much about those $100 bills, and that's when I can get them to do just about anything I want."

Such was the case when Puggy came to confront Eric Drache in a Seven-Card Stud showdown at the Aladdin back in the early 1970s. Freshly arrived from New Jersey and a hitch in the army, young Drache had big ideas about making it as a professional poker player, and he idolized Puggy Pearson in the same way that Pug once idolized Minnesota Fats—the famous pool hustler who was at the peak of his powers when Puggy was just a boy. Drache had a mod haircut and an easygoing disposition. He was thrilled just to be sitting at the same table as Puggy, but when the more seasoned player made a big bet and there were no more cards to be dealt, Drache found himself stymied. He admitted as much.

"I've got two Aces," he said to Puggy, not yet sure he wanted to call with his last $200, but hoping he'd be able to read something in Puggy's reaction.

Puggy, sitting tall on three extra seat cushions, trying to gain a height advantage that would translate into an intimidation factor, gave away nothing. He stared back at Drache with a totally neutral expression. Then his face softened and he appeared to take pity on the younger player. "Son," he said, "you seem like a nice kid, so I'm going to speak to you like your father. Fold the Aces, save your last $200 and go play in a less expensive game. I've got you beat, and I don't want to see you go broke. You're going to be a winning poker player one day. But today's not that day."

Drache thought about it for a second. Then he mucked his Aces. Puggy raked in the chips and squinted at Drache. "You stupid donkey," he brayed, exposing his hand to show that he was holding nothing but rags.

Winning with the worst of it, of course, is the mark of a great poker player, and Puggy was masterful at that. Against seasoned professionals, however, all the talking in the world won't bring you the pot. In those cases the requirements are more subtle, far grittier, and multidimensional. Puggy displayed a skill for this in a hand he once played against Johnny Moss, nicknamed the Grand Old Man of Poker and three-time World Series winner.

Though Moss's skills deteriorated with age, this particular confrontation took place in the 1960s, when the hardened Texas gambler was still sharp and scary. They were playing a Five-Card Draw game called Kansas City Lowball (a low-only game in which 2-3-4-5-7 is the unbeatable hand), and Puggy was dealt 2-3-4-7-Jack. After the first round of betting, three players remained in: Puggy, Moss on his left, and a third player on his right. The third guy raised $1,000, Puggy raised him back $2,800, and Moss raised an additional $5,000. The third guy called that bet, and Puggy pushed his entire stack of $25,000 into the pot, hoping to scare everybody else out.

With $53,000 on the table (including $200 antes from five additional players who never called any of the bets), Moss pushed in his remaining $15,000, figuring that the guy to Puggy's right would also go in for $25,000. This would give Moss the potential for a 2-to-1 return on his money. It's what poker players call good value. But then the guy to Puggy's right did something unexpected: He folded. Now Puggy and Moss were playing heads-up, and the potential return on Moss's investment became quite a bit less than what he had been anticipating—about 3-to-2.

What did Puggy do? With split-second timing he reconfigured his strategy, well aware that Moss must have had him beaten. "I immediately announced that I had a pat hand, that I wasn't taking any cards—even though I knew the Jack does not make for a particularly good low," says Puggy, explaining that his goal was to make Moss draw and run the risk of picking up a bad card. "He figured I had to have a strong hand, because I didn't take anything. I figured him for something marginal." Moss considered things long and hard, and, finally, he sacrificed his 10 low to get a new card. It was a King. Puggy revealed his hand and announced, "Johnny, you made a mistake."

Not needing to work through the math, Puggy had quickly realized that, if he was correct about putting Moss on a marginal hand, at best, there were 24 cards that could hurt Moss (either by pairing one of his four cards or giving him a worse low than Pug's), 15 that could help him (by giving him better than a Jack low), and three that would be neutral and could possibly lead to them splitting the pot. "If I drew a card," explains Puggy, who now says he was better than 50 percent sure that Moss did not have a playable hand, "he wouldn't have drawn and would have been a big favorite. Instead, I made him into an underdog, and won the pot with actions that forced him to believe things were different than they truly were."

That kind of multitiered, bluff-intensive play made Puggy a wealthy man and kept him in the Vegas poker rooms—often to the chagrin of his wife, who tossed many a pot roast in the trash or against the wall—for four or five days at a time, usually with little sleep. "The games would be too good to quit," he says. "Or else I'd be big loser in a game and need to get my money back. Either way, I couldn't get to sleep. Then, after poker ended, I'd finish up and go to the Las Vegas Country Club, where we'd play $100,000 rounds of golf. Things were real high and real fast back then."

PROBABLY THE MOST astonishing thing about Puggy Pearson and his evolution as a gambler is the very fact that he evolved at all.

Jack Binion, who helped create the World Series of Poker at Binion's Horseshoe, describes Pug as "completely self-invented," and marvels over the process. "Most of us grow up, more or less, the same way," says Binion. "We have mothers and fathers and similar value systems on which we base the way we live. It wasn't like that for Puggy. He was on his own from a young age and had to figure out everything for himself. Along the way he's devised unique styles of thinking and looking at the world. It's all reflected in the way he approaches poker."

The fourth of nine children, Puggy was born in poor and rural Adairville, Kentucky, in 1929. His parents worked as sharecroppers and his mother was picking peas along a fence row when she went into labor with Puggy. "There was no birth certificate; I always felt a need to prove that I existed," says Puggy. "We were so poor that I ate molasses on cornbread every day for lunch. I didn't even know what white bread was; the first time somebody handed me a piece, I thought it was cake." Puggy estimates that he lived at 19 different addresses before his tenth year, when the family finally settled down in Nashville. "We would move right when the rent came due," he says.

In Nashville, Pug immediately quit going to fifth grade. He began peddling newspapers and shining shoes outside an expanse of pool halls downtown, where he was seduced by the insular world of con men, cardsharps, hustlers, and suckers. He noticed a steady influx of soldiers, fresh from Fort Campbell in nearby Kentucky. They sauntered into the pool rooms, their pockets full of government-issued cash, and frequently exited broke. Young Pug dropped his shoe-shine rag and followed them inside. He became fascinated with the minidramas that enveloped games of craps and poker and pool. He learned his biggest lessons firsthand, by getting hustled himself, right alongside those soldiers.

It shocked his younger brother J.C., who also sold papers but found the gambler's life to be less appealing (though he, too, eventually settled in Vegas and took up poker as a profession). "Big brother," J.C. said to Puggy one afternoon in the early 1940s, "why do you keep going into those places and letting those suckers take your money off of you?"

"Don't you worry about it none," Pug advised. "I'll get this money back with interest."

While J.C. used his newspaper revenues to pay for movies and popcorn, Puggy bought an education, learning the rudiments of separating people from their cash. Putting a master plan into action, on his 17th birthday he had his father sign him up for the navy—not out of patriotism or a need for adventure but because he figured it would be a good venue for his already considerable hustling skills. "I noticed those fellows from the armed forces, and I wanted what was in their wallets," says Puggy.

During his final hitch in the service, Pug was stationed in Puerto Rico and operating as a one-man bank and casino. Like a cold-blooded Bilko, he mopped up the poker games, ran football pools, and Shylocked cash to the sailors he busted ("I loan you 10, you give me 15, baby!"). He regularly wired home, to his mother and big sister Bertha, transfers of hundreds of dollars at a time. It's estimated that, over an

18-month period, he sent them approximately $10,000. The money went to good use. By the time Puggy was discharged in 1952, Bertha had bought a gift-shop and café. Puggy was driving a brand new Hudson, and he converted the gift-shop into a house before opening a second café and a pair of pool halls. Gambling had taken the Pearsons from destitute to respectable in less than three years.

Though a pool hall had its appeal—as proprietor, Puggy waited inside and got first dibs on the pigeons—Pug was far too restless for the day-to-day management of a business. He frequented poker games in the backrooms of Nashville's restaurants and strip joints, like the Uptown Club and the Rainbow, both situated in the famously con- and crime-intensive Printer's Alley. And when things slowed down in Music City, Puggy took to the road, where he had a route as defined as a milkman's.

Sniffing out the action, he would drive from game to game, going from a Celina, Tennessee, bait shop to the home of a numbers runner in Hollywood, Florida, and back to a steel-roofed houseboat docked in a lake near Nashville and filled with lousy players. "Poker back in those days was almost all business people playing as a pastime; there were very few professionals, which made it good for Puggy," says Doug Hall, a Nashville running buddy and a frequent partner in Pug's golf-gambling ventures. "I remember him driving to Kentucky to play in an old shack, taking the backroads to Miami once a week, going out to Louisville and Chicago. Puggy didn't have a lazy bone in his body. If there was money to be made somewhere, he'd drive there to make it."

Road gambling was a profitable but hazardous proposition. "You always had to worry about getting heisted," says Puggy. He once lost his bankroll stashed inside a hotel room pillowcase (the chambermaid, who might well have swiped the money, swore that she never saw it), but he usually kept cash underneath one of his car's tires (if you wanted to get at Puggy's dough, you needed to move his Caddy first). "Most of the games seemed to be on the upper floors of bars in run-down neighborhoods. We primarily played no-limit Five-Card Stud or Draw. Pretty basic. You'd press the buzzer outside, they'd look you over, and let you in."

Through it all, there was continual talk of Vegas. Gamblers described it as a kind of Shangri-la with chips, where the gaming was legal and the action was soft. On the way back from a poker trip to Gardenia, California, in 1957, Puggy took a detour through the desert. And like so many poker players after him, guys who were accustomed to living under the radar and crisscrossing the country in search of games, he was immediately seduced by Vegas's easy, endless, relatively above-board action.

Winning in Glitter Gulch proved to be a cinch for Pug—and, best of all, there was a nonstop procession of tourists, criminals, businessmen, and professional gamblers coming through town and eager to take him on. "I told people that I was just like a strawberry picker who had become accustomed to harvesting only in springtime," says Pug. "Then I came to Vegas and picked ripe strawberries all year 'round."

Indeed, following his first big run of success, after he got backed in the Major Riddle game, Puggy took to calling the Dunes his own personal strawberry patch—full of sweet suckers, ripe for picking and consuming. Through the 1960s and into the '70s, it fed Puggy Pearson's bottomless hunger for action. But, as he would soon discover, the ugly cousin of hunger is greed, and greed can lead an ambitious poker player down the road of ruin.

WHEN PUGGY PEARSON gets to philosophizing, which he is prone to doing these days, he likes to talk about riding a line. He calls it "the line that separates good and bad," and he's referring to fortune, rather than morality, residing on either side of that line. The way he puts it, "It's about managing your highs, your lows, and your emotions. In doing that, you need to stay as close to that line as possible. Nobody can stay *on* it, but you need to stay *near* it. If you could quit every time you started to cross that line—that is, quit while you're still at your high point—you would be a billionaire. The problem is, nobody can do that. The successful gambler is the one who stays close."

One night at Binion's Horseshoe, in the mid-1970s, Puggy first laid eyes on the man who would push him farther from that line than he'd ever been pushed before. And if he were able to read the tea leaves a little better, maybe read himself a little better, he'd have known that he was ripe for pushing. Though Puggy had won Binion's World Series of Poker in 1973, beating Johnny Moss for the winner-take-all prize of $130,000 (after outplaying the world's 12 greatest players, who had each put up $10,000, Puggy flashed a V sign, stared down piles of $100 bills, and disingenuously declared, "Glory is worth more than money"), his life was spiraling out of control.

Even as Puggy busied himself with corralling all of the $500 and $1,000 bills in Vegas—he kept them in lockboxes spread between L.A. and Nashville—smarter and younger poker players began emerging on the scene. They outfoxed Puggy in much the same way he had once hustled Johnny Moss and Major Riddle. And considering Puggy's riches—on one memorable evening, he had his wife bring $250,000 cash from their home to the Tropicana in order to tide over its cage for a night—he was a fat and juicy goose to get. "I saw new people coming in and sensed things changing," says Eric Drache. "I just knew that those $500 and $1,000 bills were going to disappear from Puggy's boxes."

Epitomizing the new breed was Chip Reese, a game-obsessed graduate of Dartmouth College. By night Reese tore up the Seven-Card Hi/Lo Split games. In the mornings he cleaned Puggy's clock at backgammon. "Pug'd call me and say, 'C'mon, baby, I'm ready to play,'" remembers Reese, who still reigns as one of Vegas's winningest poker stars. "I lived around the corner and wouldn't even bother to get dressed. I'd call a cab and come over in my bathrobe. We'd play backgammon for hours at a time, and when we got hungry, Puggy ordered in steaks from the Golden Steer. I'd beat him for $25,000 and lend him $5,000 so he could go out and win another 20 at poker, then I'd take it away from him again."

But even the card action was starting to run dry. For the first time in his life, Puggy found it hard to turn around a losing streak. And it was about to get worse. One night at the Horseshoe, while being hammered at honeymoon bridge by Jimmy Casella, a gray-haired and deeply tanned ex-bookie from New York, Puggy noticed a short, dark-haired, well-muscled thug staring at him. In no mood for the attention, Puggy snapped, "Stop looking at me, you little wormy-eyed motherfucker."

The man smirked, shook his head, and walked away. A few minutes later, Puggy got up to go to the bathroom. A friend followed him in. "Pug," the friend said, "do you know who you were just talking to?"

"I don't give a fuck," said Puggy. "I don't like the way he was eye-balling me."

"That was Tony Spilotro."

Immortalized by Joe Pesci in the movie *Casino*, Tony "The Ant" Spilotro was sent to Las Vegas by Chicago mob bosses. Diminutive but vicious, and suspected in more than 20 murders, he was perhaps most notorious for once allegedly impaling a 320-pound man on a meat hook and slowly torturing him. Spilotro's job in Vegas was to oversee the skim from mobbed-up casinos and serve as the outfit's enforcer out west. One of Spilotro's money-making schemes involved putting together cheating rings to take down the high-stakes poker players. Puggy was an early target.

At the Flamingo, where Johnny Moss (who, ironically, had been run out of Vegas in the late 1950s for cheating) oversaw the poker room, Puggy's run of good fortune derailed. He was targeted by Spilotro and his posse of players, who isolated Puggy, sent signals to one another, and teamed up against him. There's speculation that it even went beyond that kind of collusion, which alone can cripple a player. "Back then, in the mid- to late-'70s, there were guys walking out of the casino count rooms with suitcases full of money," says Dario Ortiz, author of *Gambling Scams* and a cheating consultant for casinos around the world. "It wouldn't surprise me at all if there were marked cards and flash-peaks, in which the dealer shuffles so that a player [who's in on the scam] can see cards that are about to be dealt."

However the cheating was done, Puggy didn't recognize it until his finances were just about depleted. The situation wasn't helped much by problems he was having at home. Sick of being a poker widow, his wife Andrea surreptitiously rented an apartment downtown. She took up with a man from Nashville, who'd come in to see her on the sly.

Only after she left Puggy, when he hired a private detective, did he find out the truth. "Puggy was always a sucker for women," says an old friend. "The guy has never broken up with a woman in his life, and

I've seen them take hundreds of thousands from him. He just lets it happen. Like he enjoys it or something."

The circumstances—Puggy's advancing age, an emotionally destructive situation at home, a greedy and aggressive mobster in the form of Tony Spilotro, groups of easily manipulated poker players with iffy ethics—conspired to create a perfect storm. "Between October 1974 and April 1975, Puggy went broke," remembers the old friend. "He had to have lost more than a million dollars in cash. Just gone. It got so bad that he emptied $6,000 from a bank account that his son had had since he was in grade school." The friend shook his head. "It happened in Moss's poker room. At the time, Moss had a partnership with the Flamingo, and there were mob guys in the poker room there. People know what happened. But it's an unwritten rule that nobody talks about it."

As the decade wore on, things went from bad to worse. Puggy's wife left him for good and sold the property in Winnemucca, Nevada, (to avoid run-ins with the IRS, Puggy had put it in her name) for far less than it was worth. Desperate for a bankroll, Puggy borrowed funds to cover the divorce and to keep himself in action. Jack Binion lent Puggy $100,000 cash, right from the Horseshoe cage. Puggy was knee-deep in debt to high-rolling poker pros, including Doyle Brunson and Billy Baxter. Most heartbreaking of all, the big games became off-limits. Puggy lacked the necessary buy-in for a seat. Suddenly, in his mid-40s, he was just another busted rounder, grinding it out in the medium-stakes world, struggling to maintain a table image, living worse than he ever had in his adult life.

By the start of 1977's World Series, he had a six-figure debt and was heading back toward being flat broke. And it wasn't like in the old days, when running out of money was standard operating procedure. "This is the most depressing racket in the world," an embittered Puggy told Barney Vinson, a Vegas-based reporter who, at the time, insisted that professional poker playing looked glamorous. "You win 18 or 19 sessions, then you lose once, and you're back where you started—or broke. After that you've got to look for a friendly face, borrow money, and start again. And, even then, you're always around the corner from someone with a paddle that fits your ass."

PUGGY FELT BEATEN-UP and broken-down by poker. But gambling was the only thing he knew. He had no other way to earn a living, nothing else to do with his life. So he reached down deep inside himself and struggled to get it up for the '77 World Series. After all, those four weeks every spring are primetime for professionals who want to win big in side-game action, and Puggy needed to take a stand.

He played hard that year, but experienced frustration at every turn. After one particularly unrewarding day of poker, he was too stuck to quit, too wired to sleep. It was four in the morning when Steve, who was living at home with Puggy at the time, woke up and realized that his dad was still out. He got dressed and drove over to the Horseshoe.

Steve walked in on a grim scene: his father sitting at a poker table, playing $100/$200 Seven-Card Stud with a Washington-based businessman who'd knocked around the scene for years and another guy, a seasoned gambler named Roger Moore. Puggy was practically down to the felt, unbanding what appeared to be his last $5,000 pack of hundreds as a fresh hand of cards was dealt.

Betting and raising and some more raising ensued. Puggy was in all the way. "Dad had a few thousand dollars in the pot," explains Steve. "He was obviously in trouble: four hearts to a flush and so committed that he'd go down with this hand. He got dealt his last card, he squeezed it out real slowly, and I think what happened next was fate. The final card was a heart. He hit his flush, he won the pot, and it saved him. After winning that hand he caught on fire. He went on to win half a million dollars in side action during the course of that '77 Series. He paid everybody off and never looked back."

Puggy changed everything about the way he played. "I think Dad learned his lesson in that he began picking his spots a lot better," continues Steve. "He stayed away from the toughest games, curtailed gambling with the Chip Reeses and Doyle Brunsons of the world, and went after less seasoned players with smaller bankrolls. Dad played more golf, made some smart real estate investments, and stayed cognizant about getting the best of it. He finally learned to keep his ego in check." Much to the poker world's delight, that lesson eluded Johnny Moss and many of his contemporaries. Moss, in his later years, became such a cash-bleeding sucker that Pug ended up owning all three of his World Series bracelets. Poker, after all, is a game of skill, and when you go up against the best players, at the highest stakes, you put yourself in a world of peril. Perhaps viewing Moss's downfall as a cautionary tale, Puggy discovered that there are plenty of smaller-stakes games, with far less skilled players, where lots of money can be made. To put it in Puggy-style terms, the sweetest strawberries are not always on the tallest branches.

From the mid-'70s on, Puggy's life has been a lesson in survival. He bounced back from a heart attack, and these days he can often be spotted playing and beating the $40/$80 games at the Bellagio—"cheap poker," as he calls it. He has been waylaid from golf due to the kinds of joint and bone maladies that afflict many 75-year-olds. But he insists he's not out of that game for good; he says he's eager to get back on the course. Two poker players, Brian Nadell and Tommy Fisher, offered in 2003 to make a wager with Puggy: $100,000 that he couldn't break 100, from the tips, on the 7,605-yard Paiute Golf Course. Hungry for the dough, but hungrier for the challenge, Puggy (who had once been a better than scratch golfer) wanted to take them up on it but wasn't sure he'd be physically able. One morning, eager to test himself out, he slipped onto Paiute and played a round for the first time in two years.

His ailing body stopped him from hitting the magic number, but he left feeling good, ready to regroup and accept the bet—once he figured out a surefire way to win it. As he explained one day not long after, "It's not what you play, it's not how you play, it's how you match up." He was standing outside his house at the time, alongside a camper emblazoned with a caricature of his face and these words: I'LL PLAY ANY MAN, FROM ANY LAND, ANY GAME THAT HE CAN NAME, FOR ANY AMOUNT THAT I CAN COUNT—above an addendum in small print—PROVIDING I LIKE IT.

Amarillo Slim Preston, 1980, at Binion's Horseshoe, Las Vegas

Two

AMARILLO SLIM PRESTON

The Talk Show

Endless bluster propels a wisecracking

Texan to the World Championship and

makes him poker's first national

celebrity. But is it enough to get him out

of a scandal back home?

IN JUNE 2004, JUST A few days after the culmination of the World Series of Poker, the man who made the event a cultural phenomenon, who invented the concept of poker celebrity, lay dying in an Amarillo hospital. One of his lungs had collapsed, doctors suspected he had prostate cancer, and—thanks to a faulty pacemaker—his 75-year-old heart was racing as high as 190 beats per minute. From his bed in the intensive care unit, Amarillo Slim overheard a doctor predict that he would not leave the hospital alive.

Although Slim had been the most celebrated poker player in the world for more than 30 years, he was always more of a hustler than a poker purist. The 1972 world champion, he spun his mantra—"If there is anything worth arguing about, I'll either bet on it or shut up"—into tens of millions of dollars and a batch of far-fetched adventures that were equal parts Damon Runyon and Paul Bunyon. So it wasn't surprising that upon hearing the dire prognosis, Slim perked up, as if he had been merely setting a trap all along. He offered to bet the doctor twice his salary that he would walk out of the hospital. The physician declined, and wisely so: Less than a week later, Slim was riding an ash-gray gelding around his 3,640-acre ranch and telling the story with characteristic relish.

"How would you like to be laying there and hear some shit like that?" he asked.

Although the temperature was north of 100 degrees and the wind made it feel like he was staring into the barrel of an industrial-strength blow-dryer, Slim hunched forward in his saddle and steered nimbly through the clumps of mesquite and cactus. When he reached the fence that marked the border of his property, he brought his gelding to a halt. After the long ride, his face was drawn and as gray as his horse. On the other side of the fence, the mesa sloped down sharply to a verdant valley surrounding the Canadian River, an oasis of color in the brown West Texas landscape. From where Slim was perched, high atop a bluff, he could see 15 miles in any direction.

"I like it here," he said, a tattered straw cowboy hat pushed back on his head. "Sometimes I'll ride up here with my dog and a pup tent and spend the night. Build a little fire. Just me and my dog and my horse."

His gambling colleagues and co-conspirators had long ago de-camped to the implausible palaces of Las Vegas, but Slim always chose to stay here, where the horizon is interrupted only by grain silos and windmills. He had often joked that he could never leave his hometown because he would then have to change his name. But now, in the twi-light of his life, he was finally thinking about splitting.

More specifically, he was being run out of town. In August 2003, Slim was indicted by a grand jury for indecency with a child, allegations that court papers indicated involved a 12-year-old girl, a family member. Several months later, despite taking polygraph tests that he said proved his innocence, Slim pleaded guilty to three misdemeanor assault charges.

While some folks around Amarillo felt the local celebrity walked away with a slap on the wrist, Slim felt the opposite. "It was a nightmare for me," he said. "Ruined my health, cost me a divorce. Cost me a couple of golf courses and a ranch, five Pizza Planets, two Swensen's ice cream joints, and a bunch of cash, 'cause [my ex-wife] knew where the boxes were." His ex-wife, whom he married when he was only 20, also took the 6,000-square-foot house, which featured an Olympic-size swimming pool and four golf holes in the backyard. He moved into a one-bedroom apartment.

Slim waited in vain for a groundswell of support in the community. He had made a career out of half-truths and tall tales—even boasting on numerous occasions that he was so good at deception and manipulation that he could beat a polygraph test—and the locals didn't know what to believe. For years, while they viewed his gambling as slightly unsavory, they were nonetheless won over by his good-natured winks and down-home one-liners. "Don't worry about ol' Slim," they'd say to one another. "He's all right." But child abuse was a different story, and many of them were not so generous with the benefit of the doubt.

As Slim made his way about town in his white Dodge pickup—stopping at Home Depot for ranch supplies, then at the Hoffbrau Steak House for his favorite meal of quail and a tall glass of milk—he was forced to endure the sidelong glances and whispers from people who thought he just might be guilty.

"That bothers me, because I've got a lot of pride," he said. "Goddamn, I was a big hero in this town."

IN 1972, SLIM was little more than a run-of-the-mill rounder when he sat down at a dingy, green-felt table on the casino floor of Binion's Horseshoe to play poker against Puggy Pearson, who was considered the best in the world at the time. Positioned on opposite ends of the table, they were the two remaining players out of the eight who entered the third annual World Series of Poker. "You better play 'em tight, you skinny son of a bitch, because I'm going to break you before the night's over," Puggy warned.

Slim held only $22,000 in chips to Pearson's $38,000, but he flashed a crooked grin that exuded total confidence. "I like you, Pug, but I'll put a rattlesnake in your pocket and ask for a match," he said.

Puggy lit a cigar, Slim a cigarette, and the battle was on. It stretched for hours, and Slim eventually grabbed the chip lead through a series of bluffs. Between hands, he gabbed with the railbirds. In the middle of hands, he yakked at Pearson, who chewed on his cigar and stewed silently.

By reputation, Slim was a less skilled ring-game player than Pearson, but he specialized in heads-up competition, when he could focus his constant banter on a single opponent. He used his words like antennae, constantly feeling Pearson out for signs of weakness or deception. His folksy one-liners also made him a favorite with fans, and, as the match wore on, veteran western actor Chill Wills led the crowd in cheers after each pot: "Who are we rootin' for?"

"Amarillo Slim!"

As Slim built his chip lead over Pearson to more than 4-to-1, Jimmy "The Greek" Snyder, a longtime rival of Slim's who also handled publicity for the event and went on to become the world's most famous oddsmaker, leaned in to Puggy and told him that he thought Slim was "stealing the pots" by making big bets even when he held marginal hands. Slim overheard the comment and decided to counter by over-selling his next strong hand. Minutes later, he was dealt King-Jack. Both players raised the pot before the flop, which came 8-8-King. Slim now held two pair, and was convinced it was the best hand. He pushed his entire stack of $51,000 to the center of the table. (The standard play would have been to make a smallish bet to keep Pearson in the pot, so by betting all of his chips he was trying to bait Pearson into reading him for another bluff.)

"It feels better in," Slim announced to the crowd.

Pearson's hole cards were two 6s, giving him two pair as well—

but not as strong as Slim's. Pearson called the last of his chips. The turn was an 8, giving Slim a full house—8s over Kings—and the world championship. Slim grinned wide, flash bulbs popped all over the room, and reporters pushed in with microphones.

In the popular imagination, the archetype of the professional poker player is a Texan with a wide cowboy hat, a quick wit, and a willingness to bet on anything, anytime, anywhere. It was practically born that night.

Following his victory, Slim wrote a book, *Play Poker to Win* (though he later admitted he didn't include anything that would allow amateurs to do just that), and the director Robert Altman gave him a speaking part as himself in the film *California Split*. Slim became one of the most popular guests on the 1970s talk-show circuit. Merv Griffin, Dinah Shore, Johnny Carson—Slim sat with them all, resplendent in patterned suits, a Stetson and ostrich-skin boots embroidered with SLIM and a colorful stream of clubs, spades, diamonds, and hearts.

Unlike most high-stakes poker players, who were either surly, borderline illiterate, or simply camera-shy, Slim was poker's equivalent of Muhammad Ali—quotable, charismatic, and utterly unconflicted about his place in society. Reporters loved him for it. One wrote that "he plays constantly, devotedly, joyously, wholeheartedly, and with passion—as certain consecrated artists practice their art."

A natural showman, Slim enjoyed the attention, but also saw himself as an ambassador for the game. In the 1960s and '70s, he says, "people thought if you were a poker player that meant you either crawled out from under a rock or you were dealing narcotics." He argued to an ever-growing audience that not all poker players were outlaws, and he was at least partly right: Not all poker players are outlaws.

But, as it turns out, some of them are.

THOMAS AUSTIN PRESTON Jr., as his mother called him, didn't actually move to Amarillo until he was in high school. He was born in tiny Johnson, Arkansas, and spent his boyhood moving from one small town to the next. His parents split when he was 11, and then he shuttled back and forth between his dad's hew home in Amarillo and his mom's place in Arkansas, where at local pool halls he first recognized his hustling skills.

By 16, he was staying with his dad in Amarillo but spending all of his free time shooting stick. His father, who managed a couple of restaurants, tracked him down when he played in the white part of town, so Thomas frequented the east side, where the Mexicans gambled just as high. He caught the eye of the local gambling bosses, who gave the youngster an Ivy League–quality education in hustling and staked him as he made the circuit across the Southwest on weekends.

In 1945, he drove to Hot Springs, Arkansas, where the country's top gamblers gathered each spring to play in the city's pool halls and barely concealed casinos. The top pool hustler of the era was Minnesota Fats, a portly legend who boasted endlessly about his pool prowess and the riches it brought him. As Slim recalled in his autobiography, *Amarillo Slim in a World Full of Fat People*, the first words Fats said to him were, "Son, every time a bird flies over my Cadillac, I buy a new one."

The kid was in awe. He watched the man manipulate the room with his homespun eloquence, goading his opponents until they couldn't shoot straight. Slim saw for the first time how verbal jousting could influence a match, and immediately patterned his hustling style after the hefty champ. The kid also told his friends not to call him Thomas anymore—he needed a proper nickname. He became Amarillo Slim.

But Slim noticed a serious flaw in his new role model. Fats treated his opponents so rudely that they often refused to play him again. Slim vowed to keep his opponents emboldened, not embittered. He wanted to take his marks not just once, but repeatedly, and so tempered his talk just enough that he didn't embarrass his opponents. As one of his backers told him, "You can shear a sheep many times, but you can only skin him once." He was also smart enough to invest some of his winnings: At age 16, he bought his first ranch, 160 acres outside Amarillo that cost him $7,500.

The next year, 1946, Slim joined the navy. Like many gamblers of that generation, including Puggy Pearson and a sharp young poker player named Richard Milhouse Nixon, Slim found the military full of suckers with plenty of money and time on their hands. He took bets on sporting events and ran craps games on four different troop carriers. That led to a profitable 22 months at sea. Shortly after his discharge, he was asked to join the army's Special Services Division. His task was to give pool exhibitions to entertain the troops in Germany, but the German economy was in shambles and Slim soon found an opportunity in the black market: He bought up (or otherwise acquired) all the excess cigarettes, gasoline, and nylons he could from the G.I.s and sold it at a steep markup to the Germans. The operation, which ultimately involved dozens of co-conspirators and vehicles, netted Slim more than a million dollars, and he wasn't even 19.

When he got back to Amarillo, Slim married and started a family, even as he resumed his career hustling pool. But he was forced to drive farther and farther from home to find pool halls where he wasn't known. He started playing poker, which was growing in popularity across Texas in the 1950s, and soon made a personal connection that rapidly accelerated his learning curve.

In the late '50s, Slim drove more than four hours to a game in Midland, Texas. There, among the oil millionaires at the ritzy Midland Club, he first encountered Doyle Brunson and Brian "Sailor" Roberts, two professional gamblers out of San Angelo. About three weeks later, their paths crossed again when Brunson and Roberts were near Amarillo for another game. Since they were in the neighborhood, they called Slim and he invited them to his house to play more poker. As Slim tells it, he broke both of them and as they were leaving he asked if they needed to borrow some money.

"Shit, Slim, you ever seen a broke sumbitch didn't want some money?" Roberts replied.

Slim slipped them a wad of cash and they promised to make good on the debt. Several days later, the money arrived via Western Union, and Slim was impressed with his new friends' honesty. The next time they met up, they formed a partnership, playing independently but out of the same bankroll. Slim joined them on the road, driving from one smalltown game to another. In retrospect, it was an amazing assemblage of poker talent: All three went on to become world champions.

In those days, every small town in Texas contained a regular game, usually at a fraternal lodge like the Elks Club, and crossroaders like Slim, Doyle, and Sailor maintained a standing invitation to play. The locals knew they brought cash, and there was always a hometown champ looking to prove his stuff against the pros. The games were no-limit, usually Hold 'Em but sometimes Lowball, played in smoky rooms with just one table. Few players drank—Slim and Doyle never did—because drunks almost always lost. (And if a drunk happened to win, he often found himself scrambling on the floor for his cash after someone "accidentally" knocked over the table.) The sheriff in the town was typically on the take, but if the game was raided, the players gave a fake name, paid a fine, and left town. It was the cost of doing business—as were the armed robberies. Bandits targeted gamblers because they carried large wads of cash and were generally not inclined to go to the police. Although Slim carried a snub-nosed .38 in his hip pocket for protection, the threesome was robbed at gunpoint on numerous occasions.

Slim and his pals crisscrossed Texas and occasionally ventured into Oklahoma, Louisiana, and Alabama. The money was consistent—Slim estimates they didn't lose on two consecutive nights for more than three years—but not extravagant. "We would drive 500 miles to win a thousand dollars split three ways," Brunson recalls. But at the end of the year, they each took home close to $20,000, an impressive sum at the time. (Their bookmaking operation, in which they took bets on high school football games around the state, was considerably more profitable.)

Beyond money, the lifestyle provided each of them with the one thing they enjoyed most: for Doyle, a never-ending card game; for Sailor, a new girl in every town; and for Slim, a string of captive audiences to entertain with his boundless bullshit. Most valuable of all, they learned from one another, and matured into the champions they would one day become.

Johnny Moss was acknowledged as the best player in the South, so if Moss went to Austin, they went to Waco. If he went to Midland, they went to Dallas. In later years, as Moss's skills deteriorated and theirs improved, the pattern reversed itself—they followed him wherever he went as he slowly gave away his lifetime of winnings.

In 1964, the fearsome threesome traveled to Las Vegas together for the first time. They showed up with a bankroll above six figures, and sat in on the big game at the Dunes that was dominated by Puggy Pearson. They promptly lost it all—although they suspected they had been cheated.

Cheating was commonplace in the 1960s and '70s, whether through marked cards, players colluding against unsuspecting victims, or sophisticated hold-out devices that enabled cheaters to produce cards on command. The unspoken rule was that you simply didn't say anything, and just walked away from the table if you felt something was amiss. "I don't know who came up with that rule, but it wasn't an honest man," Brunson says.

Slim, unlike Brunson, didn't mind that poker attracted a fair number of con men and petty criminals who viewed it not as a game but a quick score. He knew that if they couldn't cheat, they couldn't beat him. And if they did cheat, he was more than willing to give as good as he got. He once caught an opponent scamming him at gin—via a camera in the ceiling, the player was viewing Slim's hand on his wristwatch—and later arranged to play the same man a heads-up no-limit Lowball match.

On the last card of one hand, Slim drew a King facedown, effectively killing his chances of taking the pot. His opponent, who was again cheating, pushed all-in, knowing he had Slim beat. But Slim called the bet, and turned over the winning hand—the King he had just drawn was nowhere in sight. Only Slim knows where it went, and he's not saying.

His opponent "turned white as a ghost, jumped straight up in his chair," Slim says. "I was thinking, A son of a bitch smart enough to make that money is smart enough not to say anything, so I said to him, 'Something wrong with you?' I knew he wasn't going to say, 'What happened to that King?' At that time, I was younger and I didn't really give a fuck if he said something or not."

The vaunted partnership broke up following its disastrous trip to the Dunes, and the three men went their separate ways. Doyle and Sailor eventually moved to Las Vegas, and further enhanced their reputations as two of the best card sharks in the country.

In the years that followed, Vegas attracted more and more of the high-stakes poker action and the circuit around Texas became less lucrative. Slim made frequent trips out west—in addition to playing in the World Series annually, he hosted Amarillo Slim's Super Bowl of Poker, which for many years was the second-biggest tournament in poker—but opted to raise his family in Amarillo.

He considered leaving only once, in 1976, when he tried to buy the Gamblers Hall of Fame, a small casino on Fremont Street in downtown Las Vegas. It was an opportunity for Slim to join Benny Binion (a childhood friend of his and founder of Binion's Horseshoe) in the casino business and further leverage his celebrity, but the deal fell apart after mobster Tony Spilotro requested a meeting at the Tropicana Hotel. Like everyone in the gambling business, Slim knew Spilotro was the most dangerous man in Vegas, so he had no choice but to take the meeting. Seated casually in a booth with his brother, Spilotro got right to the point: Once Slim took over the casino, Spilotro expected 25 percent of the profits; in exchange, Slim could borrow an unlimited amount of money if he ever needed it. It was a classic mob shakedown. Slim lied and told Spilotro that Binion was his partner in the deal, then stepped outside to call Binion and tell him what was happening. Within minutes, a group of Binion's associates showed up and took Slim away. "I looked up and you've never seen so many big hats and bulges in your life," says Slim. "Binion sent a whole fucking army out there after me."

With Slim safely back at the Horseshoe, Binion called down to the Tropicana and asked for Spilotro's booth. "Let me tell you dago motherfuckers something," he told the mobster. "You are fucking with a friend of mine. I want you all to pray that the next time I see you there is a woman or a kid in between me and you or I'm going to kill every fucking one of you on sight. If that suits you, fine. If not, just say it doesn't and we'll come right now."

Spilotro backed down. Slim's deal for the casino fell through for other reasons, he says, but he didn't consider leaving Amarillo again for almost 30 years. And he stayed out of the business end of poker, refocusing his energy on talking his way through outrageous bets.

SEVERAL YEARS AFTER Slim's 1972 victory in the World Series, NBC came to Las Vegas to film a $10,000 buy-in tournament at the Aladdin. Slim busted out early, and spent the next couple of days squiring around a pretty young producer while the game plowed on day and night.

Early one morning, Sailor Roberts and fellow Texas gamblers Jack "Treetop" Strauss and Crandell Addington slipped away to get some breakfast. The producer happened to be in the dining room and joined them at the table. She was not interested in talking about anything other than the abundant charms of Amarillo Slim.

Finally, she asked, "Mr. Roberts, what is it about Amarillo Slim that sets him apart from the rest of you world-class players?"

Sailor replied, "Well it's the fact that he talks more and doesn't play as well."

Sailor was playing a joke at his old friend's expense, but it summed up Slim's standing in much of the poker community. He was good for poker, everyone knew, but many top players resented that his fame so far outstripped everyone else's. As one top player puts it, "Never has a person made so much out of winning one eight-person tournament"—the 1972 World Series.

That resentment created a backlash of sorts, leading some of those who didn't see him play at his peak to believe that he was never actually very good. His peers say that this is grossly unfair. "Slim could play, make no mistake about that. I don't think he was ever in a class with Doyle, but few people were," says Addington, who finished second in the 1978 world championship to Bobby Baldwin. Brunson himself says Slim is "vastly underrated."

Slim was at his best playing short-handed and heads-up, where his verbal skills were most effective. (Case in point: He took first place the first four times he reached the final table of an event at the World Series, before finally finishing second to young superstar Phil Ivey in an Omaha tournament in 2003.) During a match, he chatters nonstop. "I'm trying to get information," he explains, "either in their mannerisms or their speech or the way they sit or the way they bet."

The banter is always amusing, and seemingly harmless. He gets his opponents talking about sports or the weather—any subject on which they have no reason to lie. Once he knows how someone looks and acts when they are telling the truth, then he can determine when they are lying. "If we get to play very long, I'll pick up something. It might not be foolproof, but I'll pick up something," he says.

In one infamous match, he squared off against Betty Carey, an ultra-aggressive no-limit player out of Wyoming, in a $100,000 heads-up match. While Slim and Carey waited for the game to begin, he asked if he could get her something to drink.

"Yeah, that's nice, Slim, I'll have some hot tea," she said.

A few minutes later, he asked her how she liked it.

"Oh, it was real fine, Slim," she said.

The match began and the players jousted for more than an hour without either taking a commanding lead before a pot came up that, in Slim's words, "a show dog couldn't jump over."

Carey pushed the rest of her chips into the pot. Slim considered the move, then asked, "You like your hand, Betty?"

"This is a good hand, Slim," she said.

"I knew right away that bitch was lying," Slim recalls. "That's not what she said about that tea. I called her with two 5s and she had exactly what I thought she had—nothing."

A few days later, they played again, this time for $200,000. Carey's backers made her wear ear plugs, and instructed her not to engage Slim in conversation under any circumstances. Stripped of his primary weapon, Slim lost in less than 15 minutes.

THE OTHER FACTOR that affected Slim's reputation was that he was never a regular in the big-money side games. He played in all the big tournaments, where his record is impressive if unspectacular, but his bread and butter was the endless supply of wealthy amateur gamblers who simply wanted to play against a legend.

"That's been what saved me," he acknowledges. "Why would I want to look at a roomful of old, hairy-legged gamblers that's trying to win when I get to play with millionaires that are showing off to their new girlfriends or their country club buddies? They anticipate losing when they sit down, and I don't disappoint 'em a damned bit."

In 1977, he hooked the biggest fish of all.

Slim had driven over to Sunland Park Race Track, just across the New Mexico border from El Paso, to watch a couple of his horses run. He also wanted to attract the attention of El Paso's Chagra brothers, whom Slim knew by reputation; they liked to gamble high and had deep pockets lined with millions from their cocaine-trafficking empire.

Sure enough, Lee Chagra introduced himself to Slim at the track. A criminal defense lawyer and the oldest of the Chagra brothers, Lee represented many of the top drug lords in the Southwest, including his younger brother, Jimmy. When Lee invited Slim over for a friendly game of poker, Slim gladly accepted. Still, although he was used to consorting with seedy characters from his years on the road, this was dangerous new territory.

One night, Slim and Lee were playing poker on a glassed-in balcony at the home of one of Lee's neighbors. Three masked men with shotguns chained to their waists threw a lawn chair through the glass and demanded the money on the table—well over $50,000. They beat Lee with the butt of a shotgun and demanded Slim's jewelry.

Slim told the thieves: "Man, this is a cool score. You've got all our money. You done whipped ol' Lee and you threatened me. Everything is still cool. But if you hurt anybody in this room or you take our jewelry, there ain't no place in the world you can go."

Apparently convinced, the men fled, with Slim and Lee emptying their pistols into the night behind them. (Two years later, Lee was gunned down in his El Paso office. The Chagra family initially suspected Sailor Roberts of the crime—he had gone to Lee's office on the day of the killing to collect a gambling debt—but three soldiers from Fort Bliss were eventually convicted. Slim believes it was the same three men who had robbed the poker game.)

But it was Jimmy Chagra, not Lee, who fancied himself the family's top gambler. In 1978, Chagra began visiting Las Vegas on a regular basis, flush with the proceeds of his smuggling enterprise. He and his armed guards stayed at Caesars Palace on the Strip, and shuttled via limousine to the Horseshoe each day to gamble against the top pros—no one more than his old friend Amarillo Slim. Chagra played

Slim heads-up poker more than 20 times, and Slim estimates he won more than 80 percent of the matches.

Slim and his cronies also enticed Chagra to play golf for higher stakes than anyone in the world had ever played. According to Slim, Chagra brought $18 million in cash with him to Las Vegas, and burned through $3.7 million of it in a long-running golf match with Doyle Brunson at Las Vegas Country Club. Slim and Jack Binion were Doyle's chief backers and shared equally in the windfall.

The final take would almost certainly have been much higher if not for a colossal mistake by Puggy Pearson. An accomplished golf hustler in his own right, he managed to worm his way into the match but got caught improving his lie—in other words, cheating. Chagra threw a fit, canceled the match and threatened to kill Puggy.

"We took a vote as to whether to let him or not," Slim says ruefully. "There wasn't no need to move the ball. All Puggy did was maybe move it three feet closer to the hole, but he moved it to take the break out of a putt and one of Jimmy's bodyguards caught him. There's no telling what it cost us."

The party ended in early 1979, when Chagra was indicted on federal drug-trafficking charges. The day his trial was scheduled to begin, the judge hearing the case—nicknamed Maximum John for his willingness to dole out lengthy sentences—was assassinated in his garage with a long-range rifle. The triggerman was eventually identified as Charles Harrelson, a card cheat and gambler (and father of actor Woody Harrelson). In front of a new judge, Chagra was acquitted of hiring Harrelson, but two relatives were convicted in the plot. Chagra eventually served 13 years in federal prison for obstructing the investigation, and is now believed to be in the federal witness protection program.

By some estimates, Chagra, who once tipped a cocktail waitress $10,000 for bringing him a bottle of water, dropped more than $10 million in the roughly 12-month period he frequented Las Vegas. For Slim, who personally took more than a million off the drug kingpin, it was one of his greatest scores. "He had about as much chance of winning against me as he did of getting a French kiss out of the Statue of Liberty," Slim says.

THE CHIEF DRAWBACK of a poker life is its never-ending sameness: the same card rooms, the same games against the same old players. Slim, though, has used poker as the springboard to a life of endless adventure. A gambling prankster, he cajoled unsuspecting marks into making outrageous proposition bets, such as the time he beat a ping-pong champion by insisting on the right to choose the paddles (he chose skillets, then Coke bottles in a second match), or the time he hit a golf ball more than a mile (over a frozen lake), or the time he rafted down the River of No Return (in a wetsuit designed by Jacques Cousteau). As he frequently told reporters, "If I tell you a goose can pull a plow, hitch him up."

An avid hunter, he bagged trophies from around the world. He attended Wimbledon and the Masters almost every year, and he flew everywhere from Morocco to Australia to play poker against well-heeled, willing pigeons. To this day, he accompanies a junket of high rollers each year from the Las Vegas Hilton to Alaska for a week of salmon fishing, gin, and poker. The requirement for attendance is a credit line of at least $2 million with the hotel. Slim says in 2003 he made more on the plane ride up than most men make in a year.

Unlike most top pros, whose bankrolls exist only to fund the next big game, over the years Slim has constantly invested his winnings. He opened pizza and ice cream franchises in Amarillo, bought several golf courses, and accumulated vast acreage throughout the Texas panhandle. (There have been persistent rumors that he remains involved in bookmaking, but he denies it, citing stringent new federal laws—though he did plead guilty in 1979 to a misdemeanor charge of failing to pay a special gambling tax.)

By the 2004 World Series, when he should have been reveling in poker's newfound respectability as the game's sage clown prince, he found himself a pariah. At the media-saturated event, few reporters sought his comment and the new generation of players snickered at the audacity it took to show his face after pleading guilty in the child-abuse case in Amarillo. Yet Slim believes history will judge him favorably. Just before the series he sold the rights to his autobiography to

Saturn Films, the production company established by Nicolas Cage, who expressed interest in playing the lead role.

Slim is convinced the prosecution of his case was political, the misplaced zeal of an ambitious district attorney who wanted a federal judgeship. But he says he doesn't have the time, or the inclination, to persuade his Amarillo neighbors of his innocence. He is shopping for a new ranch far away from his beloved hometown.

"It's embarrassing for me, but the people who know me know how it was," he says. "I think I might just buy a place in Utah and live out the rest of my days there. I'm looking at a ranch up there in Price, next to Robert Redford's place. He rode down there last time I flew up to look at it. I didn't disappoint him. He said, 'We heard you was coming—you'd be a good neighbor.' I said, 'Hell, Robert, don't you know I'll steal all your cattle?' He thought that was all right. That's what he expected me to say."

Doyle Brunson, 1980, at Binion's Horseshoe, Las Vegas

Three

DOYLE BRUNSON

The Great One

A fierce competitive streak and an analytical mind take a former star athlete from dusty West Texas to the Big Game—along the way revolutionizing poker with a systematic approach.

EARLY AFTERNOON AT THE GOLDEN Nugget. Bikini-clad women reclined by the pool and sipped piña coladas in the brilliant May sunshine. On the other side of a plastic partition, in the temporary poker room the size of an airplane hangar, the world's greatest poker player sat alone eating a bowl of pasta. His name was Doyle Brunson, and he was in the hole—"stuck," in poker lingo—for more than a million dollars. He twirled spaghetti on a fork and dismissed a reporter who pressed past a security guard to ask about a good time for an interview.

"Son, I don't think there is going to be a good time," he said. For the past three weeks, while the 2004 World Series was in full roar across the street at Binion's Horseshoe, 70-year-old Brunson had been ensconced in the back corner of the Golden Nugget's poker room, where a table was cordoned off for the high-rolling elite of the poker world.

Each day the routine was the same: Shortly after noon, Brunson would arrive, motoring his 300-pound frame through the room on an electric scooter, and have lunch delivered to the table. The others filed in while Brunson ate: Bellagio president Bobby Baldwin, hall-of-famer Chip Reese, two-time world champion Johnny Chan, young superstar Phil Ivey, and millionaire businessman Lyle Berman, who founded the World Poker Tour. They collected chips from the cage—the buy-in was a minimum of $500,000—and settled in around the table. They wore baseball caps and sweat suits, but the air hummed with the intensity of a Wall Street trading desk for the next 12 to 14 hours. Pots routinely stretched into six figures. Fortunes were won and lost with the turn of a card.

In the early morning hours, the pool long since dark, the players either sleepily drove home to their suburban mansions or adjourned upstairs to the complimentary rooms provided by the hotel. Brunson, 15 years older than his oldest competitor, was almost always the last to leave.

The high-stakes gathering, a semi-annual affair known simply as the Big Game, represents the greatest challenge in poker today. Not only is the money nosebleed-inducing—a $4,000/$8,000 structure when they play limit poker, meaning the second-best hand usually costs upward of $50,000—it is a mixed game (i.e., the variation of poker changes with each hand). On one round, they play Seven-Card Stud. The next, Texas Hold 'Em, and then Triple-Draw, then Omaha Hi/Lo, and so on. If you are weak at only one of the games, you get clobbered. The average professional who specializes in one or two types of poker wouldn't even think about putting his feet under the table at the Big Game.

In fact, only 15 or 20 people in the world have the money and the poker expertise to sit down with Brunson and company. Most of those players are professionals, of course, but there are a few wealthy amateurs who like to join them, and the game is openly centered on these men. Berman is one, as are *Hustler* magazine founder Larry Flynt and Celine Dion's husband/manager, Rene Angelil. When one of them is in town and wants a game, the pros make time to play. The amateur, almost always a very skilled player in his own right, can certainly win, but it's expected that over several sessions he will spread a million or two around the table to the pros. Only on rare occasions will you find Brunson and the others playing without a "live one" at the table. (Brunson explains those occasions by saying, "If you want to attract customers, sometimes you've got to open the store.")

For more than 35 years, Brunson has been the anchor of the Big Game while other players have come and gone. His contemporaries Amarillo Slim and Puggy Pearson quit playing at the highest levels years ago; Reese, who is 20 years younger, stopped playing for almost 10 years when he got bored with the endless repetition; a continual stream of younger players have come into the game, but none has had the bankroll or the talent to endure. Brunson has always been there, hand after hand, day after day. The game has moved periodically, from the Dunes in the 1960s and '70s to the Mirage in the '80s and the Bellagio in the '90s. During the early 2000s it was briefly played in a small off-Strip casino called Sam's Town. Wherever it has gone, Brunson has been there. No one in the history of poker has played in the world's highest game as long as him.

But even the world's best lose on a regular basis, and when this particular edition of the Big Game broke up in early June 2004, shortly after the World Series ended, Brunson remained mired deep in red figures. He says he was just running unlucky, that the previous five weeks had been one bad beat and missed draw after another, but he refuses to dwell on his misfortune. "Money lost is money gone," he says. "If you can't handle that, you can't be in the business."

Still, why would he continue to play day after day when he had nothing left to prove and everything to lose? The answer lies in the fact that Brunson plays poker less as a business than as a sport. And, like most athletes, he enjoys it too much to walk away when he believes he can still compete.

"Doyle loves what he does more than anybody in the world," says his friend Dewey Tomko, a former schoolteacher turned gambler. "He wants to play poker and he wants to eat. He doesn't want to do nothing else."

Tomko is among a legion of old-school pros who speak of Brunson in tones approaching reverence. Brunson is the gold standard, not only because of his skill, success, and longevity, but also because of his character. Or, as they say in the poker world, his "gamble." Poker players talk about a man's gamble the way athletes talk about heart. A cousin to courage, it is an intangible asset, yet it is constantly being measured. There is no more damning assessment of a poker player than for another to say, "He doesn't have any gamble in him," which usually means he is timid and doesn't want to put his chips at risk unless he is confident he has the best hand. A player with lots of gamble bluffs and raises, sticks and moves. He gives lots of action and takes lots of action, in a calculated manner that stops just short of degeneracy. He is not scared of losing or going broke.

"Let me tell you something about Doyle," says his good friend Jack Binion, Benny's son. "Doyle's got more gamble in him than anybody."

Binion tells a story about when Brunson was a young man in his 20s, just beginning to make his name in Fort Worth as a gambler. Brunson arranged a golf match with a local hustler named Curtis Skinner, whom everyone called Ironman because he was partially crippled.

The bet was for $3,000 for each nine holes. Ironman won the front nine; Brunson paid him the $3,000, but said he was quitting before the second nine.

"What do you mean?" Ironman asked. "You can't just quit."

Brunson explained that the $3,000 was all the money he had to his name.

"That was Doyle," Binion says admiringly. "He bet all he had on the front nine."

IN THE EARLY 1970s, Benny Binion hired Jimmy the Greek to handle publicity for the World Series. The Greek liked to needle Brunson and call him "Texas Doy-lee," but several reporters mistakenly believed

Snyder was saying "Texas Dolly." After they identified Brunson that way in their stories, he was stuck with the nickname.

Texas Dolly received his poker education on the brick-paved blocks of Fort Worth's Exchange Avenue, in those days a lawless stretch of dilapidated saloons, whorehouses, and underground gambling dens, not far from the city's famed stockyards. The area had been known as Hell's Half-Acre when it was frequented by outlaws such as Butch Cassidy, and its denizens managed to grow even more unsavory in the 1940s and '50s, when the livestock industry abandoned railroads in favor of long-haul trucks.

In 1955, as a newly hired salesman for an office-supply company, Brunson walked in on a Seven-Card Stud game during one of his first sales calls and pocketed a month's salary in less than three hours. He promptly quit the job and fell in with a hard-living group of criminals who populated Exchange Avenue's gambling scene. "There were about 35 or 40 of us," he recalls. "I was 23 years old and most of them were even younger. They were thieves, felons, a lot of them had been to jail. By the time I was 40, everyone but me and one other guy were either dead or in the penitentiary."

Brunson saw five people get killed on Exchange Avenue, including one player who was sitting at the next table in a two-table room. It was spillover from a fight about a woman, and the shooter simply walked in and literally blew the player's brains all over the wall. "It was just part of the life," Brunson says.

It was certainly not the life he had envisioned growing up during the Great Depression in Longworth, a dusty West Texas hamlet that consisted of a church, a school, and five businesses. His father worked steadily as a farmer and cotton-gin manager, but earned just enough to afford a four-room house without indoor plumbing. For Doyle, the middle child, sports was the best way to avoid a career of chopping cotton or working in the gypsum plant that served as the town's commercial hub.

A fierce, if undersize, competitor, Brunson established himself as the star of the basketball team after he sprouted from five-seven to six-three before his senior year. He led the squad to the state championship tournament in Austin, a feat that was not matched by his high school for almost 50 years. When basketball season was over, he ran track to keep in shape. He was a natural runner—the best in the state, as it turned out—who clocked a mile in 4:38.

Brunson received scholarship offers from around the country, but settled on little Hardin-Simmons University. He wanted to go there for two reasons: It was located in nearby Abilene, and it was a Baptist school, which appealed to his God-fearing parents. The lanky left-hander with a soft shooting touch was a star there as well. During his junior year, he was voted most valuable player in the conference, which included big state schools such as Arizona and Texas Tech, and the Minneapolis Lakers contacted him about joining their team after graduation. In addition, his mile time was down to 4:18, fast enough to make him a contender for the national track team.

Then, one day during the summer after his junior year, Brunson was unloading a massive stack of sheet rock at the local gypsum plant when the load began to shift. He moved his lower body against the pile in an attempt to stabilize it, but more than 2,000 pounds of sheet rock toppled over and collapsed on his right leg, snapping it in two places. His first thought was, I'll never play basketball again. He stayed in a cast for more than two years due to complications in setting the fractures, and even after the cast was removed, he walked with a marked limp.

His dreams of professional basketball shattered, Brunson opted to stay at Hardin-Simmons, get a masters degree in education and look for a coaching job somewhere in West Texas. An avid poker player since high school, he turned to the game to cover his expenses and satisfy his competitive desires. Poker was expressly prohibited at Hardin-Simmons, but Brunson dominated the clandestine games on campus and began driving to other colleges around the state on weekends, ostensibly to visit friends but primarily to sit in on their more lucrative games.

Upon graduation, he was offered a coaching position in Dalhart, a town of about 5,000 at the tip of the Texas panhandle. The starting salary was $4,800. He couldn't believe it; he made more than that playing poker. So instead of coaching he took the short-lived job selling office supplies in Fort Worth.

On Exchange Avenue, when he managed to steer clear of the cheats and robbers, he scraped together a couple of hundred bucks each week playing dime-ante Lowball and Seven-Card Stud. Slowly he moved downtown to the dollar-ante games against doctors and lawyers, and then started making the circuit around the state. (The games were always no-limit, as was the custom in Texas.) Brunson relished the life of a professional gambler, betting on sports, pool and golf when he wasn't at the poker table. He befriended Brian "Sailor" Roberts, and the two became partners in a bookmaking business. They set up shop in San Angelo and soon thereafter expanded the partnership to include Amarillo Slim.

The men "faded the white line" across Texas and the Southwest for six years, playing all night and sleeping all day. Brunson recalls one summer in which he rarely saw the sun. He approached the experience as more than an adventure and a living; it was an invaluable classroom for studying the intricacies of poker. Following each night's game, he and Slim would rent a room at the local Roadway Inn and painstakingly evaluate their play. "We discussed almost every hand that we played every night," Brunson says. "We didn't have any computers or books, so we had to figure it all out ourselves." After one game, for example, Slim and Doyle disagreed about how to play a pair with an inside straight draw if they suspected an opponent held a pair of Aces. So if the flop was 10-8-7 and Slim held Jack-10, he had a pair but still trailed the Aces. Since he could still pick up two pair, three of a kind or maybe make the straight, Slim liked to play the hand aggressively. Brunson preferred to fold and get out of the way of the Aces, reasoning that there was a less than 50/50 chance of making a hand better than a pair of Aces. Back in the motel room, they dealt out the hand hundreds of times to determine the probability that the Aces could be beaten. As it turned out, Doyle was right.

In 1960, in the midst of his partnership with Slim and Sailor, a newly married Brunson awoke with what he thought was a bad cold. Two weeks of antibiotics did not help, and a doctor scheduled him for surgery to remove the suspicious lump on his neck. When they opened him up, surgeons found that cancer had spread from the base of his brain throughout his chest. He was given four months to live, and made a list of pallbearers for his impending funeral. "Doyle made a lot of tough collections [for the bookmaking operation] in that period," Slim recalls. "It's hard to say no to a man who tells you he is going to die."

Then a funny thing happened on the way to the grave: Brunson flew to the acclaimed M.D. Anderson Cancer Center in Houston for a radical neck operation that was supposed to prolong his life by a few more months. During the surgery, the doctors were astonished to find the cancer was completely gone.

Doctors couldn't explain the spontaneous remission, but Brunson credited his wife, Louise, a deeply religious woman who prayed constantly for his survival. Brunson had grown up in a religious home and believed in the power of prayer, yet he saw his recovery at the time as more of a mystery than a miracle. Either way, he won 54 sessions in a row after he returned to poker and made enough money in the process to pay off his medical bills. He later wrote, "I was reading my competitors more accurately and I felt a self-assurance I had never experienced. My brush with death had apparently triggered innate abilities I never knew I had."

Before his scrape with death, Brunson considered himself merely an above-average player and pondered a return to the nine-to-five world. After his recovery and amazing winning streak, he gambled ever higher and his play grew increasingly audacious. He pushed the envelope as far as he could because, in his mind, he was unbeatable.

THE PARTNERSHIP WITH Slim and Sailor broke up in 1964, but not before Brunson perfected a daring approach to no-limit Texas Hold 'Em that transformed the way it was played. Brunson was naturally aggressive, but he also understood from his years dealing out thousands of hands manually in dingy motel rooms that his style was strategically sound. He understood the game intellectually in a way few players did at that time. Puggy Pearson, to name one, was also extremely aggressive, but about as capable of articulating his strategy as a jungle cat is of explaining his hunting techniques—he simply acted on instinct. Brunson, on the other hand, crafted a game plan, one that he believed created a mathematical and psychological advantage for him over his opponents. It was essentially this: Raise at almost every opportunity, and in so doing steal dozens of small pots. It took guts, as it virtually required him to enter the majority of pots with bad cards. But it made sense mathematically, because when an opponent challenged him, he could afford to gamble even without the best hand since he had the financial cushion from having picked up a succession of small pots.

"I'm reaching out and picking up small pots all the time," he once wrote. "I'm always betting at those pots . . . hammering at them. And I don't want anyone to stop me from doing that. I don't want anyone to defeat my style of play."

Brunson also found opportunities in the game that less curious minds had overlooked, most notably demonstrated in his attachment to so-called baby connectors, which he considered his favorite type of starting hand. Baby connectors are small suited cards that, with a favorable flop, could make a straight flush, a flush, or a straight. For example, a 6 and 7 of clubs: Most players would see little cards like that and immediately fold. Brunson played them whenever it was reasonably cheap to do so (less than 5 percent of his available chips was his general guideline). The reasoning here was that a good flop gave him an above-average chance to beat players who were sitting on big pairs. If the flop didn't substantially help his hand, he could easily fold without having invested a mountain of chips. "They never used to play hands like that," Brunson told writer A. Alvarez in his 1983 book, *The Biggest Game in Town.* "When they raised, they always had big cards. So if you came in with small cards for a low amount of money, you could just break them. It was only a matter of time. It was so easy, it was like stealing."

In 1977, Brunson decided to codify his poker principles in a book geared toward advanced players. He recruited five other leading pros to write chapters in the book, which he called *How I Made $1,000,000 Playing Poker.* Mike Caro, the "mad genius of poker," who went on to write a handful of well-respected books on the game, took on the draw poker chapter; Chip Reese, considered by many the best all-around poker player in the world, wrote Seven-Card Stud; the late Joey

Hawthorne wrote Lowball; David Sklansky, who eventually became the game's premier theorist and the author of nine books, tackled Hi/Lo Split; and Bobby Baldwin, the 1982 world champion and future casino executive, handled limit Hold 'Em. Brunson himself wrote the final chapter on his specialty, no-limit Texas Hold 'Em.

Brunson told his co-authors not to sign on if they planned to withhold any secrets, and they didn't. Each chapter is considered the definitive manual for how to play that game. The overall approach was summed up in the introduction: "Timid players don't win in high-stakes poker." At almost 600 pages, the book is not for beginners, but it's an exhaustive guide to finding and creating edges in the toughest games.

Predictably, Brunson gambled—aggressively—even in his approach to publishing. He spurned the New York conglomerates that wanted to publish the book and instead rented a suite of offices, hired a staff, and started his own publishing company. The book took a year to compile and a $400,000 investment from Brunson. When it was released, he placed ads in every American newspaper with a circulation above 100,000 and charged an astronomical $100 per copy. After the first edition sold out, he changed the title to the slightly catchier *Super/System: A Course in Power Poker*. Over the next 27 years it sold more than 200,000 copies and, in 2004, the year poker exploded as a pop-culture phenomenon, spent most of the year in the top 50 of Amazon's sales rankings.

For Brunson, though, the success of the book was a mixed blessing. He had spelled out his secret strategies, and the newcomers who came along in the 1980s and '90s played loose and aggressive, just as he recommended. He was forced to change his game as a result, but fortunately he could turn to his own book for advice: "Play mostly tight in a loose game and mostly loose in a tight game."

TIRED OF THE hazards of the crossroader's life, Brunson moved his family to Las Vegas in 1973. During his time traveling across the Southwest, he had been robbed three times at gunpoint, once at knifepoint, and beaten several other times. Making matters worse, in 1961, the federal government passed a law making it a felony to carry gambling equipment across state lines, so he could conceivably go to prison if caught with a deck of cards while traveling from state to state. Still, he didn't see Las Vegas as anything more than a safe haven.

"It was just a place to play," he says. "I was never into casino games. There were a lot of women, but I was married and didn't get into that. Never was a drinker, never did drugs. To me, it was just another poker game."

In Las Vegas, though, the game never ended. Brunson savored the marathon battles that tested his will as much as his ability. Sometimes his injured leg would begin to ache when he sat in certain positions, but he refused to shift, and stoically absorbed the pain just to see how long he could do it. For more than 10 years, he went to the Dunes poker room almost every day. "It felt like an office," he says. "I remember Sarge [Ferris] saying he started up his car each day and it went straight to the Dunes. That's the way it was."

The poker games lasted most of the night, and Brunson spent his days on the golf course, where he rarely teed it up for less than $50,000. He was a solid player with a single-digit handicap, but was renowned as a clutch performer, at his best when the match was on the line. "It's like you have a quarterback with all the talent in the world and he never becomes a great quarterback. And then you see a guy who wins the Super Bowl because he just makes the right play at the right time," Tomko says. "Some people have the ability to do things and concentrate at the important times. That's what made Doyle great."

His competitive streak—in cards, golf, and business—served him well throughout his career, but on rare occasions it got the best of him.

One afternoon in the mid-1970s, he played golf with Chip Reese and the high-rolling gambler Billy Baxter at the Las Vegas Country Club. After the match, the three retired to the clubhouse to play seven-card knock rummy, a form of gin. Baxter and Reese were both excellent at the game, and while Brunson was good, he was not in their class. He quickly got down about $60,000. He wanted to double the stakes and before long he was in the hole almost $400,000.

"I know you all got to be fucking me some kind of way," Brunson complained. He made Baxter and Reese take off their pants and got down on the floor to inspect them for wires or a signaling device in case there was a camera in the ceiling.

When the manager came by to say he was closing the clubhouse for the night, Brunson convinced him to lock the doors and leave them there until morning so they could continue their match. The manager agreed, which ultimately cost Brunson another $400,000.

Brunson's high-risk, high-reward lifestyle earned him awe and admiration around Las Vegas, but he was painfully aware that the straight world still perceived him as a scoundrel. His father, who died in the late 1950s, strenuously disapproved of Doyle's vocation, as did many of his friends and family back in West Texas. So although Brunson was considered the world's best no-limit Hold 'Em player, and therefore was a favorite to win each year he entered the World Series, he wanted no part of the notoriety that went along with the championship. In 1972, he bowed out of the tournament after making it to the final three along with Puggy Pearson and his old partner, Amarillo Slim. Publicly, Brunson claimed he was sick. The truth, he now acknowledges, is that he simply saw no value in winning. "I didn't want to embarrass my family, because people looked down on you. The common working guy looked down on gamblers," he says.

After Slim captured the title that year and became something of a national celebrity, poker gained at least a degree of respectability. Brunson then felt free to show the world his talents, and in 1976 and '77 he became the first back-to-back champion. (Sort of: Johnny Moss actually won back-to-back World Series the first two years the tournament existed, but the rules were different for him. The first title was awarded after a vote from the players, rather than in a freeze-out, as in ensuing years.)

Amazingly, both of Brunson's World Series–winning hands came when he made a full house after holding the same two marginal cards, a 10 and a 2. Each time, Brunson basically just got lucky, but only because he had put himself in position to win big pots by constantly pressuring his opponents. In 1976, he was heads-up with Houston car dealer Jesse Alto and had just taken a giant pot. Alto was known as a steamer—a player who gets upset after losing a big pot and lets it affect his play—so Brunson called Alto's pre-flop bet with 10-2. The flop came Ace-Jack-10, and Alto bet again. Brunson called, not knowing Alto held the Ace-Jack. The turn was a 2, giving Brunson two pair. Alto pushed the rest of his chips into the middle, and Brunson called with the weaker hand. A 10 came on the river.

The next year, against 26-year-old Gary "Bones" Berland, Brunson was in the big blind when dealt the 10-2 and got to see the flop for free when Berland didn't raise. The flop came 10-8-5, giving Brunson the top pair but giving Berland two pair, 8s and 5s. Both players checked, hoping to trap the other. The turn was a 2, giving Brunson the better hand, but Berland moved all-in and Brunson called. The lucky 10 came on the river once again. A 10-2 starting hand in Hold 'Em is now known as "a Doyle Brunson."

Though he long ago quit playing in the vast majority of World Series events, Brunson ultimately compiled a record nine bracelets, a feat later matched only by Johnny Chan and Phil Hellmuth, both of whom played many more tournaments to get there. Brunson has earned more than $1.8 million in the World Series during his career, a hefty sum, but a mere fraction of the money he's accumulated while presiding over the Big Game.

THERE WAS SPECULATION that 2004 could be Brunson's last showing in the World Series. (He had put in only a cursory appearance in 2003, and before that had not played in it for several years, out of respect for his good friend Jack Binion, who was forced out of the family-owned Horseshoe after a dispute with his sister, Becky Behnen.) Thirty-four years earlier, Brunson had played in the tournament when it consisted of eight players and received virtually no publicity; now here he was again in 2004 and it boasted more than 2,600 players and a flood of international media.

It had been a tough month for Brunson, one of his all-time worst performances in the Big Game, and he was starting to question whether he could compete with the young bucks who swarmed the tournament room. For one, he was in poor physical condition. His

round, jowly face and ample midsection over the years had long rein-
forced his stature as a sort of poker Buddha. He always hated being
overweight—he concocted elaborate proposition bets as incentive to
shed pounds, and even once won $1 million by losing 100 pounds—
but he was a notoriously prodigious eater, with a special craving for
sweets. Now, due to a combination of his weight and bad leg, his physical stamina was diminished and he was forced to commute the 100
yards from the Golden Nugget to the Horseshoe on a motorized
scooter.

Of course, poker also requires a level of mental stamina uncommon to men Brunson's age. He says he wants to play until he is 80, but
knows that even the slightest reduction in brain power can be fatal at
the table. He saw it firsthand when Johnny Moss lost a lifetime of
poker winnings in his twilight years. "I have asked my best friends, 'If
you think that I'm losing it, please, please tell me.' Because most people, after they turn 50, they start declining," Brunson says, not men-
tioning that the only people in a position to tell him are the very ones
who could most benefit from his lost abilities.

In spite of all that, Brunson was still very much in contention on
the fifth day of the tournament. With a crutch by his side and a World
Poker Tour cap sitting crookedly on his head, he took his place at the
table with a group of unknowns who were playing in the most important poker tournament of their lives. Wives and friends whispered
hand-by-hand updates into their cell phones, and ESPN cameras
rushed around the room to capture the drama as players were eliminated one by one. Brunson, meanwhile, seemed unimpressed by the
prospect of winning the first prize of $5 million.

"I'd just as soon be across the street [at the Golden Nugget in the
Big Game]," he groused to the kid seated next to him. The kid, with a
hat pulled low and mirror sunglasses covering his eyes, didn't seem to
understand. He nodded, as if that were an option for him too. Struggling for conversation, the kid remarked that he was mentally and
physically exhausted from a week of sustained intensity. "I was playing 12 to 14 hours a day for a month before this. I was wore out before
I even started," Brunson replied, as he raked in another pile of chips
that got caught in his orbit.

With each exit from the tourney growing in importance, tournament director Matt Savage began giving a play-by-play over the public address system each time a player's all-in bet was called. Shortly after the dinner break, a player at a table adjacent to Brunson pushed all his chips to the center, and a crowd gathered to see if the field would lose yet another combatant. In the midst of the commotion, Brunson looked down to find pocket 10s in his hand. He moved his entire chip stack, almost $200,000, all-in.

The player in the small blind at Brunson's table, a bearded youngster named Brad Berman, was distracted by the tumult at the next table and didn't hear Brunson's bet. Had he known the legend was all-in, he would have folded, but instead he announced a raise. When Berman realized his mistake, he immediately tried to rescind his bet. Chaos ensued, and the dealer called the tournament director for an opinion.

Brunson sat silently as the officials discussed the situation over his left shoulder and players from around the room rushed over to coffee-house about the right decision. Brunson knew his hand was probably better than Berman's but also that Berman almost certainly held at least one high card that could pair on the flop and end his tournament. After several minutes, the tournament director issued his ruling: Berman was obligated to call the bet. The reasoning was that his raise had signaled his intention to play the hand, and that intention held true regardless of the size of Brunson's bet. Sheepishly, Berman flipped over Ace-7. Brunson was still a slight favorite to win the hand, but when he saw Berman's Ace, he grimaced.

The dealer dealt out three cards facedown, and then turned them over and spread them across the felt. The first card visible was an Ace. Brunson could survive only with a 10 on the turn or the river, but it didn't come. He was eliminated in 53rd place, good enough for a prize of $151,000—or about 20 big bets in the Big Game. He later said the incident was "the strangest thing that's ever happened to me."

Brunson got up from his chair and wedged his crutch under his left arm as Savage announced his departure to the crowd. Play stopped, and the assembled spectators and players alike rose to their feet for an extended standing ovation. Brunson tipped his hat and smiled broadly. It was like Babe Ruth leaving Yankee Stadium.

"It was nice to know that all those guys in there knew me, and they were appreciative of the contributions I had made," he said afterward. "It was kind of a touching moment for me. Could be the end of an era. Who knows?"

Following the ovation, Brunson got on his scooter and drove across the street to the Golden Nugget, where he played Chinese poker heads-up against Phil Ivey until three in the morning.

Chip Reese, 2004, in Tunica, Mississippi

Four

CHIP REESE

Golden Touch

An Ivy League whiz kid outwits the old

guard, survives Vegas's dark side,

and proves that the game in your head is

as important as the one on the table.

THE LAS VEGAS STRIP PULSED with the irrepressible riffs of Elton John's "Crocodile Rock" as record numbers of tourists motored up and down the eight lane boulevard, slowing to gawk at Caesars Palace, the opulent resort that had set a new standard in town for themed excess. Viewed from the Strip, the Palace's towering marble statues, 18 spurting fountains, and driveway lined with imported Italian cypress trees provided just a taste of the Roman decadence inside. A few blocks away, secretive billionaire Kirk Kerkorian was planning the groundbreaking of his monstrous MGM Grand, the largest hotel in the world. And downtown at the Golden Nugget, an ambitious young entrepreneur named Steve Wynn was laying the foundation for his own empire of glitz.

It was the spring of 1973, the dawning of a new era for Vegas. But across the street from Caesars, in the nondescript poker room of the Flamingo, 23-year-old David "Chip" Reese remained blissfully unaware of the monumental changes underfoot. He just wanted to get into the Big Game, the highest game in town, which was hosted by Johnny Moss and played under a cloud of cigarette smoke against the back wall. With cherubic Midwestern features and blond hair draped fashionably over his ears, Reese looked like a young man with the world at his fingertips—and he was. A recent Ivy League grad, poised to attend Stanford Law School, he stood out like a choir boy alongside the wily Texans and furtive New Yorkers who populated Moss's room.

In rapidly transforming Vegas, the Flamingo was stubbornly old-school: Red Buttons and Connie Stevens played the showroom, the gambling floor was more functional than swanky, and mobster Meyer Lansky, who bankrolled the property at its inception, was reputed to be still skimming profits. Management let Moss run his tiny five-table poker room however he pleased. White-haired and curmudgeonly, Moss didn't care much for outsiders. He kept a pistol in the top drawer of a desk at the front of the room, and set aside three of the five tables for so-called "snatch games," in which dealers raked as much as 75 percent of the pot from unwitting tourists. When the Gaming Control Board finally required Moss to post a sign explaining the room's exorbitant rake policy, it read: RAKE: ZERO TO 100 PERCENT.

As Reese approached the Big Game, he was predictably shooed away by one of the shift bosses and forced to spy the action from his seat at a $10/$20 Seven-Card Stud table. Even from there, Reese could see that Moss and his compatriots casually splashed $100 black chips around like quarters, while the grinders in his game handled chips as if they were manhole covers. Joining Moss were poker luminaries Doyle Brunson and Puggy Pearson, along with pool hustler and high-stakes gambler Nicky Vachiano. They played Seven-Card Hi/Lo Split, meaning the best high hand and the best low hand shared the pot evenly. It was a relatively new game in Las Vegas, but Reese had played it frequently during his years at Dartmouth. To his astonishment, he noticed that Moss and the others were playing the game unwisely. The surest strategy, Reese knew, was to consistently aim for the best low hand and throw away most candidates for the high, since it was much harder to get outdrawn with a strong low hand. He watched a while longer and became convinced that he was right; these poker legends didn't know what they were doing!

Reese called Danny Robison, his partner from Ohio, and said he wanted to take a shot at the Big Game. The two friends had been scorching the low-limit tables during their first weeks in town and they had run their bankroll up to $80,000.

"Danny, you're not going to believe this," Reese said. "You've got to come look at this game." He pleaded with Robison to bring him $15,000 so he could buy in.

"Chip, they're playing $400/$800—we could go broke," said a groggy Robison, who had been sleeping away the early morning hours.

"The way these guys are playing, I honestly don't think I could get unlucky enough to lose," Reese replied.

Robison reluctantly acquiesced, and a few minutes later Reese steeled his nerves and approached the table, a naive young David stepping into a circle of Goliaths.

Moss and the others gladly made room; they had seen his kind before. "Our games consist of hometown champions," Brunson said later. "One guy is the best in Albuquerque, and he says, 'You know, I beat everybody back home.' So he comes here to play. There's a guy from Dallas, a guy from Santa Fe. The guys who are the best in their towns all come here to try their luck against the best. Most of them don't make it."

Reese, his heart flailing against the walls of his chest, put up his $15,000 and the dealer pushed several towering stacks of $100 chips in front of him. He warned himself to think just about the game, not the amount of money at stake.

Once the cards were dealt, he proceeded cautiously, sticking to his strategy of playing mostly low hands. Within the first two hours, he built his stack to more than $20,000. Robison sat behind him, anxiously sweating each hand.

Then Reese was dealt Ace-2-3-4 of hearts, and a 6 of another suit—an almost unbeatable low hand. Moss and Brunson were fighting for the high hand, with Moss representing a flush, and Brunson three of a kind. Pearson showed 8-7, ordinarily a strong low hand, and he dared Reese to beat it. All three bet fast and furious—raise, reraise, reraise. Though Reese was a lock for the low hand, he couldn't build the pot any higher because the betting was always capped by the time it got around to him.

The dealer dealt the last card and Reese placed it horizontally in front of him, face down. Once again, the table bet aggressively—raise, reraise, reraise. With five low cards already in his hand, the last card could not hurt Reese, but there was one card in the deck—the 5 of hearts—that would allow him to make a straight flush and scoop the entire enormous pot. He squeezed the card and turned its edge up slowly until he could see a glorious red heart perched in each of the two corners. It was the 5 of hearts. Reese made an Ace-to-the-5 straight flush, known as the wheel, the best possible hand, because it's guaranteed to win the low and will almost always win the high.

He called the final bets and proudly displayed his cards. Moss, Brunson, and Pearson could do little but gape—and watch him take their money.

Reese scooped more than $35,000 from the center of the table, and 30 years later, after literally millions of hands, he says that remains the only time he caught a straight flush wheel in a Hi/Lo Split game.

In one amazing hand, Reese more than tripled his money. But he was not done. That game was on a Thursday. By the end of the weekend, he had run his $15,000 buy-in up to $390,000. And for the next six months, he and Robison torched the Las Vegas poker scene like no one before or since.

"Everything we touched turned to gold," Reese says. "We just couldn't do anything wrong. Whatever we played, we won."

The old-timers came up with a nickname for the dynamic duo: the Gold Dust Twins.

BY 2004, AT age 54, Reese was no longer a wunderkind—more like an elder statesman. Aside from Doyle Brunson, he has played for more money for a longer time than anyone. Though largely unknown to the poker groupies who judge the best players by how often they appear on television, he is recognized by many as the best all-around poker player in the world. He was the youngest player ever inducted into the Poker Hall of Fame, and is renowned for his ability to play virtually all games well. In addition to poker, he is among the world's best at backgammon and gin.

"I've never walked up to a game and said, 'What are you playing?'" he once said. "I don't care what the game is. I walk up to the game and say, 'How big is it? Deal me in.' I don't care who's playing."

Reese's unshakable self-confidence stems from a lifetime of almost painless achievement. He was the homecoming king, debate champion, and football star in high school. He breezed through Dartmouth despite putting in more hours in the fraternity card room than the classroom. In Las Vegas, even after his precocious start, his trajectory was consistently upward.

To his peers, Reese is the perfect player. His style is impeccably smooth, to the point that it's almost boring. He rarely bets with the worst hand and, when he runs a bluff, he almost never has to show it. "Chip makes it look easy," says rising star Daniel Negreanu. "It is so effortless. He doesn't make any mistakes—ever. When you watch him play, it's not spectacular. It seems almost blasé. He plays the game properly."

Reese may be admired less for what he does than what he doesn't do: He doesn't steam. When a player steams, he loses his cool. Everyone does it to some degree after suffering a bad beat or making a critical mistake. When some players steam, they play hands they ordinarily would not. Other players fold competitive hands because they assume their luck is running bad and they'll just get outdrawn anyway. The trick is to play as consistently as possible regardless of streaks, and Reese does just that almost every day.

"The worst I have ever seen him do is rap the table a little hard

with his cards and say, 'You got it,' " says Jennifer Harman, the only female regular in the Big Game. "That's the worst I've ever seen him do.
I don't know if it slides right off him or his stomach is in knots, but you
would never know it."

Reese takes great pride in his steadiness at the table. He says,
more than any other factor, it is the secret to his success. Maybe that's
why, instead of rehashing a career of seven-figure triumphs, he likes to
talk about his losses.

In 2003, Reese joined the poker elite in the Big Game at Sam's
Town, an off-Strip casino with a low-limit poker room that hosted the
heavyweights so that Bobby Baldwin, president of the Bellagio, could
play without a perceived home-field advantage. For three weeks, while
the room's regulars pushed chips around in the $1/$2 games, the
world's best players slugged it out in a corner. Reese endured an endless run of bad cards and worse luck that led to six-figure losses almost
every day. When the game finally broke up, he was down $2.5 million.

To hear him tell it, he had played some of the best poker of his life.

"I really believe that if someone else had my cards, they would
have lost $7 million," he says. "It's one of the great things in gambling
that you learn. If you are the greatest player in the world, you might
win 65 days and lose 35. If you let if affect you every one of those 35
days, you are not going to have a very happy life; and when you do
have those bad days, you are going to be playing at your worst if you
can't walk away. It's going to be a disaster. I've always said that if you
took the eight best players in the world and locked them in a room for
10 hours every day for a year, there are probably two or three of them
who would wind up with all the money—not because they are the
best players but because they have the most character. When things
are bad, they are going to hang in there and play close to 100 percent
of their game. A great player might play at 98 percent and his drop-off
is down to 90 percent—you just can't help it, when you never catch a
card and you never make a play. Some guys who are 98 percent players
might drop down to 65 or 70 percent.

"I don't outplay anybody or make these giant superstar plays that
no one else can understand. But at the end of the day or the end of the
year, if you played a videotape back, you'd see not necessarily that I

am doing something so much greater than someone else when I am at my best but that I am deteriorating less when I am not."

Those are lessons learned from a lifetime of gambling.

WHEN HER FIVE-year-old son was in kindergarten, Reese's mother answered the door at her suburban Dayton, Ohio, home to find the next-door neighbor, a fifth-grader named Sherman, standing outside.

"Mrs. Reese, I have to talk to you," Sherman said.

"What is it, Sherman?"

"It's about Chip. I think you should know that he's been gambling with all the kids."

Mrs. Reese dismissed Sherman, saying her son didn't have any money, but Sherman explained that they played for baseball cards on a front porch down the street.

"Well, that's good, Sherman," she said. "This is a valuable lesson to him: You teach him not to gamble. You go ahead and take all his baseball cards, and that'll be a lesson to him."

Sherman shuffled his feet. "Well, really Mrs. Reese, that's not why I'm here. He just beat us all and he has all our baseball cards. We'd like to get them back."

The next year, the young hustler contracted rheumatic fever. Doctors prescribed a year of bed rest, and he spent much of that year playing card and board games with his mother, developing an ability to "see" moves two and three steps ahead and feel out his opponent for strengths and weaknesses. That year, he says, created the foundation for his career as a gambler.

Reese matured into a precocious teenager, both socially adept and wickedly smart. He won the Ohio state debate championship for Centennial High School, starred in the school play, and started both ways on the football team. On Friday nights, after dropping off their dates, Reese and his friends gathered for all-night poker sessions, where Reese was the usual victor.

As a high school senior, Reese met Danny Robison on the putting green at the city-owned Community Golf Center. Robison, at 24, boasted a lifestyle that would be the envy of any red-blooded American male with a healthy dose of gamble in him. A one-time city golf champion, Robison played golf by day, cards by night, and strutted around town in technicolor clothes and drove a mint-green Lincoln Continental with a push-button drop-top. When he wasn't hustling, he chased girls and partied at a go-go bar in Dayton owned by a small-time smut peddler named Larry Flynt.

Enticing the youngster into a modest wager, Robison beat Reese in a putting contest (Robison agreed to putt left-handed), and later schooled him at gin. Robison drove Reese home so he could collect his $35, but Reese ran inside and refused to come out, knowing that the older Robison did not dare confront Reese's parents about a gambling debt he'd hustled out of their underage child.

Reese eventually paid the debt, and Robison took him under his wing. After getting wind of this, Reese's conservative parents hired a private detective to find out more about Robison (it wasn't hard—he had a lengthy rap sheet of gambling arrests), and eventually their son was forced to sneak out of his bedroom at night to go explore Dayton's thriving underground poker scene with his new friend.

In the 1960s and '70s, Dayton was a poker hotbed, with as many as a dozen regular games in a city of slightly more than 100,000. (In addition to Robison and Reese, the city produced Mike Sexton, future host of the *World Poker Tour* and a World Series bracelet winner.) And, significantly, the game of choice was almost always Seven-Card Stud. The best game, hosted by a good friend of Robison's, started on Friday night and ran continuously until Monday morning.

Even as the youngest player in the room, Reese stood out.

"He was a real likable kid, and I recognized his talent in poker before he even knew about it," Robison says. "He had the ability, which most poker players don't have, to win when he didn't have the best hand."

One night Robison staked Reese with $100 in a game and then went out drinking. When he returned, Reese was almost out of money and involved in a big pot. Reese paired Deuces on his last up card and bet aggressively, down to his last $2. His opponent showed two Aces, but folded. Reese only held the pair of 2s.

"That's the mark of a great player," Robison says. "It was purely instinctive."

After high school, Reese moved on to the bucolic Hanover, New Hampshire, campus of Dartmouth College, where he joined a minority of middle-class overachievers amid a sea of pampered blue bloods. On only a partial scholarship, he worked in the school cafeteria to cover his tuition and got by on a weekly $12 spending-money check from his father.

Early in his freshman year, he learned of a $50 buy-in game held in Brown Hall. For a month, he saved the weekly checks from his father to get in the game, but promptly blew his bankroll within 20 minutes of sitting down. While many 18-year-olds would have been discouraged, Reese was undaunted. He returned the next month and walked away with $500. He later pledged the Beta Theta Pi fraternity and dominated the regular games in the frat house card room. By his sophomore year, he maintained a wrinkled notepad with lengthy lists of the debts from his fraternity brothers.

Few actually paid him in cash, but he established a barter system that allowed him to live like a Rockefeller. If he wanted to borrow a car to visit a girlfriend, he hit up one of his debtors in exchange for knocking a few dollars off the tab. His favorite perk came on Friday nights, when he liked to eat dinner while watching his favorite TV show, *Wild Wild West*, starring Robert Conrad. According to fraternity rules, only the seniors could use the kitchen in the house, so Reese would have the seniors who were in debt to him prepare elaborate dinners. Then he'd have them present the food for his inspection; he would choose among the offerings and adjust the debts in his notepad accordingly.

After graduation, the fraternity renamed its card room the "David E. Reese Memorial Card Room."

REESE INITIALLY PLANNED to be a lawyer, but got wait-listed by Stanford Law School. He expected to eventually be admitted—the father of one of his college roommates was a top Stanford official—but opted to spend a year in Phoenix, living with another college friend and selling real estate. On weekends, he drove north to Las Vegas and blew his earnings at the blackjack and craps tables.

Before long Reese convinced Robison to come taste the action out west as well, and soon the two of them were sharing an $8 room at the Stardust and splitting their winnings from the $10/$20 tables. They quickly found that the level of Seven-Card Stud they were used to playing in Dayton was far superior to that in Las Vegas. Starting with a meager $800, they played in 12-hour shifts with the same chips: Robison would play for 12 hours, then Reese would take over for another 12 while Robison slept. The pattern continued for several weeks, and they built their bankroll into almost $80,000.

Then Reese struck gold in the Hi/Lo game at the Flamingo. After that, the sharks lined up to take a bite out of the Gold Dust Twins. Reese and Robison played for bigger stakes, but continued to play in shifts against all comers. "What happens in this town is that when a new talent comes in, until you prove yourself or are accepted, everybody thinks it's just short-term luck and they are convinced they can beat you," Reese says. "That's what happened with Danny and me. They didn't mind that we played in shifts, because we were young kids and we won all their money and they wanted their money back."

On more than one occasion, Reese and Robison played Amarillo Slim and Doyle Brunson in a tag-team match—Doyle matched up against Chip at one end of the table, and Slim squared off with Robison at the other, and vice versa. Even the two wiliest veterans were no match for the whiz kids.

"What they did to this town was unreal," Slim says. "They did the same thing that we did, only years later."

The action inevitably dried up as the competition got sick of losing. Card rooms changed their policies to forbid playing in shifts, a rule that remains in effect to this day. In retrospect, this marked a fork in the road for the two pals. While Robison had long shown a taste for drugs and hookers—he had even convinced Reese to let him fund his dalliances out of their combined bankroll—he now sunk deeper into the Vegas underworld, content to party and ravage the few who would take him on in Seven-Card Stud or gin. Meanwhile, Reese made a conscious effort to broaden his market.

"Chip loved learning new games," Robison recalls. "I didn't care about learning new games. All I cared about was getting high."

In order to entice action, Reese negotiated deals with opponents: He would play 30 minutes of Seven-Card Stud and then 30 minutes of Deuce-to-Seven Lowball, Razz, or whatever the other guy wanted.

Reese wanted to be able to play wherever the stakes were highest—regardless of the particular game. He took some lumps during the learning process, but, as he had as a rheumatic child with no entertainment except a deck of cards, he eventually mastered virtually every form of poker.

NOT LONG AFTER Reese arrived in Las Vegas, Doyle Brunson asked him to write a chapter on Seven-Card Stud for his seminal strategy book, *Super/System*.

In his chapter, Reese detailed the strategies he had learned in the card rooms of Dayton, methods that had not yet been adopted in Las Vegas when he arrived. Most of the top Vegas players at the time were veterans of no-limit Texas Hold 'Em, and carried over the same tactics to Seven-Card Stud: waiting for big hands, bluffing only on select occasions. "People were like open books," Reese says. "They didn't put a lot of deception into their play."

Reese advocated an aggressive approach—Robison describes it as a style with "a lot of motion"—that required playing a lot of hands and changing tactics constantly to confuse the competition.

"You want to do the wrong thing enough that it makes people aware that you will do those things," Reese says. "You have to be a little bit of an actor. The idea is to create an image of yourself over time, and then when you do things that are not part of your image, they work and other players never see them."

Reese stresses two seemingly contradictory principles: the importance of forcing other players out of the pot early in a hand, and the importance of squeezing extra bets out of your opponents late in a hand.

To illustrate the first point, Reese details his strategy for playing a split pair of Aces (that is, one Ace showing and one in the hole). This is obviously a strong hand and most gamblers would play it aggressively.

But Reese advises making the strongest move possible—check-raising—on the second betting round (Fourth Street) and then leading out with a bet on Fifth Street. The idea is to eliminate as many players as possible early by signaling strength. The reasoning: There is little chance that someone else has a better hand at this point, but a decent chance that someone can make one if they stay in the hand until the end. As for the opponents who elect to stay in the hand, you've at least forced them to pay the maximum price to see additional cards. You've also laid the groundwork to perhaps see free cards later in the hand, because your opponents might check to you in anticipation of a raise. If you haven't improved your hand, you can also check and see the next card without investing more money in the pot.

In contrast, Reese advocates playing rolled-up trips (when your two hole cards match one up card) much more slowly. He says to check or merely call on Third and Fourth streets to avoid tipping the strength of your hand. The goal is the opposite of the previous situation: You don't want to eliminate players by giving away the strength of your hand. More often than not, three of a kind will be good enough to win, and you want to keep as many players involved as possible. On Fifth and Sixth streets, you then raise aggressively, knowing any remaining opponents are likely to call in order to try to make their draws or improve on a big pair. The danger to this strategy, of course, is that by slow-playing the trips you allow your opponents to take a lot of cards and perhaps make a big hand. That's an acceptable risk to take in your quest to build as big a pot as possible. "Remember, you are only going to get so many hands each session," he wrote, "and so you must maximize the profit from each of them. Figuring out ways to get double bets (a bet plus a raise) out of your opponents on Fifth and Sixth streets is the best way to achieve this end."

IN 1974, REESE won a Seven-Card Stud tournament at the Sahara with a first prize of $100,000. A writer from *Sports Illustrated* covered the event, and included Reese in a profile of the new breed of young gamblers, along with Robison and Baldwin. When Reese's dad saw the piece, he flipped out—he believed his son was living in Phoenix selling real estate, not consorting with low-lifes and degenerates. The two men did not speak for two years.

Reese, though, was in paradise. He gambled at everything—golf, gin, poker, backgammon. He even learned to count cards, which got him banned from most blackjack tables in town. But one shift boss at the Alladin refused to believe that card counters could beat a two-deck shoe. Along with a new running buddy, a New York mathematical savant named Stu Ungar, Reese became a regular player during the shift boss's midnight-to-10 shift. Before the boss got wise, Reese and Ungar had made hundreds of thousands of dollars.

With some of that money, Reese and Robison (who remained close despite their increasingly different priorities) bought a house together in a fashionable Las Vegas neighborhood five minutes from the Strip. They converted the carport into a party room, outfitted it with a pinball-machine and a pool table, carted in a stockpile of booze, and then opened it up to an endless parade of showgirls, gamblers, and hangers-on. Eventually cocaine was added to the menu as well.

In the 1970s and early '80s, cocaine was as prominent in the poker rooms as bottled water is today. To poker players, it was the perfect drug: It kept them awake for days at a time and made them feel bulletproof. Those are among the qualities, of course, that also make the drug nearly impossible to manage on a strictly recreational basis. Even Reese got sucked in—though not to the extent of some of his pals. On one occasion, according to Robison, several of them (including Ungar) holed up and played an epic gin rummy match that lasted more than three weeks. They sent out for cocaine, under the condition that the losers would ultimately pick up the tab. The final bill, just for coke, was more than $90,000.

Las Vegas at the time was rife with wise guys and shakedown artists who salivated over gamblers' vast winnings. Benny Binion looked out for his old Texas cronies like Moss, Brunson, and Amarillo Slim, but the Gold Dust Twins, with their Midwestern background and fast lifestyle, were sitting ducks. They first encountered the dark side of Las Vegas after Robison beat Nicky Vachiano out of $15,000 playing gin. The next day, Vachiano left a message in verse on their answering machine:

There were two guys named Dan and Chip
And they decided to take a trip
Out to Vegas, they came to play
And they won, day after day
Their play became known as being quite tricky
But they better not fuck with gray-haired Nicky

Unbeknownst to Robison, Vachiano was connected to a low-level Mafia soldier out of Florida known as Dominick. Not long after Robison's score against Vachiano, Dominick called Robison and asked to borrow $50,000. The subtext was clear: the $50,000 bought them a little protection, but they shouldn't expect to get paid back. Robison spoke to a connected friend about the situation, and the friend said he might have a solution. He said he would reach out to Tony Spilotro, the mob enforcer who'd previously menaced Puggy Pearson and Amarillo Slim.

"I'm scared," Robison said.

"I don't blame you," the friend said. "I'm scared of [Spilotro] too. He's a killer."

According to Robison, he and Reese feared the consequences if they said no to Dominick, so they authorized their friend to speak to Spilotro. Several days later, the Gold Dust Twins showed up as agreed at a Denny's next to the Dunes hotel to discuss the "loan" with Dominick. Just as Dominick began to talk tough, Spilotro arrived.

"Okay, here's the way it's going," Spilotro told Dominick. "These boys are with me. You don't ask them for money, you don't demand any money. If I hear of you ever opening your mouth and even indicate that you might not pay them any money you lost gambling, you answer to me."

Dominick predictably backed down. When Spilotro asked him if he still needed the $50,000, Dominick said he would manage to get by without it.

Robison says Spilotro then demanded 25 percent of his and Reese's poker winnings, in exchange for his protection from the cheaters and the other Mafia muscle in town. Robison says it took them more than a year to break free of the extortion.

"We were never good friends with him. We acted like we were," Robison says. "But we were terrified, terrified of what he could do."

To most top pros, like Reese, the mob influence of the 1970s is an unpleasant chapter in poker history, especially given the newly cleaned-up image of the game. As a result, Reese refuses to discuss Spilotro. "I had a lot of trouble with [Spilotro]. Everybody did," he says.

In 1978, Spilotro was placed in Nevada's Black Book of people barred from entering its casinos (he challenged his inclusion, saying the Black Book was unconstitutional; his attorney was the future Las Vegas mayor Oscar Goodman). At about the same time, Reese was appointed to run the poker room at the Dunes, which meant that, by order of the Nevada Gaming Commission, he was not allowed to associate with anyone listed in the Black Book. Still, Spilotro continued to pester him for favors. When Reese politely declined, according to Robison, Spliotro replied, "Have a real nice life, as long as it lasts."

Spilotro never carried out the implied threat. The Chicago mob bosses wearied of his increasingly high profile and, in 1986, his body was discovered in an Indiana cornfield along with that of his brother Michael. An autopsy later showed that he had been buried alive.

As part of his new job at the Dunes, Reese was given a suite at the top of the hotel, so he and Robison sold their party house with its disco garage. Adrift from his longtime partner, Robison fell deeper and deeper into addiction. He spent less of his time playing poker and more time chasing drugs and hookers. Reese, on the other hand, quit cocaine cold turkey and reconciled with his parents. He got married and attended Bible study at the encouragement of his new best friend, Doyle Brunson. The former wunderkind matured into a poker icon.

ACCORDING TO MOST poker insiders, few people, if any, made more money than Reese playing cards through the 1980s and early 1990s. So accustomed to carrying bundles of hundreds and playing for tens of thousands each night, he forgot the value of money in the real world: He once paid a monthly water bill of more than $2,000, not knowing—or caring, it seemed—that the inflated charges were due to a broken pipe beneath his house. But even as he accumulated millions, he questioned the social value of his profession and considered walking away from the career that had made him wealthy. He called his father, the man who had once disowned him, and explained his dilemma.

"I really feel a little selfish," Reese told his father. "I don't feel like I am giving anything back to anybody. I am really thinking of going to law school."

Reese's father asked if he enjoyed what he did, and Reese said yes.

"Well then don't be an idiot," his father said. "All my friends have spent their lives working and doing things that they haven't enjoyed. They idolize you because you are doing something that you love and something that you're good at."

Reassured, Reese accepted his lot as a gambler, but drifted away from the poker scene. He shifted his emphasis to sports betting, and teamed with a Cornell-educated computer programmer who runs simulations of upcoming baseball games to find discrepancies in the lines set by bookmakers. The arrangement allowed Reese to spend more time with his children, as he could work from the comfort of his Summerlin mansion, placing his bets in the morning and coaching Little League in the afternoon. (During this time, Reese also paid for his old friend Robison to attend rehab on multiple occasions and the cure finally took hold in a radical way: Robison, who still plays poker for a living, is now a born-again Christian, and devotes most of his considerable energies to teaching Bible studies.)

Reese took a poker sabbatical in part to create a better lifestyle for himself and his family, but also because he had essentially outgrown the game. The highest stakes at the time were generally $1,000/$2,000 limit, which he says were "a pittance" in relation to his daily wagers on sports. He embodies the old saying that, in gambling, it's no fun to play unless it hurts to lose.

"I didn't have anything to prove, and the game wasn't big enough for me. It's boring to me now unless I play big," he says. "I think you have to like living on the edge to be successful at this. If I had to go play $200/$400 limit, I couldn't play, even though I know I could win. There has to be the fear of disaster on the other side. That's what makes me tick."

When the Bellagio opened in 1998, Reese returned to the Big Game, drawn by the higher stakes offered at the luxurious new property. He slipped easily back into his old role. Whereas Brunson is the grand poobah of the Big Game, Reese is its social chairman. With his natural Midwestern amiability, he is almost universally well-liked, in part because his opponents know he will not pout when he loses nor gloat when he wins. He is a master of managing table dynamics, complimenting opponents on their winning plays and assuring losers that they simply got unlucky. It's a table persona that flows out of his natural charisma—a writer once described him as "friendly as a small-town mayor"—but also rooted in pragmatism.

"I like people, and I like to have fun when I play. To me, it's a game," he says. "But if you are a person who is just taking people's heads off all the time, no one is going to want to play with you."

Reese is particularly skilled at drawing in rich "live ones"—the celebrities, Hollywood producers, and corporate titans who have millions in disposable income to gamble away. His compatriots have a word for the way he massages the egos of such wealthy marks: Chipping. On more than one occasion, he's whisked a vacationing millionaire away to his home or a private hotel room so he can have exclusive access. The whales don't mind—they enjoy playing with him.

In the summer of 2004, for example, a handful of top professionals were playing a weekend-long game of $2,000/$4,000 Seven-Card Stud with Larry Flynt in Southern California. Reese was scheduled to play but did not show. He called shortly after the game began, and Flynt's bodyguard handed the porn mogul a cell phone so Reese, ever the gentleman, could explain his absence. The other players sat quietly while Flynt chatted with Reese. "C'mon, Chip, I'll send my plane for you," Flynt said, adding that he would extend the game an extra day if Reese played.

The other players, who were waiting for the next hand to be dealt, chuckled and silently shook their heads. Reese flew in the next afternoon, after setting one condition: The stakes had to double.

Stu Ungar, 1980, at Binion's Horseshoe, Las Vegas

Five

STU UNGAR

To Live and Die in L.V.

The game's brightest prodigy takes aggression to new heights, sets a World Series record, and blows his mind on a lethal cocktail of poker and cocaine.

STU UNGAR'S POCKETS BULGED WITH $100 bills. He dressed in Versace and kept a closet full of custom-tailored silk slacks. Tens of millions in cash passed between his manicured fingernails and dropped into the pockets of hustlers, drug dealers, and whores.

During his first time on a golf course, Ungar gambled away $80,000 before getting off the practice green. On the streets of Las Vegas he wrecked five Jaguars and a Mercedes-Benz. He turned down an invitation to the White House ("I wouldn't know which fork to use"), and once proved to be of drinking age by slapping $20,000 down on the bar. "What kind of teenager walks around with all this money in his pocket?" he demanded. The barman promptly poured him a Scotch on the rocks.

Back in the late 1970s, when Ungar began cutting a wide swath through Vegas card rooms, other poker stars around town nicknamed him "The Kid"—largely because he resembled a child as he took huge sums of money away from middle-aged men. Ungar's card counting skills were suitably deadly that he got himself banned from every blackjack pit in Vegas. He once short-circuited a computer that had been programmed to beat him at gin rummy—"The fucking thing went through shock," he said. "It was hysterical"—and was widely acknowledged as the best in the world at that mathematically ball-busting game. But it was in the more publicized arena of high-stakes poker where Ungar made a name for himself: He won 10 of the 30 major tournaments he entered, raking millions of dollars and setting a standard that few players have come close to matching.

In 1997, Stu Ungar became the first person to win three World Series of Poker championships. After claiming a jackpot of $1 million, he vowed to mirror his back-to-back series victories from 1980 and '81 by winning again in 1998.

For one year, the poker world held its breath, waiting for Ungar to fulfill his audacious, Namath-style guarantee—and hoping the Kid could hang in there and do it before his inevitable crash.

ON MAY 11, 1998, 30 minutes before the World Series championship kicked off, Binion's Horseshoe was a crush of big-money players. Guys who hadn't been together since the previous year's series greeted one another with hearty handshakes and bear hugs. Debts got paid off with thick stacks of $100 bills. Posing alongside Doyle Brunson and Puggy Pearson, Amarillo Slim grinned big and fanned out a straight flush for a local newsman's camera. Actors Matt Damon and Ed Norton, playing in the World Series as a publicity stunt to promote their movie *Rounders*, were trailed by a dozen gushy teenage girls and half as many elbowing photographers.

Only one hotly anticipated player was missing from the pregame festivities: Stu Ungar, poker's reigning champ. The Binion's people, surely frantic behind closed doors, played it cool for the public. No matter, they insisted. He'd be down to defend his title. In a profession where character is as prized as talent, the very idea of someone failing to defend the World Series crown was unthinkable. However, as game time neared, Ungar remained conspicuously absent.

Most concerned about the potential no-show was the nattily turned-out professional gambler Billy Baxter, who had put up Ungar's $10,000 entry fee in exchange for 50 percent of his potential winnings. The year before, he and Ungar had had an identical arrangement, and it paid off magnificently—to the tune of $500,000 for Baxter. Now he was rocking from the toes to the heels of his shiny black loafers, looking around the room every few seconds. "Where's our man?" he wondered aloud. The question was returned with quizzical glances.

At about 12:50, 10 minutes before the first hand was to be dealt, Baxter reached for a Horseshoe house phone and caught Ungar in his room. "Come on down, Stuey," he said. "They're getting ready to play here."

"I'm resting," Ungar replied.

"Resting? You've had the last three weeks to rest."

No response from Ungar.

"If you don't show up, I'm gonna take the money down."

"Take the damned money down," Ungar shot back. "I'm too tired to play."

Baxter got his entry fee refunded just in time and a lame announcement poured out of the poker room P.A. system: "Stu Ungar will not be participating in the World Series of Poker championship. He is not feeling well."

A mix of groans and laughter resonated from the crowded tables, and above it all the cry of a frustrated woman: "Stueeeey!" The voice belonged to Cyndy Violette. Ranked among the top female players, she's a Meg Ryan look-alike who idolized Ungar for his skills and once had a bit of a crush on him. She remembered sitting behind the Kid during a game, looking over his shoulder, being entranced by the beauty with which he played cards.

She wasn't alone. "There is nobody in poker history who has been able to calculate quicker than Stu Ungar," says Mike Sexton, a respected high-stakes player in the '90s and now a commentator on *World Poker Tour*. "You have no concept of this guy's mind—above a genius-level IQ."

If he had made it down from his room, Ungar realistically could have pulled off his second back-to-back World Series victory. "He takes poker to a whole other level," Baxter said after recouping his 10 grand. "He's a brilliant guy. He has a knack for zeroing in and putting you on a hand. He understands how to win a pot where no one else would even attempt it. Through a process of elimination, analyzing betting patterns, and understanding how people play the cards that are out there, he can pigeonhole hands. If he figures you have the second- or third-best, Stuey will try to take the pot away by betting big. But then Stuey is also very good at estimating the amount of heat you can stand, how much he needs to bluff in order to make you so uncomfortable that you fold—with anything but the best possible cards. He judges the precise amount required to get that job done without betting any more than is necessary."

Puggy Pearson summed up Ungar's X-factor thusly: "He's unafraid of risking his chips to take advantage of weakness. It's harder to do than it sounds; it's wired into your heart or it isn't, and that is one thing that makes him a great player. If you show him weakness"—by playing slow or hesitating while making a bet—"shame on you."

By midnight, Ungar's absence was still a major topic of discussion, and everybody had a Stuey story to share. Mostly they were anecdotes of card-table genius colliding with amazingly stupid self-destruction—like the time he won $3.6 million playing poker and was broke three weeks later. Or when he bought a top-of-the-line Mercedes-Benz, never bothered to change the oil, and was surprised when the thing seized up on him. Then there were the outlandish rumors floating around: Somebody said that Ungar's skin was peeling off. One British journalist insisted that dealers were ferrying eightballs of cocaine up to his room. A friend of a friend swore that the room's walls had been smeared with days-old food.

Baxter's got one of the greatest Ungar stories of all, and he told it with dramatic relish, pointing out that the afternoon's no-show was not exactly unique. "In the '80s Stuey didn't come down for the second day of the Series, even though he was close to being chip leader. I backed him that year too, my money was on the line, and I was pissed. Turns out that he had been carried out of his room at the Golden Nugget on a stretcher [apparently overdosed on drugs]. So I tracked him to Sunrise Hospital, over near the Las Vegas Country Club. That's where I saw him laying there, unconscious, like a little bird, in what appeared to be a crib of some sort. I started shaking him, telling him to wake up. The doctor came in and asked if I was a relative. I told him, 'Not exactly.' I told the doctor that Stu needed to get up and finish playing in a poker tournament. The doctor said, 'I have bad news for you. He won't be going anywhere for a couple days.' He didn't play, they kept anteing him off, and he had enough of a chip lead that he still got to within five places of the money."

Somebody asked what had made Baxter reinvest in Ungar for the '97 series. "Nobody would have anything to do with him at that point," he said, not needing to mention the fact that drugs had hobbled Ungar's poker skills and crippled his reputation. "But he wanted to get into the tournament and asked me to stake him. I said, 'Stuey, please, leave me alone. Last time I did that, you wound up in a fucking hospital bed.' He waved his hand and said, 'Stop it with that bullshit, Billy. Just give me the 10,000.' I was playing Lowball at the time, and must have been winning, because a day later I put up the entry fee for Stuey and we split a million-dollar prize. Now he's broke again, but I just couldn't turn the guy down this year—not after he won for me."

BY THE START of the 1998 World Series, the five-foot-five Ungar had wasted away to less than 100 pounds. His skin was gray, his pupils were pinned, he looked half-dead. The bottom row of his front teeth had gone missing, and his lower lip curled over enflamed gums. He was 45 years old, and he walked with the hunched shoulders and stuttery gait of a frail old man.

As the championship tournament unfolded at the Horseshoe, Ungar sat alone, upstairs, in room 1208. He watched television, did drugs, and obsessively stacked Pringles as if they were $1,000 chips. Over a baggy white T-shirt, he wore a black satin World Series of Poker jacket that hung like a tent. As a young man Ungar had come off like the Mick Jagger of gambling, with his confident swagger, puffy brown hair, and hyped-up mannerisms. Now his right nostril had caved into the center of his nose due to excessive cocaine use. The cartilage had literally worn away and collapsed, despite a recent rhinoplasty (which he destroyed by snorting lines of cocaine soon after the procedure was completed).

Players who visited Ungar in room 1208 would have happily given odds on his dying within days. But they'd have lost. Six weeks after pulling his Howard Hughes act at the series, Ungar was alive and astonishingly well. An old girlfriend had mercifully taken him in, kept him off drugs, and nursed him back to health.

On a sunny afternoon, during the final days of June 1998, he stood near the entrance of the buffet at Arizona Charlie's, an off-Strip casino that caters to locals. Having bounced back from the World Series debacle, Ungar had put on some pounds and filled in his missing teeth. Black hair, flecked with gray, was neatly swept to the left side of his head. Clean-shaven and charismatic, he wore a tropical-weight, black-and-white button-down shirt and gray slacks. The cuffs broke beautifully over soft Italian loafers. His demeanor was like that of a little boy who wants to impress.

Stepping up to the buffet's carving station, Ungar loaded his plate with roast turkey and prime rib. He sat down at a corner table and settled in for a long interview. Over the next several hours, Ungar would open up and reflect, sometimes pausing and thinking for long periods, as if he were a much older man unspooling tales from a rich and varied life. He began by leaning forward and recounting his introduction to gambling as a kid growing up in New York.

"My father, Isador, was a bookmaker, a Shylock, a big man; I was eight years old and helping him to figure out what the parlays paid at Belmont," Ungar said. His voice was gravelly, and he spoke with the rapid-fire timing of a stand-up comic. "My father managed Fox's Corner, a bar on Seventh Street and Second Avenue on the Lower East

Side, and had a million dollars in lockboxes around the neighborhood. I was born in 1953, and I grew up alongside Italian Mafia guys and Hasidim with payis. They were all tough."

Like many New York Jewish families, the Ungars—Stu, his parents, and his older sister Judy—spent summer, Hanukkah, and Passover in the Catskills, usually at the Raleigh Hotel. That's where Stu first displayed his excellence at gin rummy, reveling in its low luck level, which tilts the game toward skillful players rather those those who are merely fortunate. "I started by watching my mother playing poker; but she was a big sucker and never went out," he said. "I knew I could do better than her, and I was only 10 years old. I'd play the waiters at gin and win $40, $50, $60. I had the fever at a young age."

By his 13th year, Ungar had lost his father, who died of a fatal heart attack while in the arms of his mistress; 12 months later his mother suffered a debilitating stroke that eventually landed her in a nursing home. Isador's millions never turned up ("The government wound up getting all of it," his son said), Ungar dropped out of 10th grade despite having skipped from sixth to eighth with apparent ease, and the young gambler took it upon himself to support his mother and sister. "I was never a kid," said Ungar. "I got a job dealing poker in a goulash joint on Ninth Street between Second and Third avenues. I was 14, but I looked like I was seven."

A natural born hustler, Ungar operated with the craftiness of a professional gambler long before he possessed the consciousness to articulate what he was doing. A friend of his recounts that, as a boy barely in his teens, Ungar would stand on the outskirts of high-stakes gin games, watching the action, while a partner played. The partner would eventually tell others at the table that he was tired, then ask if he could have his nephew sit in for him. He'd nod in Ungar's direction. "Of course, the opponents were always happy because they figured they'd be gambling against a child," recounts the friend. "Then Stuey would sit down and beat them all."

Ungar played gin in a manner that foreshadowed his greatest skill as a poker player. "Stuey had the imagination to put other people on certain combinations," says Chip Reese, who learned gin from Ungar in exchange for teaching him the finer points of Seven-Card Stud. "He told me about this old man, this guy he played when he was about 12 years old, back in New York, who taught him a secret to looking at the first seven discards in a game of gin, then looking at your hand and creating a picture"—an actual visual image of what an opponent's cards looked like. "It's one thing that he never showed me."

After outplaying New York's most legendary gin professionals— eccentrics with nicknames like the Bronx Express and Leo the Jap—the teenage Ungar established himself as a nervy kid who needed to be put in his place by the game's elders. The person who seemed poised to do it was a superior gin specialist from Canada named Harry Stein. "They called him Yonkie," Ungar remembered. "He was imported to New York to play me. We played 27 games of Hollywood. I won $10,000 from him and became a marked man who nobody wanted to play without a spot. You have to understand that $10,000 was a lot of money back in the '60s."

What did Ungar do with his winnings? "Of course I took the cash and went to the racetrack. Whoever said that money burns a hole in your pocket was talking about me. I once played ping-pong for $50,000 against some Chinaman in Tahoe. I played this old Italian game called Ziganet. I went to Aqueduct and bet a guy $2,000 on which horse would come in last. I'm an action freak. I'd bet on a cock- roach race."

The thousands were virtually meaningless to Ungar. It was as if he had taken one of Amarillo Slim's aphorisms—"To be a successful gam- bler, you need a healthy disregard for money"—and perverted it to the unhealthiest possible extreme. More specifically, as an old running buddy of Ungar's has said, "Money was the cheapest commodity in Stuey's life." He could always get more of it from backers (eager to buy 50 percent of his action). "Stuey never cared about winning," says Reese. "He only cared about playing. One reason he was so good at gin was because you have to play every single hand."

Ultimately, though, in 1978, Ungar's reckless wagering got him into more than just debt. "I was betting a bookmaker who was hooked up with the top guy in the city, and I ended up owing him $60,000," Ungar remembered.

The top guy in the city?

"I was sick," he said. "Give me a phone and I'm going to bet. I don't care if it's fucking Al Capone on the other end."

Not exactly eager to pay off 60 grand, Ungar quietly lit out for Los Angeles.

He explained that Victor Romano, a masterful bridge player and Mafia soldier with the Genovese crime family, had been looking out for him in exchange for 20 percent of his winnings, so he hadn't been too worried about what might happen to him if he skipped town to dodge a debt. "Victor could have straightened it out," said Ungar. "Besides, there's no use killing someone who owes you money. Everybody knew that I had good earning power—I was an oil well for Victor and those guys. I just didn't want to face the pressure. It would've been embarrassing. And I might have got a beating if I stayed in New York."

From L.A., Ungar made a trip to Las Vegas for a gin-rummy tournament at the Union Plaza Hotel. He put up the $1,500 entry fee and cashed for $50,000, with which he paid off a chunk of what he owed back in New York. An additional payment came out of $100,000 that he won from Danny Robison, who was then regarded as Vegas's top gin player. Two months later, Ungar was free of the mob debt and a million dollars in the black. He settled into the Vegas Jockey Club with his New York girlfriend, a former cocktail waitress named Madelaine Wheeler, and her son, Richard, whom Ungar would later adopt. "In New York, I didn't have the confidence that I developed out here," he said. "This town is heaven for a degenerate, for a sick guy like me."

Just to keep things cool and protect his investment, Victor Romano dispatched his nephew Phil "Brush" Tartaglia to Vegas. Uncle Phillie, as he became known, looked after Ungar and fended off guys to whom his young charge owed money. "Stuey always wanted to gamble with me, but it became impossible," says a Costa Rica–based bookmaker who used to operate out of Vegas. "Whenever he lost I had to take it up with Phillie, and he would never pay me. It got to the point where I told Stuey that we should be friends but stop doing business together."

HIGH-END PLAYERS in Vegas were thrilled by the arrival of Ungar, who was virtually unknown outside New York and more than willing to gamble with anyone at gin rummy. He angled for sky's-the-limit stakes and, in order to attract action, always offered to be in the dealer's position. This meant that opposing players received an extra card and threw out the first discard to begin the game—a huge advantage for them. To hustlers like Amarillo Slim, that setup was irresistible. Slim came into town with a satchel full of cash, ready to break this little freak from the Lower East Side. "I said, 'Don't let him leave. I'm on my way,'" recounts Slim. "Well, I brought enough $100 bills to burn down the whole fucking Horseshoe."

Slim left $40,000 poorer.

According to Ungar, it's his ability to remember past hands, past games, past actions that helped make him so successful at cards. That ability led him to turn poker into a series of complex numerical problems. What made his performance so stunning, though, was that, unlike the mathematically inclined players who came after him—highly educated guys like Chris "Jesus" Ferguson who were aided by computer science and sophisticated theories—he had no access to computers or college professors. Ungar instinctively incorporated a crude version of high-level math without ever formalizing—or even fully understanding—what he was doing.

And he muscled-up his mental game with a steroidal dose of machismo. "When it comes to *mano a mano* stuff in cards, I take it personally; my ego is at stake," said Ungar. "If somebody challenged me, no matter how nice the guy might be, I'd find a flaw in him. Maybe there'd be something about his eyebrow that I hated. I take it very personal that somebody wants to beat me. I got to hate somebody to play him."

What about Amarillo Slim and his $40,000? What had Ungar found distasteful about Slim? "I hated him for being so fucking tall and lanky," Ungar said. "And he's a cocky guy. He thought he was conning me, and I wanted to wipe that smirk and everything else off his face in the worst way."

As word of Ungar's acumen spread, the gin action in Las Vegas dried up for him. Hotelier Steve Wynn once said, only half jokingly, that Ungar would need to dig up someone who'd been living in a cave in order to uncover an opponent who hadn't yet heard about his talents. Ungar had no choice now but to find a game he could beat without completely turning off the competition. Poker, with its reasonable degree of luck and abundance of weak players who view themselves as losing to the table rather than to an individual, was perfect.

In the early spring of 1980, the 27-year-old Ungar, who had never before played no-limit Texas Hold 'Em, asked Fred "Sarge" Ferris, a high-rolling poker stud, to back him in the upcoming World Series. Sarge, who died of a heart attack in 1989, naturally hesitated. "He figured that I'd be burning up $10,000," said Ungar. "But then Jack Binion said, 'Let him play. I'll put up 25 percent.'" Sarge relented. The young prodigy went on to storm through the tournament and take the title. "Doyle Brunson had laid 100-to-1 odds against my winning that series, and I beat him heads-up to take the title," Ungar said. "So that was doubly satisfying."

In 1981 Ungar won the World Series for a second time, and became a disruptive force at the no-limit tables. "Back then there were a lot of Texans who were used to dominating the games—and Stuey would put these guys on tilt," says fellow New Yorker Jay Heimowitz. "He would raise an awful lot of pots and play a lot of crap. Then, all of sudden, he'd totally change his style by tightening up. They couldn't handle the continual adjustments—but I loved it."

While Ungar described himself as a "buzzsaw" and insisted, "They got a skeleton out of the closet when they put me in a no-limit game," the reality is that he was a big sprayer of money in cash contests. "Especially when it was his own money," says Danny Robison, who played a lot of Stud with Ungar. "The consensus is that he did better with other people's money than with his own. Maybe that's because he cared more about his ego than he did about his bankroll."

When people discuss Ungar's drawbacks as a player, the conversation invariably shifts to the very quality that made him successful: the reckless aggression of an amphetamine-crazed pit bull. On a rush, when he was getting cards and making hands, that style of play worked in his favor, allowing him to steamroll the table; when Ungar ran cold, however, this same strategy was a recipe for financial ruin. "The thing you never hear about Stuey is that he made a great lay-down," says Barry Greenstein, currently considered the winningest player in poker. "Any time he had top pair, he just moved in. But if he ran into a real hand, he would lose." Reese, who seems to understand Ungar as well as anyone, adds, "Of all the people I've played with over the past 30 years, Stuey could be the best and the worst. But that is no formula for success. What you get when you're the best does not nearly balance the losses you accrue when you're the worst."

Whatever the case—even those who are critical of Ungar's overly aggressive cash-game style describe him as being fearsome, not to mention fear*less*, in heads-up and tournament play—he appeared to be living every one of his dreams during the early 1980s, taking both his high and low ambitions to their extremes. He married Madelaine in '82, then bought a large Tudor-style home and filled it with fine fur-nishings. The couple's daughter, Stephanie, was born that same year, and one day his new wife went out and purchased his-and-hers Jaguars—on a whim. However, no amount of domestic perfection could get Ungar to settle down. He routinely blew through massive amounts of cash and spent nights bedding a rotating cast of poker groupies who hung around the high-stakes card rooms with dollar signs in their eyes and bottomless appetites for drugs, sex, and fame.

Though Ungar seemed to be living the life of a rock star, was he happy? "That's a good question," he said. "I think back on those years and I don't know. If I liked it so much, why did I escape reality all the time?"

PRIOR TO MOVING to Las Vegas, Ungar said, drugs played a very small role in his life. Before the age of 22, he hadn't even smoked a joint. He didn't drink. He didn't party. His vices at that point were gam-bling and chasing girls. "If there were 58 massage parlors in New York, [Stuey] knew all 58," card player Teddy Price told a reporter from *New York* magazine. "And he was a big tipper. He'd walk in the door and the girls would yell, 'Stuey's here!' "

Ungar first snorted cocaine on the afternoon he sent his stroke-addled mother to a nursing home, in 1975. "She was crying like a baby and she broke me up, but I couldn't handle it no more, to be playing cards, trying to scratch out a living, and my mother calls me to get her a bedpan," he remembered. "I started very moderately, like a gram a week."

By the time he won his second World Series, in 1981, his drug consumption had spiked precipitously. But Ungar insisted that it was rooted in practicality. "I did the coke to keep up," he said. "You use it as an excuse to stay awake and play poker. But then you take it home with you." Ultimately, of course, the cocaine went beyond recreation or practicality. "When you have access to it and the money don't mean nothing and people keep calling you with it . . ." His voice trailed off, implying that there's nothing you can do to fight the temptation. "It's a sickness. I don't even like to think about it. I guarantee you, it's taken 10, 15 years off my life. I don't look like it, but I feel beat up." Actually, whether he wanted to admit it or not, he looked plenty beaten up. It was as if the pain that he felt inside had leaked out, erasing what once seemed like indelible youthfulness from his poker face.

The coke-fueled '80s were the decade when Ungar's sports betting spun completely out of control. "The figures were exorbitant," he acknowledged. "A regular person wouldn't even be able to relate to it. Winning a couple hundred thousand playing poker was nothing compared to what I would lose in sports."

Vegas's golf courses were another sinkhole for Ungar's card-room millions. "Stuey's a big sucker at a lot of things," Puggy Pearson said in the late '90s. "Because he's so good at certain things, he thinks he should be good at everything. This is his downfall." Puggy recalled that, as a golf handicap, Ungar was allowed to tee up all of his shots. "That's a huge advantage, and he had all kinds of tees—big long ones, itty-bitty short ones. Hell, I seen him tee the ball up in a lake one time at the old Sahara golf course. But he still lost every damned thing he had. He'd lose his shoestrings if he needed a couple dollars. That boy can't be still. He's got to have action."

During one memorable two-week period, Ungar went on a massive winning streak at the card tables and then laid it all down on a long Thanksgiving weekend of football games—Thursday through

Monday. "I had a million in cash going into that weekend," Ungar said, "and at the end of *Monday Night Football*, I owed $800,000." He lost $1.8 million in a weekend? Ungar nodded. "I was betting $100,000, $150,000 a game. That was nothing to me. I had no sense of the value of money."

He hesitated a moment. "Sometimes I think that I wanted to lose, so that I could get mad and go back to the poker table."

Drugs and sports betting combined to leave Ungar financially and spiritually destitute. The dual demons created a vicious cycle that wreaked havoc with the one thing he could have done brilliantly: play poker. "He was always under pressure because he went through so much cash," remembers Billy Baxter. "Stuey's money management was a joke, and he kept himself against the blade all the time. He never got into a comfortable financial position. He had to win every day just to support his lousy habits. Then he'd run bad a couple days in poker and be busted again." Indeed, when Ungar was losing and strung out, says Greenstein, he became so scared and so desperate "that you were able to push him around like a little girl."

In the mid-1980s, Madelaine left him and took his beloved Stephanie with her. Several years later, a poker-playing friend carted a dining-room set out of Ungar's home to settle a gambling debt. In 1992, he sold his house for approximately $270,000. "I needed money," Ungar remembered. "I borrowed $150,000 against the house. It was one of those hard-loan shit things, you know, and I had to pay the guy back." Ungar considered the circumstances for a moment. "I had a nice house."

It didn't get better. Throughout the '90s, Ungar slept where he could and occasionally surfaced when he needed to win or borrow money. There were flashes of the old brilliance, but he spent most of his time away from poker, caught up in a world dominated by drug dealers, hookers, con men, and petty thieves. He scraped by with occasional low-profile action, through financial support from benevolent friends, and by calling in the many loans he had made to other players back when he was flying high. But for the most part, nobody wanted to get involved with an unrepentant, unreliable drug addict. Even Uncle Phillie Brush, Ungar's minder from New York, began to distance himself.

By all appearances and opinions, Stu Ungar was completely finished as a competitor in the heady world of no-limit. He seemed like
the Brian Wilson of poker—a brilliant guy done in by drugs and his
own strange, unmanageable form of genius. Then, during the early
months of 1997, Ungar hit some kind of emotional nadir, and it compelled him to resurface, initially through occasional appearances at
$20 buy-in tournaments around town. "People were saying how I'm a
has-been and washed-up and all that," Ungar explained. "Finally, it got
to me real bad. My pride was hurt. So I tried to eat right, got some
sleep, put myself into shape to play."

Some of it, however, was involuntary. Following a couple of busts,
one for possession of drug paraphernalia, another for trespassing, Ungar was legally compelled to remain clean. Nevertheless, his changes
slowly became evident during the 1997 series. If his presence initially
seemed like a sick joke, by day two nobody was laughing. On the third
afternoon of play, local newspaper reporters, contemplating their
leads for Thursday's paper, had already rechristened Stu "The Kid" Ungar as "The Comeback Kid." "If they wanted to do a clinic on no-limit
Hold 'Em, they would have filmed me from day one to the final hand,"
Ungar said in 1998. "You can't play more perfect than I played. It was
just a thing of beauty, what I did in '97. I was reborn."

At the start of the fourth and final day of the series, Ungar had almost $1.1 million stacked in front of him, dwarfing his nearest com-
petitor by more than $300,000. He was confident and cool, diminutive
and flashy, with blue-lensed granny glasses and a densely patterned
shirt. He played with such confidence that it was as if he could see
through the backs of his opponents' cards. "It might have been the
greatest performance ever in a World Series of Poker," says Mike Sexton. "He just dominated the tables."

ESPN cameras stalked Ungar as if he were a movie star, and he rev-
eled in the attention. When it finally came down to Ungar and John
Strzemp, then president of Treasure Island Hotel and Casino, for the
championship, it was clear that Ungar was the superior player by a
wide margin. "But," says Sexton, "John was smart enough to recognize
that he couldn't play with Stu Ungar. You can't sit there and play with
the guy and let him take your money slowly but surely as you go

along. John realized that the only chance he had of beating Stuey was to get all his chips in the pot as quickly as possible and gamble with them."

The miraculous resurrection culminated with Ungar pulling a tournament-winning straight on the final card of the last hand. Smiling broadly for the cameras, telling reporters how vindicating the victory had been, holding up a photo of his daughter that he had kept close to him throughout the contest, Ungar seemed to be his old self. "He was in his element again," says Sexton. "He was put back in that throne of destiny, where he would have a new chance to start fresh. I really thought he would do it."

Ungar, posing before a fortress of banded $100 bills, a freshly minted World Series of Poker bracelet in front of him, became the first player to win three championships. He promised to keep himself in shape for the next year's Series. "I was sleeping for 15 years," he announced. "I've decided to wake up."

But just a couple of months after netting $500,000 (the million-dollar first prize, minus Baxter's cut), Ungar was broke. He apparently blew the money on all his old vices: sports betting, drugs, and hookers. A poker-playing friend who popped by the apartment where Ungar was staying in late '97 remembers a refrigerator with nothing in it but Tang. Propped against one wall was a beautifully framed collage, filled with laudatory press clippings from Ungar's glory days. "I'm reading the collage, and there's something in there that says, 'Talent will get you to the top, but you need character and discipline to stay there,'" recounts the friend, one of Stu's old coke buddies. "I said, 'Stuey, we ain't got that fucking shit. We have character and talent, but we don't have discipline.' He heard me, but he didn't say nothing."

Whatever Ungar's problems, his decision to pull out of the '98 Series was still impossible for anyone in the poker community to comprehend. He checked into the Horseshoe on April 17, intending to rest up and get acclimated for the Series' final event three and a half weeks later. Billy Baxter suggested he get himself warmed up with a couple preliminary tournaments, but Ungar waved him away and said, "I don't need that shit."

On the morning of May 11, the day the world championship event was slated to begin, Ungar's cocaine addiction was in full flare, leaving him emotionally depressed, strung out, and physically wrecked. His right nostril was practically flush against his face. The tips of his fingers had been burned black from handling the hot end of a glass crack pipe. Bob Stupak, casino entrepreneur and occasional backer of Ungar's, had offered to provide a hairdresser and makeup artist to ensure that the drug-addled star would look presentable, but Ungar never green-lighted them to come upstairs.

Even minutes before the tournament's starting time, he said, he still intended to play. "I got showered and dressed. I put my clothes on. And then I looked at myself in the mirror. I looked terrible. I looked like I came from Auschwitz. That's when I knew I couldn't sit there and play for four days, for 10 hours a day, and put in a good performance. I wasn't geared up. I was physically out of it. The year took a toll on me."

Ungar stopped speaking for a moment, maybe to replay the World Series nightmare in his mind. "Look, it was criminal what I did. I honestly think I could have won back-to-back if I was in decent shape. But I thought it would have been more embarrassing to have gone down there looking the way I did than for me to stay in my room and not play. In the end, though, I disappointed everyone and, what's worse, I made everybody who's jealous of me happy."

But maybe the horrible experience had given him perspective. If he walked away from the Horseshoe with a realization that some things are more important than the primitive act of winning money— like not letting down the very people who care about you—then it all could be worth it in the long run, couldn't it? Ungar considered the theory for a split second. "If there is more to life than gambling," he said, "I don't know that I'm able to enjoy it. And what I'm afraid of is that gambling ain't stimulating me lately. That's a bad sign."

A WEEK AFTER opening up in his lengthy interview at Arizona Charlie's, Ungar was having dinner with his ex-wife, Madelaine, and daughter Stephanie at the Sahara Casino and Hotel, a mid-level place on the Strip with a low-stakes poker-room. Stephanie, 16 at the time, was a lovely, intelligent girl who had endured a lot of disappointment and heartache from her father. At that moment, though, she was thrilled to be with him. "We've spent a whole week together," she gushed. He appeared to be completely straight. "People introduce themselves to my dad and say that it's a pleasure to meet him. We walk around holding hands, and everybody is so happy to see my dad with me."

When they strolled into the Sahara's poker room, Ungar's dentist was there, messing around in a low-stakes, 30-person freeze-out with a $22 buy-in and a first prize of a few hundred dollars. Just for kicks, maybe showing off his star patient, the dentist requested that Ungar pull up a chair and enter the event. Considering that Ungar's more obvious poker milieu would have been the Horseshoe or the Mirage, where, at the time, games ranked among the highest in town, this was a bit of a comedown. But, as a favor to the man who had built a bridge for the front of his mouth, Ungar dispatched his ex-wife to the blackjack pit and accepted the invitation.

He wound up signing 40 autographs, and a crowd of some 200 railbirds formed around a tournament that would ordinarily have generated no interest whatsoever.

Goosed by the crowd and glad to be back in action, Ungar played aggressively and hard, as if psychologically making up for the World Series he had missed. "It came down to me and this old man," Ungar recalled. "I had $12,000 in tournament chips in front of me. He had $400. Then he outdrew me for seven pots in a row and won the thing."

Ungar was initially upset about losing. Then the man told him, "You made my life, Mr. Ungar. I can tell my children, my grandchildren, and everybody else that I beat you."

After shaking the man's hand, Ungar said to him, "If I can make your life, I'm tickled that I lost."

It was a rare glimpse at Ungar's sentimental side, but, sadly, didn't auger long-term change. A couple of weeks later, he convinced a doctor to prescribe narcotic painkillers and found himself backsliding into drug dependency. Following a disagreement with his girlfriend, he bashed her in the face with a telephone. She kicked him out of her house and called the police. He went to stay with a friend, someone said, but nobody seemed able to find him.

Mike Sexton hinted that Puggy Pearson might have a lead. Puggy had met Ungar two days before at Sam's Town Hotel and Casino, and had lent him $500, "He didn't look too damned good," Puggy said. "Stuey was sitting there on the bench, next to a guy who claimed to be his plumber. Stu gave me his word, on his daughter's life, that he would pay me back $500 in two days, which is today. I lay 100-to-1 that I don't hear from him until he needs me again. But that's okay." Puggy sighed. Then he added, "Stuey's all right."

A day later, Ungar was back at Binion's Horseshoe, registered on someone else's credit card. Speaking over the phone and sounding lucid, he said, "I'm gonna start playing. I'm waiting to see a friend of mine who's got money for me. Then I go to the Mirage."

DESPITE VOWS TO resume his once-brilliant career, Ungar maintained a ghostly poker-room presence during the summer and into the fall of 1998. Billy Baxter lent him 25 grand and he used it to play $30/$60 Hold 'Em. But his heart was no longer in it. Inferior players beat him in heads-up matches, and cocaine retook its place at the center of Ungar's life. He continually phoned the Mirage poker room, trying to scare up money from old friends, but nobody would take his calls.

Then, in November, things seemed ready to turn around yet again. Ungar signed a contract with hotelier Bob Stupak, agreeing that Stupak would pay off Ungar's debts and finance tournament-play in exchange for a piece of Ungar's future winnings. Stupak even assigned a bodyguard named Dave to look after Ungar and make sure he stayed away from drugs. Quickly, though, Ungar convinced Dave that he had to take his daughter to a birthday dinner.

Dave cut him loose for the afternoon, and Ungar checked into the Oasis Motel, a notorious short-time sex joint on the northern end of Las Vegas Boulevard. He paid cash for a single night and claimed the Mirage as his permanent residence on the check-in form. Earlier that day Stupak had given him a $10,000 advance, as "walking-around money."

The next morning, after Ungar failed to check out of his room on time, an Oasis employee knocked on the door, entered the room, and found him lying facedown in bed, shaking. Apparently in no condition to leave, Ungar asked to see the hotel manager, then slipped the manager a $100 bill for a second night. "Can you close the window?" Ungar asked. "I'm cold." The manager looked up and noticed that the window was tightly shut.

Twenty-four hours later, Stu the Kid Ungar was found lying in the same facedown position on the mattress—but this time he was dead. Eight hundred eighty-two dollars, all that Ungar had to his name, was found in his pants pockets. The room was clean of drugs and paraphernalia.

According to a Clark County spokesman, the official cause of Ungar's death was coronary arterial sclerosis brought on by his lifestyle. Essentially, the arteries around his heart hardened and would not allow blood to circulate. Ungar's passing was ruled accidental, even though cocaine, Percodan, and methadone were found in his blood. Maybe the dope in Ungar's system reflected a final binge before he checked into the hotel with the intention of kicking his habit for good. Maybe he sensed that the end was near and wanted to die alone, in peace. Or maybe something more nefarious transpired.

A longtime friend of Ungar's claims to know what happened. "Stuey bought a bunch of crack and picked up two hookers who like to troll near the Oasis," says the friend. "Once they found out how much money Stuey had on him"—presumably a good chunk of Stupack's $10,000—"he was as good as dead. They pushed him to smoke enough so that he went into convulsions—which Stuey was prone to do. The convulsions came, they took most of the money, and left Stuey for dead."

Ungar's funeral was presided over by a rabbi and financed by Bob Stupak. The ceremony was a who's-who of no-limit players, and Stupak reportedly hit them up for donations to help cover the burial costs.

Days later, at the big-money tables around town, cards were dealt, millions were won and lost, and the games rolled on unabated by the passing of poker's ultimate supernova.

Erik Seidel, 2004, at Binion's Horseshoe, Las Vegas

Six

ERIK SEIDEL

Card Room Chameleon

A former Wall Street trader and teenage

backgammon champ beats the odds at

poker by constantly shuffling strategies.

A BULLET-COLORED SUBWAY TRAIN rumbled to a stop at Manhattan's West 79th Street station. Its double doors slid open and Erik Seidel stepped in, joining a dozen commuters in a scramble for seats. Dispirited by the very notion of dressing up for work—"It kills you a little bit each day," he figured—Seidel grudgingly wore a white shirt and striped necktie underneath his zip-up windbreaker. It was Monday morning, October 19, 1987, and he had that day's *New York Times* folded to reveal a headline that

summed up the past week on Wall Street: IN THE AFTERMATH OF MARKET PLUNGE, MUCH UNEASINESS.

But, like just about everyone else, Seidel wasn't worried. Despite recent losses, the economy still seemed robust. Coming in the midst of a five-year bull market, this dip resembled another buying opportunity. Even David Rockefeller, retired chairman of Chase Manhattan Bank, told the *Times*, "I don't think there is reason to be alarmed."

Tall and skinny, with a mop of dark brown hair, and a hawkish nose, 28-year-old Seidel got off the train when it reached the World Trade Center station. He rode an escalator up to the street—clogged with its daily rush-hour snarl of Town Cars, taxis, stretch limos, and pedestrians—and proceeded to the monolithic American Stock Exchange building. He walked inside, cleared security, donned his blue trading-floor jacket, and waited for the opening bell.

This was an unexpected world for Seidel, who lacked the college credentials that paved the way for most of Wall Street's buy-and-sell cowboys. Unlike virtually everyone else on the expansive but crowded trading floor, Seidel got to where he was—earning six figures a year and seeing nothing but blue sky ahead of him—by gambling.

Prior to taking a straight job, he had earned his money on the high-stakes backgammon circuit, traveling from New York to the Caribbean to Monte Carlo and Rome, playing big-money games against multimillionaires such as William Bartholomay, chairman emeritus of the Atlanta Braves; and the late Angelo Drossos, a lanky, down-to-earth Dean Witter executive who went on to own the San Antonio Spurs. It was a good life: Seidel won the 1985 Backgammon Championship, an annual event held in St. Moritz, Switzerland; prior to that he beat European champ Joe Dwek during a big tournament in Florida. Lucrative side action led to a reliable income of more than $1,000 per week—not exactly a fortune, but plenty of money for someone who devoted his life to playing games.

Soon after Seidel beat Dwek, backgammon's popularity began to swoon among the jet set (in part because all the bad rich players got tired of losing and returned to the less demeaning games of tennis, polo, and golf). "It got to the point where backgammon became more of a hustler's game," explains Seidel. "You had to be able to find live

ones and create an atmosphere that was fun for them. I was only good at playing, not so good at the schmoozing." Eventually he began to dabble in poker, but it was nothing serious—just a new game to learn in the wake of backgammon. With fiancée Ruah at home on the Upper West Side, and a child on the way, he was happy to apply his game-playing chops to a high-paying job with stability—neckties be damned. Instead of hustling up action with rich rubes wearing Ralph Lauren cashmere, Seidel now placed bets against market volatility as an options trader, focusing on stalwart stocks like Sara Lee, Hecla Mining, and Walt Disney.

He worked for Roger Low, a tall, good-looking former backgammon pro himself—one of the world's best in the early 1980s—who traded options with a multimillion-dollar bankroll and firmly believed in fiscal order. "A lot of people were speculating on calls"—betting that stock prices would go up—"but stocks were historically over-priced," explains Seidel. "So we figured that the value was in betting against volatility. We weren't hedging much, and it was clear that any kind of a big swing could hurt us."

Seconds into the trading day on October 19, in the wake of sell-offs around the world, negative trends quickly gained momentum. Millions of stock shares immediately went up for sale on the U.S. exchanges, but they failed to move—and everyone seemed to be losing money. Sam Walton, then the richest man in America, would drop $1.3 billion over two days of plummeting prices. Automated trading programs kicked in and retreated out of investments with lightning speed. Values dropped so quickly that the exchange's computers could not track all the losses. Beige-boxed monitors flashed strings of tiny green question marks instead of stock quotes. By lunchtime pension funds were dumping off at an alarming rate. Panic set in. Seidel received a call from Roger Low: *Sell everything you can.* He tried, but there were no buyers—at any price. By 4 in the afternoon, when the market closed for the day, it had shed 508 points—or 22 percent of its value—in just six and a half hours.

Cocky traders, still wearing their designer suits and eyeglasses, went slack-jawed. High-flying stocks had become virtually worthless. Risk-taking millionaires found themselves broke. Lives were ruined.

People started using the word *crash*, and the day was dubbed Black Monday. A local pub, popular with traders, marked the debacle by reducing drink prices 20 percent.

"Everything has been wiped out," a despondent Roger Low told Seidel in an office upstairs from the trading floor a day later.

Seidel himself had invested $50,000, the bulk of his savings, in Low's trading portfolio. Now, for the first time in his life, he had pressing financial problems. His job had evaporated. Backgammon, once his steadiest source of income, was moribund. Within a couple of weeks he'd need to generate cash flow, and unemployment wouldn't cut it. "I think the world has irreversibly changed," Seidel told Ruah, now his wife, during a grim dinner in their one-bedroom apartment that night. "I don't know what kind of shape the economy will be in for the long term."

Over the next several days, Seidel felt rudderless. Wall Street offered no opportunities. And he lacked marketable skills in anything other than options trading. Instinctively, he retreated to a place of comfort: the Mayfair Club, a tatty, yellow-walled gambling joint carved out of three hotel rooms on the second floor of Manhattan's elegantly seedy Gramercy Park Hotel. The heart of the club was an unadorned expanse of backgammon tables and a couple of poker felts. The air swirled with smoke. Wall Street's bloodbath had surprisingly little impact on business at the Mayfair, with its parallel universe of professional gamblers, wealthy amateurs, and risk-addicted degenerates. Strangely, though, this odd club, in a hotel that had seen better days, was where Seidel believed he could rebuild his life. In playing poker, he instinctively applied a trader's mentality—quickly putting values on his cards, unemotionally bailing when risk outweighed reward—and tracked raises as if they were numbers on a fast moving ticker. Best of all, he discovered that he could exercise degrees of control and influence over poker that he could never impart upon the bigger, more unruly stock market.

Action at the Mayfair revolved around a $25/$50 game of no-limit Texas Hold 'Em, and Seidel began to spend his nights waiting alongside the table, observing and carefully timing his entry for opportune moments—like when a weak, superloose player called Phil the Rabbi

(he worked as a financier, not a clergyman) happened to be sitting down. "Phil had a secondary nickname that was one of the all-time greats," Seidel remembers. "We used to call him Gefilte Fish. It conveyed three things about him: the fact that he was Jewish, that his name was Phil, and that he was a fish. Everybody loved when he played—especially me. I didn't have a lot of money saved up. I was scared to death of losing."

During Seidel's early poker days at the Mayfair, he approached games gingerly, as if every table were a field full of landmines. He evaluated situations as if they were potential buying opportunities on the stock exchange, and he jumped in only when he believed the price—or, in poker, the competition—was right.

UNLIKE DOYLE BRUNSON, Chip Reese, and Stu Ungar—natural-born risk takers—Erik Seidel entered the world without a whole lot of obvious gamble in him. Both of his parents worked in the film business, and he was a regular city kid, living in a racially mixed neighborhood near Harlem, amid big apartment buildings with doormen on the northern reaches of Manhattan's Upper West Side. By his own admission, Seidel was not a particularly good student, inept with the girls, an unskilled athlete, and not even very good at poker. But long before he understood the financial value of observing people and absorbing their characteristics, he was doing it.

Between the ages of 10 and 13, he and his friends hung out in front of the building where he lived and played endless games of handball, smacking a pink Spalding—a "spaldeen"—against an exterior wall. "Handball was the first thing I did that clicked," remembers Seidel. "Other kids in the game had moves that freaked you out. I didn't have those moves. But what I did have was a natural ability to *observe* those moves, pick up on them, and practice till I was as good as they were." He was a human sponge—not a particularly artful or original player, but an effective one. Sly and the Family Stone blasted from a primitive boombox as Seidel adroitly mastered slappy maneuvers like the *killer* (a hard slice that came back at the opposing player with a kooky spin) and the *baby*. "The kid who invented that one would hit the ball with such a tiny arc that you couldn't return it. I'd adapt all the moves, use them, figure out how to play against them, and employ specific strategies when they would be helpful."

A couple of years later, as a teenager, Seidel moved up a notch on the urban food chain when he began running with a cross-cultural crew of graffiti artists. They slipped into rail yards at night, carrying cans of Krylon spray paint, and bombed vacant trains with bursts of color. He tagged subway interiors with stylized letters that spelled out his self-appointed nickname: VOTE. At the same time, Seidel and his brother Jed, now a TV writer, wandered through Manhattan's theater district, sneaking into hit Broadway shows like *Pippin* and *Equus*. They earned money by buying discounted coupon books of movie tickets and selling individual admissions for full price to people waiting on line at the Embassy Theater on 72nd Street and Broadway. Erik Seidel lived a broad, curious, self-invented life, and he was open-minded enough that anything was possible.

During one of the Seidel brothers' wanderings, they came upon a cavernous place called Chess City. It was one flight above an old movie theater, around the corner from where they lived. The two boys walked upstairs to check it out. For 15-year-old Erik, it was like falling down a rabbit hole. Chess City patrons paid a few dollars per hour for table time, and grand masters—including, on one occasion, Russian champ Boris Spassky—would come in to square off against dozens of players at once. Erik found chess to be mildly interesting—and, like the world of graffiti bombers, this scene was freaky enough to be intriguing—but what really turned him on was a small cluster of backgammon games being played near the front of the club. He started spending evenings at Chess City, just watching, spying on the good players, gleaning an understanding of what they were doing right, blowing his mind on the realization that there actually *was* something to do right.

Seidel's earliest introduction to backgammon had come a couple of years earlier, when he was messing around with friends, playing on a board that his mother had bought at Bloomingdale's. He originally believed that the game was all about getting lucky rolls of the dice. At

Chess City he discovered that the best players usually won. Then he yearned to be one of those players.

Just as he had when he played handball against 10-year-old friends, Seidel instinctively adapted his game to beat specific opponents. When someone played conservatively, Seidel turned aggressive, leaving checkers unguarded and invading the other guy's side of the board. "I liked the idea of learning moves that would allow me to beat my friends for lunch money," he says.

Seidel, it was clear, had a natural instinct for the game and a dormant aptitude for gambling, both of which were so much more interesting than sitting in a classroom. "After graduating high school, I led two lives: going to Brooklyn College during the day and trying to make a living at backgammon each night," he remembers. After winning a tournament in Puerto Rico, he became so renowned on the circuit that an article in the *Boston Globe* dubbed him "New York's teen sensation." "I came home from that Puerto Rico trip with $12,000. It was a lot of money for a kid my age. How could I continue with school? I was totally intimidated by girls and felt like a complete outsider. But the backgammon scene was filled with social misfits. I was one of them."

Forgoing college, Seidel graduated to Chess City's highest stakes, playing for $25 or $50 or $100 per point and risking as much as $3,000 in a single match. Seidel lived with his mother—she and his father had divorced—and worked hard to keep his home life and his gaming life separate. But one afternoon, in 1981, the two worlds collided. Seidel came home and found his mother playing Scrabble with Teddy the Kid, an overweight, high-voiced backgammon gambler from the club. Seidel's mother, an attractive redhead, played reasonably well when the board came out at family gatherings, but she was no match for a hardened gamesman. He wound up winning $176 from her, and Seidel was livid. "Teddy clearly hustled my mother," he says. "This was real money to her. She's not used to gambling. She didn't realize what was going on. It was pretty sickening."

How Mom and Teddy the Kid hooked up was a mystery, but Seidel became obsessed with avenging his mother's loss. For days afterward, he hung around the game room, keeping an eye out for his adversary. Then, one snowy night, Teddy walked in, promptly lost $150 to Seidel, tapped his pockets, and admitted to being out of money. But he desperately wanted a rematch. Seidel, displaying a kind of gambler's ruthlessness that, for the first time, felt natural, refused to extend credit. He wanted to keep his opponent off-balance and desperate, leaving the guy broke, without a chance to recoup. Then Teddy pointed to his Timberlands and said, "I'll play for my boots."

Seidel, for whom the boots would be worthless, accepted the terms, willing—even eager—to humiliate an opponent in a way that he had never before done. At 2 in the morning, Teddy the Kid lost his boots. A crowd had formed around the game, and Teddy could not bring himself to begin undoing the laces. "You don't want these boots," he told Seidel. "Next time I see you, I'll pay you $100."

But the crowd was having none of it. Men pushed in around the backgammon board and started a slow chant: "Boots. Boots. Boots." Teddy scanned the room, grimaced, realized he had no choice. He pulled off the Timberlands and handed them to Seidel, who suddenly had the level of heartlessness necessary for any gambler who needs to take large sums of money from financially troubled opponents. "I got the satisfaction of watching Teddy the Kid walk through the snow in his socks; I wanted to punish him, and I did," says Seidel. "I gave my mother the $150, and I still have one of his boots. It's in my garage somewhere. I'd get it framed and mounted and hang it up on my office wall, but my wife won't let me."

ORGANIZED POKER GAMES have been illegal in New York City for generations. But that's rarely stopped them from thriving. Every neighborhood has its regular games behind bike shops, up in windowless second-story card rooms, even in apartments that double as casinos. They've always had evocative names—the Diamond Club, Gerty's, Play Station, Rounders, the Commodore Club—and run the gamut from semiposh to seedy to downright uncomfortable. But during the mid- to late-1980s there was something special about the Mayfair. It was founded by bridge master Alvin Roth in 1957, originally as a backgammon and bridge club, with a heavy emphasis on the latter, but with the highest-stakes wagering on the former. The Mayfair is where New York gamblers were first exposed to no-limit Texas Hold 'Em after a group of backgammon specialists returned from a scouting trip to the 1985 World Series.

In 1987 many of the best game players on earth happened to operate out of Manhattan, and they all gambled at the Mayfair. Guys like the professorial Howard Lederer, action hungry Billy Horan, and the brilliantly tight playing former lawyer Dan Harrington were all mastering the fine points of Hold 'Em on the Gramercy's second floor. Jay Heimowitz, an avuncular beer distributor from upstate who was a regular at the club, went on to win six World Series bracelets; bizarrely creative Noli Francisco, a World Series finalist, introduced odd concepts like the negative bet, in which each player would take a certain amount of money *out* of the pot. "There was a family feel to the Mayfair when people weren't hustling and cutting each other's throats," says semiprofessional gambler Wendeen Eolis. "People took a lot of delight in discussing who was losing—much more than in discussing who was winning—and it provided a way of humiliating the fish."

Poker's equivalent of the Algonquin—New York's famed, rakish literary watering hole—the Mayfair was an island of lost, but very bright, boys. They played against one another, but they also educated one another. "Their poker rapidly improved," says Eolis. "and they made big differences in each other's lives."

Between all-night sessions at the Mayfair, Seidel bolstered his skill and his confidence by playing endless strings of $50 no-limit freeze-outs—that is, mini-tournaments where each person plays until his $50 is gone—with options-trader/horse-handicapper Bob Banish and sports bettor Steve Zolotow. "I was the live one in that game—and I knew it," admits Seidel. "Banish and Z. weren't trying to tutor me or help me. I was essentially paying them money to see how they played. It was like paying tuition. I was losing but learning, and I knew I needed to do that if I wanted to get better."

SLOWLY, SEIDEL GOT the hang of poker. His confidence improved and so did his play. After the Wall Street crash, he earned enough at the Mayfair that he stopped concerning himself with getting another job as a trader. Already able to make quick decisions and assign value to abstract concepts—such as an opponent's two cards that you can't see—Seidel proved to be a quick study. One thing working in his favor was an instinctive ability to sublimate ego—or, as he puts it, "A lot of people think they're better than they are; it gets them into situations they can't beat"—and accept the fact that he was often not the strongest player in a particular game. But, as he learned, he didn't need to be: As long as there was someone Seidel could beat, he could extract positive results out of tough games. Employing the financial ruthlessness that had coalesced at Chess City and the stock exchange, he isolated the weak and vigorously attacked when he spotted an advantage.

Though Seidel lacked the kind of advanced math skills you learn in college, he had a good sense of how to reason things out in terms of their odds and expectations—instinctively understanding whether or not a bet was worth it, based on the cards he had and the hands he'd be capable of making. Seidel describes this as "real world mathematics," and he used it while carving out his ever-expanding advantages against specific opponents. "I was willing to be more versatile than other players," he explains. "I could play tight if I needed to, and I could play splashy when the situation called for that. I'm good at adapting my style to suit the circumstances. Maybe this comes from backgammon, where you play one-on-one and need to make quick adjustments, but I've always been able to focus on people and figure them out."

Seidel was so attentive at the table that, under the right conditions, he even studied bad players—like a guy named Jerry who went from being a fish to a winner, seemingly overnight, even though his overall play did not obviously improve. "I wanted to see what he was doing well," says Seidel. "On the surface he suddenly added a layer of unpredictability to his game—but you couldn't immediately see where it came from. Then I watched him and saw that he had devised a special technique for picking off bluffs. Certain patterns would become visible to him, and he would react to them in unpredictable ways"—maybe raising back when it seemed an unlikely thing for someone in his position to do. "It was a great lesson to see that a guy who's not a particularly good player can do a couple of things right and win."

After only six months of intense cramming at the Mayfair, Seidel became a consistently winning player. He went on a rush and raked in $78,000 over a two-week period. Suddenly he was reading tells, reacting to them, and focusing more intensely on newly transparent opponents who weren't expecting to be read so clearly. By May 1988, Seidel had gotten good enough that fellow Mayfair habitué Howard Lederer urged him to go to Las Vegas and take a shot at the World Series of Poker championship. Several Mayfair regulars wound up buying a piece of Seidel—that is, they contributed to the series's $10,000 entry fee in exchange for a portion of whatever Seidel might win. Having held onto only 30 percent of his potential profits, he was, as they say, "cut up like a boardinghouse pie."

Judging by the way things began in Vegas, however, it seemed a good bet that there would be no slices of Seidel for his investors. Soon after checking into the Golden Nugget, right across from the Horseshoe, he promptly lost nine single-table satellite tournaments, blowing through $9,000 of his own money. Hours before the World Series began, he started wondering what he was doing in Vegas and whether he was good enough to play in this league. "If I had had to buy into the series on my own, I don't think I would have done it," he says now. But, once the tournament began, Seidel shook off the early losses and surprised himself by surviving the first and second days. "I played each hand as it came. I didn't think about getting knocked out. I just thought about playing individual cards. What I remember very clearly is that I felt lucky to be at tables that weren't as tough as they could have been. But I also capitalized on the advantage of being an unknown in a tournament. People had no idea of my capabilities. I employed intense aggression against tight players after absorbing their styles and figuring out how to work them. Plus, I didn't come up against any supergeniuses for the first couple days, and that gave me a chance to build up a reserve of chips."

Seidel made the final table, but he squeaked in with the shortest stack—just $131,000 as compared to chip leader Johnny Chan's $529,000. Despite being a total underdog, Seidel called his wife Ruah and suggested she fly from New York to Vegas to watch—though he warned, "By the time you get here, I will probably be knocked out. I'm going in shooting."

Next day, wearing a long-sleeved black jersey, jeans, and a cock-eyed visor, Seidel played like a pro but looked like an outsider. Surrounded by cameras and TV lights, sitting alongside the astute Texas road gambler T.J. Cloutier ("I was so clueless that I had no idea who T.J. was," Seidel says), seasoned Costa Rican star Humberto Brenes, journeyman Ron Graham, and defending champion Johnny Chan, he was clearly the least experienced person at the table. "I began to wonder what was wrong with this picture," says Seidel, who surprised himself when his lack of final-table experience began working in his favor. "I was this goofy kid from the east, playing very fast." Often, during the early stages of a final table, people like to take it easy, feeling out the other players, preserving chips and enhancing their chances for survival. "I was raising a lot, but raising the same amount all the time, and, conversely, not putting enough pressure on people when I should have been. I played like a maniac, and it's hard to play against someone like that. I wound up frustrating a lot of people."

By the time Ruah's plane touched down in Vegas, the remaining players had contracted to three. Miraculously, her husband remained among them. She arrived in time to watch him square off against Ron Graham. He had been playing tight and began to steam a little as Seidel kept running over him, raising him out of hands. When Graham resolutely pushed all his chips to the center of the table, an opportunity availed itself. "I thought I had a read on him," remembers Seidel. "I thought he was sick of having this young kid stealing pots." The young kid was right; with 10-5, Graham was running a stone-cold bluff. Seidel, however, had only Ace high—not the hand you want to risk a tournament on. Ruah held her breath as the cards on board helped neither player, and Seidel just about doubled his stack. Graham stepped back from the table, leaving his opponent perfectly positioned to win the Series.

When it came down to two people, Erik Seidel and Johnny "The Orient Express" Chan, chip percentages had just about flip-flopped from the start of final-table play: Seidel had $1.2 million to doughy faced Chan's $470,000. But despite his lead, Seidel hardly looked like a clear-cut favorite. Even discounting the fact that Chan had won 1987's World Series, the pompadoured pro came to the table with a fear-inducing presence.

Over the course of the next three hours, Chan slowly chipped away at his less experienced opponent, letting Seidel play fast and loose while he kept things slow and conservative, not allowing his game to be bullied into reckless patterns. Ultimately, Chan grabbed the lead and built it to $1,374,000 in chips versus Seidel's $296,000. Then the flop came Queen-8-10. Sitting behind the dealer button, Chan made a tiny $40,000 bet. Seidel, who had hit top pair, interpreted it as weakness. He quickly called and palmed two additional stacks of chips, raising $50,000. Chan lazily rested his face in the palm of his hand, observed and re-observed his cards, and finally called. When the next card, a Deuce, seemed unlikely to help either player, Chan timidly checked. True to form, Seidel played the aggressor and pushed his chips all-in. Chan called and turned over his cards: Jack-9, which gave him the nut straight, an unbeatable hand that held up against Seidel's pair of Queens. Chan had won the Series by inducing Seidel to bet with the worst hand. Seven hundred thousand dollars in cash was promptly pushed toward Chan.

Facing a battery of reporters, Chan made it sound like Seidel's strategy was completely readable. "He played fast and bluffed off his chips," said Chan. "My whole game plan was to set a trap and make him bluff." Minutes later, Seidel, who walked away with a not-too-shabby $280,000 second prize, looked a little sick as he candidly responded to a TV interviewer's questions. "My inexperience [hurt me]," he acknowledged. "He outplayed me."

Later on, Seidel would reason that he probably should have played even faster than he had, and forced Chan to take risks that would have made him uncomfortable. "It was awful to be in such a great situation, but totally unprepared for it," Seidel told poker writer Dana Smith. Though he later acknowledged an upside: "The experience made me realize that maybe I could make a living from poker."

DURING THE ENSUING 17 years, that is exactly what happened. Weeks after the World Series, Seidel won a $1,000-buy-in tournament at the Bicycle Casino, near Los Angeles; it netted him $100,000 and the realization that he could shut down a table. He went on to earn six World Series of Poker bracelets, maintain a stable home life (complete with wife and two kids), become independently wealthy through sharp playing and shrewd investing, and relocate to Las Vegas, where he lives in a sprawling home on a golf course.

For a while Seidel was a regular presence in the big-money cash games around town—especially when a freewheeling gambler known as George the Greek came around—and he's clearly earned the respect of his peers. "Erik's obviously a great no-limit player and a great tournament player," says veteran gambler Billy Baxter, winner of seven World Series of Poker tournaments and one of the more venerable high-stakes specialists.

In Baxter's view, Seidel's human-sponge approach is most effectively applied after the flop, when the key to winning is in figuring out what your opponents are doing and reacting in a way that will draw them into the hand or push them out. "Preflop is a no-brainer," continues Baxter. "The real betting skill comes after the flop: determining what the other guys have, the best way to extract funds from them, when they are bluffing, when you should bluff. The way I see it, his strength is in reading the board and quickly determining a strategy for the rest of the hand." Seidel does it by analyzing what a player does preflop, then looking at the flop, watching how the player reacts to those new cards, and puzzling together an approximation of the opponent's hand and impending strategy. Then he adjusts his game to work around that opponent.

Seidel's current level of skill and sophistication would have come in handy in 1988, the year he lost the World Series championship to Chan. And though Seidel has built an enviable career for himself, his inability to beat the Orient Express in '88 will always be a lingering regret. But it goes a few levels beyond a merely missed opportunity. To begin with, in order to make the final table and reach the point where there is only one player between you and the bracelet, things have to line up perfectly—and, as the World Series championship field gets increasingly dense, that becomes more and more of a longshot, even for the best players. You need cards at the right moment, you have to play exceedingly well, and your opponents need to get unlucky. Realistically, there is a good chance that Seidel will never again find himself one seat away from poker's greatest achievement.

Making matters worse is a brief but memorable reference to Seidel in the movie *Rounders*. It comes during the scene in which Mike, played by Matt Damon, is watching a video of the 1988 World Series with his poker moll girlfriend Petra, played by Famke Janssen. The final hand between Seidel and Chan is being dealt, and Petra says, "Look at the control. [Chan] knows his man well enough to check it all the way and risk winning nothing. He knows him. Poor Seidel. Kid doesn't know what hit him."

Never mind that "poor Seidel" went on to become one of the most consistently winning players in poker—and is stable enough that he will never go broke. Anybody from outside the game would watch that scene and figure he's a big fish. The misperception irked Seidel, and he hungered for a chance to set the record straight. In 2001, at the World Series of Poker's $3,000 no-limit Texas Hold 'Em tournament, with a first prize of $411,300, it came down to two players: Seidel and Chan. Again. Sitting at a Horseshoe card table, with an ever-growing crowd pressed in behind him, Seidel, short-stacked with $200,000 in chips, looked across the table at the tournament's only remaining contender. "I guess we have a rematch," Seidel said.

"Yep," replied Chan, sitting with $950,000 and sounding unenthused. "History repeats itself."

The implication, of course, was that Seidel would again lose to Chan. And five hands into the showdown, the two-time champ seemed to be prognosticating correctly. Seidel made a couple of bets, failed to call an all-in wager from Chan, and was quickly down to $130,000. Over the next few hours, though, Seidel built-up his stacks—during a pair of critical hands, in close succession, he pulled down a total of $792,000—snagging the lead a few times before letting it shift back to Chan. "At the start, after that first hand, because he had me out-chipped, Chan played very cautiously," Seidel explains. "He didn't want me to get lucky and win the thing. But as I started to take the lead, he woke up, turned around, and played very aggressively. It was a total reworking of his strategy. But I changed mine as well."

After three hours of heads-up play, the tournament room was packed. Spectators began making bets with one another on the outcome. Seidel had developed a miniscule chip lead and Chan had slipped into the aggressor's role when a juicy hand unfolded. Following an initial bet of $40,000, the flop rolled Jack-5-King. Chan checked. Seidel, with King-2, made a $35,000 bet. Chan raised it $100,000. By this point, Seidel believed that Chan could easily raise with nothing. So he called the bet.

When a 2 came on the turn and Chan went all in, Seidel (now with two pair, Kings and 2s) suddenly got a funny feeling. Maybe he had misread his opponent. Maybe Chan wasn't bluffing at all. Maybe Chan had once again shifted his strategy, becoming more conservative, but doing it so quickly that it slipped below Seidel's radar. Seidel thought for a moment and decided that his hand was too strong to get away from, so he called. He stared down at the table. Chan showed his cards: Queen-7. It had been a total bluff. Seidel won the tournament and earned his revenge.

"Calling early on with that King and a Deuce kicker shows how fast I was playing," says Seidel. "It was a matter of my figuring out that he was playing differently, and now, all of a sudden, I had to gamble more. He might have been steaming a little bit, and I think he overcompensated with the aggressiveness."

That flexibility is broadly indicative of Seidel's playing style and a key to his success. In a game where each player usually maintains a signature style, Seidel is a chameleon. He shades his strategy to suit his opponent. Against Chan he slowed down his betting but not his play, and let Chan bluff himself out of the tournament. "Winning any World Series event is special," says Seidel. "But winning one against Chan, in light of our history—well, that made it even more special."

THREE YEARS AFTER the rematch, Seidel was sipping from a glass of early morning orange juice on the front patio of his house, blowing off a day of tournament poker so he could watch his daughter play volleyball in the afternoon. No longer the restless backgammon kid searching for thrills, he now appeared quietly content, possessing the kind of confidence that comes only from wide experience and success. He rocked back on his wrought-iron chair and remembered an anecdote that grew out of a game he played in at Paris's Aviation Club, a private poker room that overlooks the Champs Elysée where the action is notoriously fast. "A friend of mine got into a conversation about me with another player," Seidel began, "and this other player said he couldn't understand how I could play so tight and win. Fine. That is what that person thinks of me. But then, a couple weeks later, someone else told the same friend, 'That Erik Seidel is such a sick maniac. He's in every hand when he plays.'"

Seidel let it sink in for moment, then he twisted his lips into a shy and knowing smile. "I like what that story says about me."

Phil Hellmuth, 2001, at Binion's Horseshoe, Las Vegas

Seven

PHIL HELLMUTH

The Poker Brat

Outrageous antics and a supertight

strategy propel an ambitious Midwestern

kid into becoming the game's most

polarizing figure—and its biggest brand.

IN THE CLUBBY, OLD-VEGAS dining room of Binion's Steakhouse, with its oak paneling and red-velvet accents, tuxedo-clad waiters pushed chicken kabobs and other greasy hors d'oeuvres on a group of reporters more interested in wolfing down the wisdom of the one and only Phil Hellmuth, the notorious "poker brat." Wearing khaki chinos, a long-sleeve black T-shirt, and his signature mirror sunglasses, Hellmuth was the star attraction here, at a press conference announcing the launch of a new software application that allows subscribers to play Texas

Hold 'Em—rather, "Phil Hellmuth's Texas Hold 'Em,"—against other live players via their cell phones.

The event, held during a brief lull in the 2004 World Series of Poker, featured all the standard bluster that accompanies the launch of any new product with a celebrity endorsement. All smiles, Hellmuth joked with the software company's chief executive, fielded questions from the press, and signed a few autographs. "This is the future of poker," he proclaimed from the podium at one point.

The scene would have seemed like a desert mirage to the grizzled old-timers scratching out a living against the tourists downstairs: Autographs? Endorsements? Historically, poker players dwelled in anonymity—and they wanted it that way. As obsessively high-rolling gambler Nick "The Greek" Dandolos once said, "In my profession, fame is usually followed by a jail sentence."

But the Greek toiled in a bygone era, from the 1930s to the '60s, when poker was a renegade profession. Hellmuth, who has ridden his "supertight" playing strategy to a record number of poker titles before the age of 40, helped make it respectable. You could argue, in fact, that the concept of mainstream poker celebrity was conceived when Hellmuth won the World Series as a fresh-faced 24-year-old in 1989. Unlike talk-show favorite Amarillo Slim or New York prodigy Stu Ungar, Hellmuth immediately registered with kitchen-table gamblers around the country as more than simply a colorful curiosity. After all, he was just a regular kid from Wisconsin with an $8 haircut and acne; if he could capture poker's most prestigious championship, why couldn't they? So what if he was a bit of a pill at times? Didn't that just make him all the more human?

As poker steadily gained traction in the culture at large, Hellmuth recognized that the game's growing respectability would translate into more money—huge money—for the top players. So he didn't just accept his fame, he embraced it.

"People like Johnny Chan or [1999 world champion] Huck Seed, who I have tremendous respect for, would almost go out of their way not to get press," he says. "I always met with the reporters because I figured, as my fame grows, my endorsement opportunities grow."

Indeed. In 1998, Hellmuth built a website, philhellmuth.com. The next year he signed an endorsement deal with ultimate bet.com, one of the first Internet poker sites (and now one of the most successful), in exchange for an equity position in the young company. When *World Poker Tour* debuted, in 2003, with Hellmuth as one of its main stars, he became even more of a commodity.

In 2003 Hellmuth also signed with Brian Balsbaugh, a former sports agent for professional golfers who was starting a management company specializing in poker players. Balsbaugh sought players that fit three criteria: They needed to be successful, attractive, and willing to sell themselves. "The vast majority are 0 for 3," Balsbaugh says. "Only two or three players in the world of poker are good at all three." Hellmuth is at the top of that short list, he says, and therefore has become the biggest brand in poker. When a startup company proposed forming a television network devoted to gambling, programming execs approached Hellmuth before any other poker player. He received offers for everything from clothing lines to instructional videos to reality TV shows within the first three months Balsbaugh worked with him. He was even paid $25,000 to speak at a Goldman Sachs corporate event. And now he's poised to leverage his poker fame into the kind of money that is not imaginable at the tables.

"It's not even close," Hellmuth says. "I might make $100 million or $200 million or $300 million in my endorsement deals. The upside is hundreds of millions."

Rank-and-file players, who are thrilled to get their hands on a few hundred thousand, can't even fathom figures like that, and roll their eyes at what they consider standard Hellmuth hyperbole. But most of them learned a valuable lesson long ago: Don't bet against him.

HELLMUTH IS A poker superstar for two reasons. There is his precocious talent: youngest World Series of Poker champion in history, a record-tying nine World Series bracelets, and a trophy case full of other major titles—all before the age of 40. And then there is his ego.

The *Sports Illustrated* columnist Rick Reilly wrote that Hellmuth once referred to himself as "the Jack Nicklaus of poker," "the Tiger Woods of poker," and "the Mozart of poker" in the course of a 30-

minute interview. He has often been compared to another supremely talented prima donna, John McEnroe, and he frequently lives up to the comparison by kicking chairs and flopping to the floor after a bad beat. His antics earned him his moniker, "poker brat"—and raised his profile among fans—but they don't always endear him to competitors.

"I've never seen a player so disliked by his peers," says Amarillo Slim. The lanky and eminently quotable Texan, of course, knows a thing or two about self-promotion, but he says Hellmuth's grandstanding is different because it is disrespectful to other players. He recalled an incident at a tournament several years ago when Hellmuth repeatedly got up from the table to pace and stew when the cards were not falling his way. Slim walked over to Hellmuth and asked him to sit down so they could resume the tournament. After tipping his cowboy hat back so he could lean in close, Slim whispered to Hellmuth, "Son, if you want some notoriety, set yourself on fire."

Hellmuth also regularly berates other players for poor play, particularly those he feels he can intimidate. Diego Cordovez, a former dotcom executive who went on to win a World Series bracelet and several other tournament titles, says that the first time he and Hellmuth played together, Hellmuth snarled, "Do you know who you're fucking with?" when Cordovez had the temerity to raise a few times in a row.

It was far from an isolated incident, as virtually all newcomers to the tournament circuit must endure Hellmuth's bullying tactics until they earn their stripes. In 2001, Hellmuth was busted from the World Series in rather cruel fashion by an unknown player from Brooklyn named Robert Varkonyi. On the tournament's third day, Varkonyi opened the betting with a small raise and Hellmuth reraised. Varkonyi, who later said he thought Hellmuth was trying to bully him and steal the pot, moved all-in. Hellmuth called the bet and turned over the Ace-King of hearts. Varkonyi held only the Queen-10 of clubs, making Hellmuth nearly a 2-to-1 favorite to win the hand. But Varkonyi made two pair on the flop and crippled Hellmuth's chances to capture the title.

Hellmuth fumed over his unlucky defeat for two days as Varkonyi proceeded to the final table. In the midst of the last day's action, as the inexperienced Varkonyi battled for the $2 million first prize, Hellmuth openly ridiculed him. He announced over the public address system that he would shave his head if Varkonyi won, a pledge he repeated on ESPN. And sure enough, when the MIT-educated Varkonyi took the title (fittingly, by making a full house out of his Queen-10), Hellmuth stole the spotlight at the awards ceremony when he submitted to the clippers in front of the jeering crowd. Meanwhile, Varkonyi, in what should have been his moment of glory, stood on the sidelines and watched. Even in loss, Hellmuth had managed to get some press. "He acts like a teenager who doesn't get enough attention," says Varkonyi. "Whether it's good attention or bad attention, he wants it."

Hellmuth's behavior is rooted in more than simple hubris, however. By all accounts, poker's Mr. Hyde turns into Dr. Jekyll outside the card room. He is uncommonly sensitive, a devoted husband and father, and gracious with fans. During the 2004 World Series, he was spotted giving $20 to a homeless man loitering in the tournament area. The man, who said his name was Robert, later explained that he was a down-on-his-luck poker player and Hellmuth gives him $20 every time he sees him. "Phil's a great guy," Robert said. "Most people don't understand that." Russ Hamilton, winner of the 1994 World Series, echoes that sentiment, as do many of Hellmuth's closest friends: "He's the nicest guy you'll ever meet—away from the table," says Hamilton.

Hellmuth himself has acknowledged that his conduct in the heat of the moment can be a problem, and admits that he's embarrassed himself at times. He's even taken steps to correct it, he says. He's consulted therapists, meditated, and issued a series of contrite mea culpas in the press:

August 1991: "I feel like the ego binges are over."

June 1996: "I'm over my ego problems now."

May 1999: "Maybe, just maybe, I've learned to control my ego now."

But it's an ongoing struggle. Shortly before the final event of the 2004 World Series, Hellmuth was asked to rank himself in the pantheon of poker greats. "I may be the greatest player in the history of poker," he replied.

A week later, during the second day of the tournament, with ESPN cameras pointed at him, Hellmuth sat with a table of unknown players, most of whom guarded stacks three to four times larger than his.

Perched on the edge of his chair with his elbows on the table and chin rested in his palms, Hellmuth was coiled and controlled, giving the impression of a man wound tighter than the inside of a baseball. He raised repeatedly, only to have other players come over the top. Clearly frustrated that he wasn't dominating in front of the TV cameras, he sighed and shifted in his seat, but continued to lay down hand after hand. "Guys, I got the bat cocked and ready and you guys keep stepping in front of me. All I gotta do is swing," he snapped.

As Hellmuth's stack continued to dwindle and no big action unfolded, the ESPN crew moved across the room. "Phil, the cameras are gone," one of the players said, "so tell me, why are you always so unhappy, always complaining?"

"I'm not unhappy," Hellmuth replied. "I count my blessings every morning. I've got my health, my family." If he had stopped there, it would have been a rare display of humility. But he continued to enumerate his blessings, clearly intent on highlighting the difference between himself and his lowly questioner.

"Fame," he said sharply. "Fortune."

The other players chuckled and filed away the comment, a good one to tell the boys back home about Hellmuth's monstrous ego.

As his chips continued to drain away, fans lined up five-deep on the rail in hopes of catching a classic Hellmuth meltdown—surely he would blow off some steam when he was inevitably knocked out by one of the bigger stacks. What the crowd didn't know was that his antics rarely stemmed from anger, but rather his intense disappointment in losing. He didn't want to win—he *needed* to win. And, here, in the biggest poker tournament in history, he was about to bust out early. Hellmuth pulled his hat down low and didn't speak to the other players or the spectators. He was still, almost serene. Behind the sunglasses, he was crying.

"WHETHER HE LIKES it or not, a man's character is stripped bare at the poker table," author Anthony Holden once wrote. It's a truism that reveals itself in a variety of forms, not least in the way a player's personality is often exposed in his strategic approach to the game.

Brash, ultraconfident players like Amarillo Slim and young Daniel Negreanu play lots of pots and give lots of action because they believe they can outplay their opponents with psychology and cunning. Chip Reese and Howard Lederer, on the other hand, are sober and businesslike, rarely making bets that are not dictated by mathematical probabilities or table position.

Hellmuth plays tight, meaning he plays relatively few hands. He frequently folds hands that most players would play aggressively. He even tries to avoid pots where he is a slight favorite, preferring opportunities where his chances of victory are almost assured, either because he is convinced his opponents will not call or because he holds a monster hand. He learned to play tight from his mentor at the University of Wisconsin, but since then he's taken it to a level all his own—the strategy he calls "supertight."

It is unquestionably successful, particularly at no-limit Hold 'Em, where one bad decision can cost you a tournament. But, if Holden is to be believed, it is perhaps not surprising that Hellmuth adopted a strategy that offers the fewest possibilities of failure. This thinking runs counter to most other pros' strategies, which all but require doing things unconventionally and therefore looking foolish on occasion. By picking his spots so selectively, Hellmuth reduced to almost nothing the chance that he'd look foolish—all the more important when you're concerned about your public image.

At nearly six-foot-six and with the face of a chubby-cheeked choirboy, it's easy to imagine Hellmuth as a high school basketball star or president of his class. But he was neither. Growing up on the shores of Lake Mendota in the heart of Madison, Wisconsin, he had few friends and spent most of his time in the video arcade. "I felt kind of like a loser," he says.

His self-esteem plummeted further his sophomore year of high school, when he contracted a severe case of warts. The bumpy lesions, more than 30 in all, covered the backs of his hands and crawled up his wrists. Hellmuth hated the feeling that his classmates were staring at his hands, so he learned to write with his palms facing up and walked down the hall between classes with his hands stuffed in his back pockets.

A doctor surgically removed one of the warts but the procedure left a scar. He said removing all of the warts would likely leave Hellmuth's hands permanently disfigured, and he advised Hellmuth simply to wait and hope they went away. So he did. After more than a year of misery, the warts finally disappeared.

The next year, though, Hellmuth's face broke out with acne. The problem stayed with him until he was 35, but as a senior in high school it further eroded his self-confidence. In a family of high achievers—his father was assistant dean of the College of Arts and Letters at the University of Wisconsin, his mother was a sculptor, and his four younger siblings already showed considerable promise—Hellmuth saw himself as a failure.

His mother encouraged him to dwell only on the positive. She posted a saying on the bathroom mirror: YOU ARE WHAT YOU THINK. YOU BECOME WHAT YOU THINK. WHAT YOU THINK BECOMES REALITY. But he wasn't buying it, at least not until, as he recalled later, "something weird happened" when Rose Gladden, a renowned psychic and faith healer from England, visited Madison.

Hellmuth's mother had an interest in clairvoyance, and invited Gladden to stay with the family while she was in town. One night, Gladden sat in the living room with the assembled clan and told them what she saw for each of them. When she held Hellmuth's hands, she announced, "You will be very, very famous and well-known throughout the world."

Hellmuth pressed her for more—famous at what? But she would not say. Gladden gave less outlandish fortunes for the others in the room. The oldest son, she said, was the one who would be famous. And he believed it.

"You could sense that she had this aura about her," Hellmuth says. "I'm not saying I believe in ESP, but she predicted some stuff correctly about me."

The next year, Hellmuth moved across town to the University of Wisconsin with a conflicted self-image. On the one hand, he was still deeply insecure. On the other hand, he was convinced he was anointed for greatness.

Hellmuth muddled along and set a half-hearted goal of going to business school after graduation. Then, during his junior year, after a pickup basketball game, he tagged along with a buddy who played in a regular poker game at Memorial Union. The game was no-limit dealer's choice with a $5 minimum buy-in and a 10-cent ante. The cast of students, cab drivers, and white-collar professionals gathered around a rectangular cafeteria table and bet with Austrian coins so campus police would not suspect they were actually gambling.

Hellmuth, who had played only penny-ante poker as a kid, bought in for $20, and quickly lost it. But he was intrigued by the game—especially the opportunities it presented to manipulate how others perceived him. "When he had a strong hand, he would try to act weak. When he had a weak hand, he tried to talk up his hand like he had a big hand," says Tuli Haromy, a Ph.D. student in biochemistry, who was originally from Las Vegas and organized the game. "He acted so primitively that it was obvious what was going on. But I could see he had potential."

Hellmuth began playing twice a week, but still lost consistently. He borrowed $100 from Haromy, and lost that, too. He eventually stopped coming around, and Haromy wondered if he would ever see his $100 again.

When Hellmuth returned, after building a bankroll through a $4-an-hour job pulling weeds for the school's agriculture department, Haromy took the kid under his wing and taught him the crucial difference between playing poker for fun and playing for money: Play fewer hands. Haromy just wanted to get his $100 back, but he instilled in Hellmuth his philosophy that "tight is right." He didn't want Hellmuth to be passive, just selectively aggressive.

"In a full game, no matter how good you are, you must throw away at least 75 percent of your hands," explains poker theorist and author David Sklansky, who frequently stresses the importance of hand selection. "If you put [the best players in the world] at a full table and require them to play at least 40 percent of their hands, I can take a run-of-the-mill $10/$20 pro and he will beat them. It's sort of like being a paramedic or an airplane test pilot. You have to sit around and do nothing, and have the patience to do that, and then be aggressive when you have the right hand. But most people who are aggressive are impatient. And most people who are patient are not inherently aggressive. Poker forces good players to combine two things that are inherently contradictory."

Hellmuth managed to do that, and finally started to win. Before long it was his sole passion in life. He was certain he had found the vehicle to fulfill the psychic's vision.

Across town, his parents were furious when he dropped out of college to pursue poker full-time. Hellmuth later told an interviewer that he once asked his father, "Would you rather I worked in a post office or became the greatest poker player in the world?"

"The post office," his father had said.

Hellmuth persisted. He didn't read Sklansky's books—or anyone else's, for that matter; he just played as often as he could. It felt increasingly naturally to him, and he supplemented his "tight is right" formula with a newfound instinct for reading other people. He moved up to higher stakes in the Madison area, routinely buying in for $500, and hosted games at his one-bedroom apartment. He drove to a game in Minneapolis, where the buy-in was $1,000, and took home $6,000.

For the most part, he was well-mannered, with few of the tantrums that would become his trademark. "He was always temperamental, but he was able to hold it because he didn't want to get thrown out of games," Haromy says. "Now he has made a name for himself and he is so famous that a casino is not going to risk barring him for something that is out of line. It's a totally different situation."

During one all-night game at Hellmuth's apartment, the field dwindled down until Haromy and Hellmuth controlled all the money. Playing heads-up, the pupil finally beat the teacher. Haromy knew Madison was a shallow pool of poker talent, so he sent Hellmuth to his hometown: Las Vegas.

IT WAS IN 1988, just two years later, that Hellmuth entered his first World Series of Poker. The 23-year-old had won a small no-limit tournament in Reno and, despite a bumpy start, had finally started to win in Las Vegas at the higher-limit tables. His confidence was soaring and he was steamrolling through the field when stone-faced defending champion Johnny Chan came to his table.

If Hellmuth, with his preppy attire and petulant behavior, was poker's McEnroe, Chan was the game's Bjorn Borg. Chan was as inscrutable as he was invincible. He favored Fila track suits and oversize Yves St. Laurent sunglasses, and placed an orange in front of him on the table as some sort of mysterious talisman.

Soon after Chan sat down, Hellmuth ran a bluff at him and Chan saw through it, taking a big bite out of Hellmuth's stack. A few hands later, Hellmuth was dealt 10-10. He pushed all his chips in. Chan called and turned over Jack-Jack. When the rest of the cards were dealt and neither player improved his hand, Chan raked the pot. Using Hellmuth's chips, Chan went on to beat Erik Seidel and take his second straight title. It wasn't a bad play by Hellmuth, but tournaments are often won by recognizing that a good hand is actually the second-best hand at the table. He felt he had to play even tighter.

At the same time, Hellmuth's incessant boasting was drawing notice from the more-established players. He approached Seidel at the Diamond Jim Brady tournament at the Bicycle Casino and bragged about winning three satellites at the recently completed World Series. Seidel had just finished second to Chan in the main event, and was understandably unimpressed. "He made a big deal over what little things he had done," Seidel recalls. "He was Phil. He didn't have the credentials yet, but he was already talking like he did."

Hellmuth proceeded to finish second to Seidel in a $1,000 buy-in event, and the next day captured his first major title in the $5,000 event, pocketing a first prize of $145,000. When he got back to Madison, Hellmuth added a bold prediction to the outgoing message on his answering machine: "Next time you talk to me, I'll be the world champion of poker."

But the road to the top went through Chan. In January of 1989 Hellmuth faced Chan in a small tournament that was little more than a prelude to the World Series. When Chan bluffed Hellmuth out of a pot, he showed his cards proudly. In a scene that seemed to predate the classic showdown between Matt Damon and John Malkovich in the movie *Rounders*, Hellmuth claimed he picked up a tell on Chan. "You'll never beat me again," he told Chan. "You showed me something there."

Chan went on to claim that tournament as well. A writer for *Esquire* magazine, on hand for a profile of Chan, asked the champ about the mouthy kid. "I let my ego get out of hand when I was younger, too," Chan said. "But Phil will be world champ one day too. He just needs to learn to tuck it in a bit."

Remarkably, Hellmuth and Chan found themselves heads-up again at the 1989 World Series. Chan was going for an unprecedented third-straight championship bracelet. Hellmuth, with a recent outbreak of acne compounding his already youthful countenance, was playing for his entry into poker history. He flew his parents in to watch, the first time they had seen him play poker.

Thirty minutes into the action, Hellmuth was dealt Ace-7 of diamonds—a very strong hand heads-up. He opened the pot for $35,000 and Chan raised another $130,000. Hellmuth, sticking to his tight gameplan, folded the hand. He sensed that Chan was trying to establish himself as the aggressor, and planned to set a trap the next time he found a strong hand. Hellmuth knew that his tight strategy did more than just minimize his losses; it allowed him to take advantage of the image he was broadcasting. In this case, he believed that, if he mimicked his earlier play (despite having a stronger hand that he'd be less likely to fold), he could entice Chan into coming over the top again—and this time take the pot. A couple of hands later, Hellmuth looked down to find a pair of black 9s in the hole. He made the same bet as before—$35,000, hoping Chan would snap at the bait. He did— Chan raised another $130,000. This time, Hellmuth didn't fold. He raised $1 million. The tournament was on the line. Chan had $450,000 left in front of him. If he folded, Hellmuth would have three times as many chips. If he called and won the pot, he would take over the chip lead. If he called and lost, the tournament was over.

After pondering the decision silently for more than a minute, Chan reluctantly called, and showed Ace-7 of spades. The remaining cards didn't help either player, and Hellmuth's pair of 9s earned him the title as the youngest champion in the history of the World Series. He raised his arms in triumph. His father hustled down to the table and embraced him.

FEW QUESTION THAT Hellmuth is among the top tournament players in the world, and many rate him as the best. In the 15 years after his 1989 title, he was arguably the most dominant player at the World Series, claiming eight more bracelets and earning in excess of $3.5 million.

But he has long been dogged by the perception that he is a consistent loser in side games. To old-school gamblers, cash games are the truest test of poker, because a player risks not just his entry fee, as in a tournament, but possibly his entire bankroll. Hellmuth certainly got off to a bad start: After his World Series victory in 1989, he took his $775,000 first prize into the side games, and lost almost all of it. His critics say he doesn't have the temperament to ride out the inevitable peaks and valleys in the marathon side games, which stretch on for hours, sometimes days. In addition, Hellmuth is regarded as a no-limit Hold 'Em specialist, and side action almost always features a variety of games, almost all of them forms of limit poker. As a result, the regular players in the world's biggest cash games say Hellmuth hasn't sat down there in years.

"I would pay him just to play," says Daniel Negreanu, who regularly buys in for six-figure sums in cash games at the Bellagio. "His fundamental knowledge [of most games] is very weak. He hasn't studied enough. When he makes claims that he is the best player in the world, it's insulting to people like Chip [Reese], Doyle [Brunson], Phil Ivey, Gus [Hansen]—it's like, are you kidding me?"

Hellmuth shrugs off the criticism. He claims he has made more than half a million dollars in cash games in recent years, but says that is beside the point. He insists that the money is merely a byproduct of his goal to be recognized as the greatest player in poker history. "Do you want money, or do you want history? Or do you want both? If you want both, the answer is not to be sitting in the side games," he says. "No one remembers that you won $300,000 in a month—no one cares." To Hellmuth, in other words, poker greatness is measured in terms of public recognition, not money—which is the opposite of how just about every other player in history has thought of it. Some may have embraced fame as a byproduct (Amarillo Slim, for example), but none has pursued it as a goal in and of itself.

Hence Hellmuth's concentration on tournament play. Tournaments declare winners, issue press releases, and now are often televised. If Negreanu claims to win a half-million dollars in side games at the Bellagio, no one outside of his accountant and the IRS knows if he actually did. If Hellmuth wins a World Series bracelet, it happens on stage and gets recorded for posterity. Poker traditionalists may snicker at this career model, but it is perfectly suited to the game's modern age.

In recent years, though, Hellmuth's tournament performance has fallen short of his lofty expectations. Although he made several final tables, he failed to win a World Poker Tour event during its first two seasons, and did not win a bracelet at the 2004 World Series. He came to believe that he needed to revamp his tournament strategy.

His new approach takes his supertight strategy and squeezes even harder. It stems in part from a hand at the 2003 World Series that still haunts him. Midway through the fourth day, Hellmuth held a pair of Queens and called an all-in bet by Jason Lester, who held a pair of Jacks. Lester spiked a Jack on the river to make a set and cripple Hellmuth. He ultimately finished 27th out of 839 entries.

Even though 98 out of 100 pros would have played it the same way, Hellmuth regretted his decision. "I was so sharp last year," he says. "I felt like I could have folded that hand and run my $200,000 into a million without ever playing a big pot."

Hellmuth pledged to stick to a new game plan that avoided confrontation at almost all costs, choosing to chop out little pots and wait until he got the nuts.

At the 2004 World Series, as he put his new approach into practice, Hellmuth folded a number of big hands. He folded pocket Kings when his opponent reraised him before the flop. Twice, he folded Queens, once to a single raise. He said later that he believed the other player held a pair of 7s, but he didn't want to risk losing to a set if a 7 came on the flop. That's a remarkable statement: If it's true, then he believed he was a 4.5-to-1 favorite—and he folded.

The ability to lay down a big hand at crucial times is one of the demarcations between the good players and the great players, as Hellmuth learned in his 1988 confrontation with Chan. But it's also true that poker contains an element of luck that is impossible to avoid at all times. The accepted wisdom is that you have to run lucky enough in tournaments to win a handful of "coin flips"—such as Ace-King versus a pair of Jacks when it is virtually a statistical dead-heat as to who is favored to win the hand—in order to survive.

Of course, it goes without saying that Hellmuth must deviate from his supertight strategy just enough to keep opponents off balance. But he insists that, on the whole, he can pick his spots so sparingly and so accurately that he will almost never put his chips in danger. "My game has to be so sharp—and the fact of the matter is I'm only sharp enough 20 percent of the time," he says. "But there will be a time in the next year or two when I fold pocket Aces before the flop."

"If you want to be the best in the world at something," he says, "sometimes you have to invent a new way to do it."

HELLMUTH NOW SPENDS more of his time building the Hellmuth brand than actually playing poker. Though he lives in Palo Alto with his wife and two boys, he rarely drives in to nearby Bay 101 casino, in San Jose. He stays home with his family, writes books—his first effort, *Play Poker Like the Pros*, briefly entered the *New York Times* best-seller list in late 2004—and evaluates offers from potential sponsors. Like Tiger Woods, another history-obsessed competitor, he plays only in the major events.

"I don't have to be the best poker player of all time in order to be a brand, in order to be a celebrity," he says. "That was coming anyway. But it just so happens that I want to be the best poker player of all time. This is what has been driving me for 15 years, and I am going to continue to drive on it. I just need to win a few World Poker Tour events, 15 or 20 more World Series bracelets, and then I will have put the records way out of reach, kind of like Jack Nicklaus with 18 majors. Let's see if someone can come along and catch me."

Men the Master, 1991, at Binion's Horseshoe, Las Vegas

Eight

MEN "THE MASTER" NGUYEN

The Vietnamese Godfather

A refugee finds the American dream at

the card table, deals in his countrymen,

and forms a controversial poker cartel.

WHEN MEN "THE MASTER" NGUYEN squared off against young Leo Alvarez one weekday evening in the fall of 2002, it resembled one of those lopsided boxing matches in which the only big questions are: How long will it last? How brutal will it be? And how much can a less experienced fighter learn from witnessing his own slaughter? Like any number of Men's heads-up confrontations, the result here was all but preordained.

They battled inside an unadorned tournament room at the Bicycle Casino in Bell Gardens, California, a smoggy, blue-collar suburb of Los Angeles. It was 10 p.m., and a crowd of 20 people—largely Vietnamese, mostly rooting for the man named Men—leaned in after every shuffle and watched the hands of Seven-Card Stud unfold. Earlier in the day, at around 3 in the afternoon, this space, which resembled nothing so much as a Holiday Inn ballroom, was full of players—118 of them, each of whom had put up $330 to enter the tournament and angle for a share of the $35,400 pot.

Inevitably, of course, it came down to two guys, holding all the chips and vying for the lion's share of the proceeds ($14,160 for the winner, $8,140 for second place, and the remaining money split among the top six finishers below them).

Men, 51 at the time, rolled up the sleeves of his white dress shirt, pushing the cuffs past his elbows. He wore black pants with yellow monogrammed letters along the legs. Lemon-colored Buddha beads rode low on one wrist, and strapped around the other was a thin gold watch that commemorated his $280,000 first prize from the 2001 Tournament of Champions poker match at the Trump Taj Mahal in Atlantic City. On Men's feet: square-toed elevator boots, custom-made in L.A.'s Chinatown. His face was a slightly pocked full moon. His hair resembled barbed wire.

Suddenly, after winning a hand with two pair to Leo's one, Men karate-sliced the green felt table-top. Aiming to pressure his opponent into ending things right here—it had been a long day and Men's stomach audibly rumbled with hunger—he looked at Leo and said, "Let's chop it," meaning that they should split the money and quit playing.

Just one problem. Leo, a 30-something hipster with slicked-back hair, a goatee, and shades, had never won a tournament in his life. He's a sharp player, and he wanted to leave with the first-place finisher's ring. But Men had more chips and, if they settled, he would be the de facto victor. "Let's take $10,000 apiece and play for the last $2,000 and the ring," Leo suggested, pumping his right knee at about 120 bpm.

Men looked at Leo. Then he shot a leer toward a young Vietnamese woman wearing a black miniskirt and sitting in Leo's corner. "We play for $2,000 and the girl," he said.

The girl, positioned a few seats behind Leo, blushed. "Men's got plenty of women. He doesn't need me," she said.

This got a big laugh from everyone except Leo, who just focused on the ring until the next hand was dealt. They would play to the finish, he declared.

And so the head games began.

At one point Leo had two high pair, and decided to bet heavily. "What are you *doing*?" Men asked, and raised right back. Leo considered his options long and hard, then folded. Men raked the pot and cackled. He revealed two 4s.

Later, when Leo signaled uncertainty by making a medium-size bet, Men raised with gusto, leaving the impression that he was running a bluff. "Yum, yum," he said, licking his chops, nervously glancing at his cards. Then, after Leo called, Men unveiled a full house. "Leo, Leo, Leo," he sighed. "You should have known better than to go in against me when I say *yum*."

It went on like that for the next hour, the Master playing like a high-stakes David Blaine, magically producing the right cards when necessary and—perhaps even more magically—winning without them half the time. Clearly, though, Men was not controlling the cards, he was controlling poor Leo. He showily bluffed without even having a low pair. He set traps, leading Leo to believe that he could win against daunting odds. He had, in short, a spookily perfect read on his less experienced opponent.

"You are making big mistakes here, losing opportunities, Leo," Men scolded, raking in chips. Piling a big stack, he added, "Now you have no chance to beat the Master."

Indeed, by 11 p.m. it was over. Men posed for Polaroids with a pile of cash and a velvet-bottomed case containing the commemorative ring. Then he put the box in his pocket and strode out.

"People see me play and say, 'He's lucky.' Or they think I talk too much and needle people. But I don't care," he says. "I came to this country from Vietnam, with empty hands. Now, I got everything I want. All I need to do is say, '*Call. Raise. Call.*' And people give me their money. Americans made me who I am today. I love America. Without America, I would probably be dead."

NEAR THE BICYCLE Casino entrance, Men huddled with half a dozen of the Vietnamese players who had been watching him in action all evening. Out here, just a few steps from the valet parking attendant, they cracked up at Men's jokes and seriously reviewed the hands he had just played. Speaking in Vietnamese, they dissected how everything went down. For Men and his cartel of Vietnamese poker players—even the ones just learning to play—the game is as choreographed as tai chi, with each situation demanding a correct move and countermove.

L.A.'s expat Vietnamese poker players love Men the Master. He is their don, their father, their teacher. Unlike most poker pros, Men rarely travels without his retinue in tow. They provide him with the kind of unquestioning respect granted to strongmen everywhere. They rise to their feet and cheer when Men enters a casino. They call him "Master" with no irony. They savor every word that tumbles from his mouth.

Westerners on the circuit view him with less exaltation. One of Europe's hottest poker stars snickeringly calls him Men the Monkey. A top pro in Las Vegas characterizes him as "a sleazy guy." And a couple of New York players suggest that Men and his Vietnamese acolytes engage in ugly forms of collusion.

To be sure, there have been suspicious incidents—perhaps none more so than what happened during a 2004 ESPN broadcast of a Seven-Card Stud tournament, when Men and one of his guys, Minh Nguyen (no relation), played at the same final table. When an ESPN interviewer asked Minh how he felt about competing against his teacher, Minh admitted, "I stay away from him [at the table]. I don't want to get involved in hands with him. He is too good." And then— early in the game—Minh folded two Queens against Men's two Jacks on board, arguably giving the appearance of soft-playing his Master and allowing him to win the pot. It was a sketchy-looking move that was difficult to ignore but impossible to nail as cheating.

Regardless, whether you view Men as master or monkey, his success is uncontestable. At poker tables in Southern California and Las Vegas, he has won more than 75 major tournaments and raked in prize money in excess of $5 million over 19 years—and he claims he's won even more in cash games. In 2003, Men ranked number one on *Card Player* magazine's list of the winningest tournament players in poker. "Men's got a special ability to read opponents' cards," says Barry Shulman, publisher of *Card Player*. "Plus, he has some kind of photographic memory." Why the derision from other players? "He wins their money and doesn't give a shit what anybody thinks."

That was evident in Atlantic City, when, while competing in the tournament he ultimately won at the Taj, Men pulled a highly unconventional move. "He had huge chips, it was late at night, we were down to two tables, desperate to get to the final table, and one person away from doing that," remembers tournament finalist Adam Schoenfeld. "The guy in the big blind might have had two chips left, but instead of raising him, or at least calling with the hope of knocking him out, Men just folded. It kept us from getting to the final table and extended the agony that any one of us, other than Men, could get busted. But it was also a very good, crafty poker move. By prolonging things, he was able to keep picking up blinds and antes at will."

Beyond his own game, Men has also proved a deft teacher, mentoring and financing a posse of Vietnamese poker pros who hit the tables en masse and operate with single-minded precision. Guys who had never before gambled, who speak broken English but have mathematical instincts, are tutored by Men in the ways of flushes and full houses. In exchange, the players that Men calls "my boys" abide by his rules: 2 a.m. curfew, no drugs, no sex with other players' girlfriends, and, most important, if Men tells you to do something, you do it.

Their success and attendant loyalty have imbued Men with riches and power that extend beyond the tables. "He's trained more tournament winners than anyone else in the business," says Benny Behnen, grandson of Benny Binion. "Men is the best money manager in poker, the only guy I know whose money is taller than he is. He's got a piece of everything going. I call him the Vietnamese Godfather."

One of Men's players, skinny Chau Lee, who has a stringy map of Vietnam tattooed down one bicep, puts it more militantly: "We are the Master's soldiers."

AN HOUR OR so after beating Leo, Men took his crowd out for a celebratory dinner. As always, Men chose where the meal would be eaten, ordered the food, and paid for everything. Try to pick up a tab, and he will say, "Please, you are my guest. This is my way." It's about Men getting off on being the host, the big man, the father figure.

On this particular night, Men's table at NYC Seafood, a big Chinese joint in Monterey Park, groaned under a lazy Susan jammed with platters of lobster, giant clams, steak with peppers and onions, sweet-and-sour pork, tuna sashimi, seaweed, fried rice, and little bottles of Vietnamese hot sauce that Men and his guys never leave home without.

Among the Vietnamese crowding the big, round table were Van Pham, a tough and blustery poker pro in his own right; Hai Tran, a scraggly haired older gent who owes his poker career to Men and serves as first lieutenant, largely because his distaste for craps makes him a good person to hold the team's money; and David "The Dragon" Pham, Men's cousin and the most convincing evidence that Men is a masterful instructor. In 2000, *Card Player* magazine named the slender, mustachioed Pham player of the year; in late 2004, he ranked number three. "I hooked up with Men in 1988," says Pham. "I came from Vietnam and worked for a dry cleaner that Men owned. Every night I see Men coming home with big money. He tells me the money comes from poker. I said, 'Teach me to play poker.'"

Beyond the game's rudiments, Men schooled Pham on something much less concrete: how to read people's hands—through body language, betting patterns, and the pace at which they play. "I read other people's cards even more than I read my own," says Pham. "Then, when I have a worse hand than my opponent, I can still win by making him think I've got something better."

Though the advice sounds simple, it's difficult to do proficiently and impossible for most players to teach; it's about having a card sensibility and savvy—the gambler's equivalent of good taste—which develops through costly trial and error. Elusive as it is, this sixth sense is essential for successful play in a game where you cannot survive simply by hoping for the best cards every day.

A key skill in high-stakes poker is the ability to sense what your opponents are doing, then telegraphing back select pieces of information and disinformation. Played strategically, poker is a multilayered game of traps and subtle deceptions (for example: raising with a strong hand, because you know your opponent figures you will bet big with a small hand, to make him *think* you have a big hand); whoever X-rays deepest gets the money. It's been said that the truly gifted poker legends, guys like Chip Reese and Doyle Brunson, can win without even looking at their cards. The best players take down pots through sheer manipulation of opponents—regardless of who really has the better cards. Which is precisely what Men did in the tournament against Leo Alvarez.

And it's precisely why the students keep lining up, why they come and beg to join Men the Master's crew. This night at NYC Seafood it was a guy named Steve, a motion-picture location manager who tries to supplement his income through poker. He wanted to be Men's first Caucasian student. In exchange for the tutelage, Men requested 5 percent of Steve's future winnings—for life. Steve thought that was a bit much. "Steve," Men began, refilling his plate with food, "the reason I don't want to take you on for less than 5 percent is because my people here, they are all Vietnamese, all Buddhist, and they all swear to our God, to Buddha, that they will not betray me." What remained implicit was that Steve is not Buddhist and therefore would have little to stop him from eventually taking Men's secrets and blabbing them to the world—never mind reneging on the 5-percent agreement, which would be logistically impossible to enforce anyway.

Not bothering to make eye contact with Steve, Men casually added, "You say that 5 percent for life is too much. But you get to many final tables and do not win tournaments. I will teach you to win." Men chewed, swallowed, and asked, "How come you didn't play today?"

Steve turned his beefy face down to his plate of food. He ran a hand through thinning gray hair and admitted, "I'm too disgusted. I'm losing a lot of money."

Men considered this, then proposed what sounded like a magnanimous offer: "Steve, you come to my house tomorrow afternoon. I will give you a free lesson. We come up with situations, and I will tell you whether you play the hand wrong or right. You'll love it."

Steve agreed to be there at two. Men turned his head and jumped into the middle of a Vietnamese conversation. Steve craned away from Men and said, "I have seen Men fold Kings, Queens, flush draws when he senses he's beaten. He lays down hands that I cannot believe. He's the best at reading other players." Another lesson for Men's students: Cutting your losses, by knowing when you're beat, is an important component of winning.

THE NEXT AFTERNOON at two, in the long, dim living room of Men the Master's modest townhouse, Minh Nguyen, Van Pham, Hai Tran, David Pham, and Steve were all there, passing around seven boxed wristwatches—Rolexes, Movados, Tag Heuers—that signified various tournament wins. The guys sat on black leather sofas and chairs, marveling at the timepieces, fiddling with poker chips, absently shuffling cards on a shiny, low-slung coffee table.

At the other end of the room sat Men's wife, Tuyet, 33, a slender woman with long black hair and delicate features. He married her in 1991, but brought her from Vietnam to the States only in 2000. ("I didn't want her to come to this country right away and change," says Men. "I like the Vietnamese way. I tell her to cook for me, she cooks. I tell her to sit, she sits. I tell her to get me a glass of water, she gets me a glass of water. She makes me happy. Other people bring their wives here from Vietnam and get divorced.") Tuyet sipped apple juice and talked on a cordless phone while keeping track of their rambunctious three-year-old daughter, Tiffany.

Men passed around a big cardboard bank. The guys slipped in $10s, $20s, $50s—each member's tithe. The money, Men said, would go toward building schools and temples in his Vietnamese hometown. On a black-lacquer shelving unit—crowded with poker trophies alongside bottles of cognac and of rice whiskey with dead cobras floating in their centers—sat framed snapshots of three single-story buildings that Men has had constructed. After eyeing each person's tribute, Men dealt poker hands, divvying cards face-up so he could critique every student's play. The session operated like a law seminar, with poker hands getting taken apart, analyzed, strategized, and absorbed.

After a few rounds of this, Men offered a Texas Hold 'Em scenario: "You have pocket 9s. The guy who raised in front of you has $30,000 in chips. You have $40,000. What do you do?"

Steve considered this. "That depends on how many people are at the table," he said.

"Final table in a tournament, six players," Men said impatiently. "What you gonna do?"

"Two 9s at the final table?" Steve paused to think, as all eyes focused on him.

"What you gonna do?" Men demanded. "He put in half his stack."

"Either I fold or raise," said Steve, believing that it would be best to retreat or else to telegraph a strong hand and encourage the other player to fold.

"What about you?" asked Men, turning to another student.

"Raise."

"You?" Men said to Hai Tran.

"I fold. If you are in the hand, he might hurt you. Why take the chance?"

Men verbally circled the room, asking each player the same question. Then he offered a proclamation: "Best thing to do with two 9s is fold. There are only six people in the tournament. Let somebody else get hurt. Or let somebody hurt the bettor."

This was followed by a flurry of Vietnamese discussion, as the guys energetically offered their own analyses. Then Men held up his hands and all talk stopped. "Okay, okay," he said. "Now we've got the same cards with a different situation: There are four tables left, the guy has $3,000, you have $2,800, and they pay two tables. The guy in front of you calls. One guy raises to $2,000. What are you gonna do?"

"Muck the hand," said one student. "I don't want to mess with that low of a pair."

"Move all-in," said another.

"Why?" Men demanded to know of the second student.

"They pay two tables, I have four tables left to play through, and I put him on a hand with two over-cards. At that point, I have the best of it. I need to gamble with the best of it. If I win, I bring a lot of chips to the final table."

Men smiled like a proud papa. "The thing to do in this situation is play," he confirmed. "You have to move all-in. This is your opportunity to double your chips and win. If he has two Jacks he will call; if he has two Queens he will call; with Ace-Queen he might not call. You move all-in, he's sure you've got the best hand. Let's say he gambles and flops the King or Queen or Aces, there is nothing you can do. You play to take the blinds and bets. You need to gamble to win. Go in there with a short stack and people run over you. Win that hand and you will have enough to play the next hand and not get hurt. If you don't go in you might not get as good an opportunity again."

It went on like this for a couple of hours. Guys proposed various scenarios, everyone contributed an opinion, and Men the Master offered his final analysis. It's a deep-think, almost Talmudic kind of schooling, and the session could have lasted through the night. But eventually Hai Tran looked at his wristwatch and said, "Master, it is time to play poker."

Conversation ceased. The guys hustled outside and sped off to the Bicycle Casino.

While it's not unusual for players to stake one another, the group dynamic Men has created is unique in the typically cutthroat world of high-stakes poker, where information, advice, and tips are guarded like precious gems. Men's cabal operates more like a family (whether or not that is with a capital *F* remains open to debate) headed up by a domineering father who controls the purse strings. He keeps track of his operation's finances in a small spiral notebook, fronting travel expenses and tournament entry fees from a bank of a few hundred thousand (and, of course, with the understanding that it all acts as an advance against future earnings).

"In exchange for putting up the money and teaching, I get 50 percent of everybody's wins," Men says. He keeps about 20 Visa cards and a half-dozen keys to casino lockboxes, which, in a tight spot, can produce hundreds of thousands in immediate cash. "Aside from the bank for my boys, I have a personal bankroll of $100,000. If I need more money, I can take it from the players' bank. But I'd be more likely to stop playing for a while. When I run bad, I take time off and let these guys play for me."

Running bad and going broke are occupational hazards, of course, but Men has built his poker empire in a way that hedges against his losing everything. Like most professional gamblers, he doesn't think twice about betting his entire chip stack on a solid wager. But at the same time, he can't justify living as extravagantly as many of his peers. He can't see paying the crippling expenses that would come with a bigger home, for instance. He won't jeopardize his bankroll.

Men is cautious enough that he's gone bust only once, back in 1994. "I lost $100,000 in a single night," he remembers. "I was playing $200/$400 Hold 'Em and got myself killed. I should never have lost that kind of money. At $10,000, $20,000, $30,000, I should have stopped." When a former student refused to lend money to Men, he turned to the credit cards and withdrew cash at usurious interest rates. "Less than one year later, I won $300,000 at a Binion's Horseshoe tournament, and I haven't looked back since. But now I'm careful not to get in the deep shit again."

MEN THE MASTER'S earliest recollections are of the South Vietnamese seaside town of Phanthiet, 150 miles outside of Saigon. During his formative years there, he saw American soldiers slicing ears from wounded Viet Cong and slipping the souvenirs inside their shirt pockets. Dead bodies, bomb blasts, midnight interrogations—those things were regular occurrences in young Men's world. "A friend was about to get married," he remembers. "The night before his wedding, a bomb dropped on his house and he died. Things like that happened all the time."

Men quit school at 13, worked odd jobs, and eventually landed a steady gig as a bus driver. But he hated living under a communist regime. In 1977, he escaped on a boat to a refugee camp on Pulau Besar, a Malaysian island; during five days at sea, he lived on handfuls of rice and sips of water.

Six months later, he was relocated to Los Angeles, where he shared a Koreatown studio with another guy from the camp. A month after that, Men found an apartment in a grungy downtown neighborhood. He attended English classes and worked as a machinist for L.A.-based Sun Net Tool. Before long, he moved in with a Salvadoran woman, they had a daughter together, and Men felt like he was part of a family. Then she dumped him and took their kid. For the next several years, Men worked hard, dated a succession of women, and felt unsatisfied with his life.

In 1984, a friend suggested that Men join him on a junket to Las Vegas. Men was making decent money with Sun Net by then, and Vegas sounded like a good break from the monotony of life in L.A. Besides, the price was right: In exchange for several hours of gambling, airfare and meals were comped. He met his friend at Burbank Airport, and they caught the charter to McCarran. Their group, mostly senior citizens, was shuttled directly to the Dunes. Numbers were slapped on their shirts, and they were expected to lose their money by playing slot machines, blackjack, craps, and roulette—all sucker games with odds tilted in the casino's favor.

By sheer serendipity, however, Men wandered into the poker room. Seven-Card Stud looked similar to Xiphe (pronounced *say*-feh), a Vietnamese game played with only 28 cards. Men watched for a little longer and decided to try his luck. "I asked how much money I would need to put down if I wanted to play," remembers Men. "They told me $300. The game was $15/$30, which is a big game for somebody who's never played before." He cashed in and promptly dropped $1,600. "But I didn't feel bad about that. I liked poker right away. I thought it was a game that I'd be able to learn and become good at."

Men junketed to Vegas every weekend. Poker-room regulars called him Money Machine. The nickname was double-edged: Not only was Men continually jumping up from the table and retrieving money from the casino ATM, but he was also *being* a money machine, literally dispensing hundreds of dollars to others at the table. "I chased cards and lost a lot," Men recalls.

But he also devoted his weekdays to endlessly analyzing hands and ironing out strategies. Other players laughed at this hard-gambling Vietnamese guy who continually got himself rousted away from the tables by junket reps demanding that he play the slots. "But then I learned poker," he says. "I got good. People played tight and I played loose. I took pots away from them. They were surprised to see this weekend guy from L.A. suddenly winning."

Men won his first tournament in 1987, pulling down $23,000 in a single day. Later that year, he cashed out for $44,000 at Caesars Palace by outplaying Johnny Chan. Men took those winnings and bought his dry-cleaning business. He worked at Sun Net Tool all day, checked in at the dry cleaner each evening, and spent his nights playing poker at the Bicycle Casino. "I never saw poker as gambling," he says. "It's about talent and patience and reading people. You don't *play* each hand; you *weigh* each hand. But the Orientals, they think of poker as gambling. I go back to Vietnam and don't tell anyone that I play poker. I told my father that I am a machinist. He looked at me and figured that machinists make good money in America."

Men soon developed a reputation in the Vietnamese community. He sold his business, quit the day job, began playing poker full time, and became the go-to guy for other Vietnamese immigrants who hungered for card-room glory. But in a game where everyone is supposed to play their own cards and keep their own counsel, Men evolved into a troubling character. "There are stories about Men's people slipping their tournament chips off the table during bathroom breaks and dumping them to other players on the team," says a former World Series of Poker champion. "That's cheating. Some of Men's tournament wins were tainted because people dumped to him. We've been unable to prove this, but it's public knowledge in poker circles. There's collusion in which he plays partners and has his guys squeeze players out of key hands. They work out signals and do all kinds of dishonest things."

The most blatant accusation against Men centers around an incident that took place in Mashantucket, Connecticut, at Foxwoods Resort Casino. Men was there with his guys for a poker tournament and, as is their norm, they arrived with coolers full of steak, fish, rice, and Corona. They shared a suite and set it up with hot plates, steamers, and a fridge.

After a team member overcooked dinner, the room filled with smoke, and fire alarms went off. Hotel workers rushed inside and asked Men and his guys to leave while they dealt with the situation. The fire was extinguished, but rumors spread that tournament chips were found in the room. If true, that's a terrible infraction of poker-tournament rules. It means that players on Men's team had been pulling chips from the table as their likelihood of getting knocked out became more and more of a certainty, and they then provided those chips to the group's winning players, who could surreptitiously supplement their chip stacks.

Men adamantly denies this and all other charges of collusion and cheating. He was thrown out of the tournament, but he insists that was because of the fire. (Foxwoods has confirmed this, but, as one player puts it, "Of course they would; the last thing they want anybody to think is that their tournaments can be corrupted.") "Cheating," Men fumes, "goes against my Buddha. It's against my religion. I cheat you once and it comes back to me. I have a family, I have a nice thing going, you think I'd cheat you to make my life better? No! God punishes people like that. Some players say things, but nobody can prove anything. If they caught me with chips, I'd never be allowed to play anywhere, not ever again. I travel all over the world, I play poker, I win. That is what I do."

Even the World Series winner who accuses Men of cheating can't argue with the Master's skill. "You still have to give Men credit for being among the top-ranked players every year," he says. "Even if he gets a little bit of help, he still needs to be a damned good player to win as much as he does. Plus, he's an excellent teacher who, [by financially backing his students] puts his money where his mouth is."

UPSTAIRS AT CIRCUS CIRCUS, a rundown casino on the northern
end of the Vegas Strip, tired acrobats swung overhead, performing
not-so-exciting feats with safety nets between them and the Middle
American tourists who thought it was the greatest thing since Liber-
ace. Downstairs, seeming oblivious to it all, wearing an impossible-to-
miss, sun-colored N'Sync T-shirt (he's not a fan, but yellow is his
favorite color), Men the Master materialized from the crowd. He wiped
sweat from his brow and struggled under a burden of half a dozen
enormous plush toys. "The casino has a game arcade upstairs," said
Men. "But they threw me out. Told me that I win too much."

Men's family had been visiting him here in Vegas for a few days,
and he was thrilled to have snagged some goodies for the kids. But
that was not the only thing making him happy. Last week, during a
series of tournaments at the Bicycle Casino, he cleared $200,000 in
personal winnings, not to mention cuts from his team members.
David Pham did so well that he also earned a bonus offered up by the
casino: a 2002 Mercedes ML500 SUV, which he sold to Men for $42,000
in cash.

Men would have liked to hang out with his family, but business
beckoned and his team awaited. He headed up to his suite at the
Horseshoe and conferred with the half-dozen players there.

Steve was nowhere in sight. Stringy-haired Hai Tran had just won
$40,000 at a no-limit Hold 'Em tournament. Men himself was having
no success during this trip to Vegas. He hadn't come close to winning
a tournament, and the cash games had been unproductive. He gave a
fey wave of his hand and said that the losses didn't dog him. "People
say I should not be happy about leaving when I am $5,000 behind [af-
ter a session of poker]," says Men. "They think I should try to get it
back. But I'm not winning. So what should I do? Wait until I lose
$10,000?" Then he reached below the coffee table and pulled out a
fancy, hard-angled liquor bottle that contained a cobra floating in rice
whiskey. A couple of his guys were spinning up tuna rolls, spiked, of
course, with Vietnamese hot sauce. Hai Tran lazily cruised the Internet, looking to find a soft game online. Men poured a healthy shot of

snake-infused whiskey. He downed it and grabbed his crotch. "It make you strong here," he said.

Minutes later he slipped on a bright yellow sport jacket, popped a piece of tuna roll into his mouth, then led his team out of the room and across the street to the Four Queens casino, on a mission to play poker and live the American dream.

Howard Lederer, 2004, in Las Vegas

Nine

HOWARD LEDERER

The Poker Professor

The cerebral son of a teacher approaches

the game with classroom diligence, aces

its most demanding tests, and proves

that years of study can be as effective

as natural talent.

SHORTLY AFTER 7 A.M. ON THE morning of December 6, 1996, 33-year-old Howard Lederer was sleeping soundly in the upstairs bedroom of his Las Vegas home, most likely dreaming about poker. He often dreamt about poker back then. He would come home in the early morning after a lengthy session at the Mirage and spend the next few hours methodically replaying the evening's hands in his mind. Win or lose, he sought to answer the same question: *What could I have done better?* He didn't just ponder, for example, whether he had acted correctly on Fourth Street based on the card that subsequently came on the river—he surveyed whether he'd acted correctly based on all the cards that could have come on the river. It was an endless exercise, and when sleep inevitably overtook him, the cards kept coming.

But on this morning the game was interrupted when Lederer was startled awake by a thunder of male voices downstairs: "Who else is in the house? Where are they?"

Lederer, built like a polar bear at six-foot-five and more than 320 pounds, pulled on a robe and rushed down the stairs to find his nanny in the front hallway holding Lederer's four-month-old son in her arms. A small army of men in windbreakers had pushed their way into the house and surrounded her, one of them with a gun to her head. The men turned their guns toward Lederer and identified themselves: Nevada Gaming Commission.

Before the agents handcuffed him and took him to jail, they turned the house upside down in search of incriminating computer files and betting slips. Across town, other agents seized more than $1.2 million from his bank accounts and from his safe-deposit box at the Mirage. The next morning, New York and Las Vegas papers named Lederer as a key figure in an illegal $400 million sports-betting operation tied to the Genovese and Gambino crime families.

The allegations were ridiculous, according to Lederer, but led to a turbulent, unpleasant year in which he tried fruitlessly to explain to prosecutors that he was merely a sports bettor, which was legal in Nevada, and not a mobbed-up bookmaker. In hindsight, it's hard to picture Lederer, one of the game's most reputable characters, at the center of such a seamy episode. But, he says now, it actually helped catapult him into poker's top ranks. Less than a year after the raid, freed from the distractions of what had essentially been a lucrative day job, Lederer was for the first time able to devote 100 percent of his energies to poker.

The top ranks of poker are full of freaks of nature, players with indomitable wills, instinctive gifts for math, or uncanny abilities to put their opponents on specific hands. Their skills are impressive, even awe-inspiring, but at the same time incomprehensible to the average home-game player striving to emulate them. Lederer, a two-time World Poker Tour champion, is a notable exception. He reached the upper echelon through more pedestrian means: He studied. He spent years dissecting the game, both philosophically and analytically, while steadily rising from the low-limits to the mid-limits and, finally, to the biggest games in the world.

"Poker is kind of an interesting game because a lot of players play on feel," says Erik Seidel. "But they don't have it as concisely laid out as Howard has it. He just has an encyclopedic knowledge of what you should do in every situation. He understands the games better than anyone else, even top players. He really approaches it from an intellectual place."

As significant, at least to his growing legion of fans, is Lederer's ability to explain the intricacies of the game, which has earned him the nickname "the professor of poker," along with a nice little cottage industry as a highly respected instructor. In 2003, he released a popular DVD, *Howard Lederer's Secrets of No-Limit Hold 'Em*, and in 2004 more than 150 novice players ponied up $3,200 to attend "Howard Lederer's Poker Fantasy Camp."

To Lederer, poker is as much craft as it is art. It's a puzzle that a reasonably intelligent person can solve by training the mind in logic, psychology, and math. It's not easy, but it can be done. "It's a gradual process where you are analyzing and analyzing and analyzing these situations, and slowly but surely you stop analyzing and you start doing. It's like, 'Wow, I did it. I played it perfectly,' " he says. "I get e-mails all the time from people saying, 'I've been playing for two months and I'm not beating these games.' Well, it probably took me 15 years."

AMONG HIS FRIENDS, Lederer is known for obsessively diving into the subjects that grab his interest. When his friends got into billiards, Lederer frequently stayed at the pool hall to practice for hours after the others had left. When he took up golf, he beat balls relentlessly on the driving range in his quest to become a scratch player. When a cabbie off-handedly extolled the virtues of being a vegetarian, Lederer researched the philosophical tenets of the lifestyle and ultimately converted. (His devotion has its limits: He once ate a hamburger to win a $10,000 bet.)

Alan Boston, a high-stakes sports bettor and tournament poker player who served as best man in Lederer's second wedding, recalls introducing Lederer to jazz. "I gave him a couple of albums," Boston says. "A couple of weeks later, we're at a concert and he turns to me and says, 'Boston, you hear that chord change?' I was just enjoying the music. But Howard had studied it. He has to know everything about the things that he is interested in."

The obsessions have come and gone over the years, most fading when a new one supplants the last, but poker has remained.

The oldest of three siblings, Lederer grew up on the tony Concord, New Hampshire, campus of St. Paul's boarding school, where his father taught English to the WASP-y New England elite (distinguished alumni include Senator John Kerry and E. Digby Baltzell, the sociologist who actually coined the term WASP). The Lederers lived in faculty housing and, by dint of income alone, did not fit in among the blue-blood campus population. They were also somewhat eccentric, as Howard's youngest sister, Katy Lederer, recounts in her critically acclaimed 2003 memoir, *Poker Face.*

Their father, Richard, was a thrifty academic with a passion for words (he later wrote a popular book—called *Anguished English*—about linguistic bloopers, and served as a regular contributor to National Public Radio) matched only by his love for all kinds of games. Richard met his wife, Deedy, while playing bridge at Harvard. An aspiring actress, she was also an avid gamer. Though she consumed copious amounts of Scotch—a source of consternation for the other family members—she regularly completed the Sunday *New York Times* crossword puzzle in 20 minutes with seemingly little effort. Howard's other sister, Annie, later studied psycholinguistics before joining her brother in high-stakes poker. "Howard's the dumbest one in the family, and he's pretty fucking smart," says Boston.

Each brilliant in his or her own way, the Lederers battled wits over chess and card games like Hearts and Oh Hell. Losing with dignity was not encouraged. Katy Lederer recalls her father pouting for days after

Howard first beat him at chess, and Howard developing the laserlike stare that would become one of his poker trademarks.

Badly overweight by his early teens, Howard shied away from athletics at school but led the St. Paul's chess team to the state championship. After graduation, he moved to New York to pursue his dream of becoming a chess grand master, with plans to enroll in Columbia University the following year.

In a matter of days, he found the Bar Point, a seedy game room on the second floor of a building near 14th Street and Sixth Avenue. The club offered backgammon and chess games in the front and an illegal poker room in the back. He soon drifted from the quiet intensity of the chessboards to the more romantic environs of the poker felts, where he latched onto a new—and lasting—obsession. He started out playing $1/$2 limit and, although the stakes were miniscule, he still managed to blow not only his poker bankroll but all of his savings. Unable to afford monthly rent on an apartment or enough for a hotel room, he slept in Washington Square Park during the day and hung around the Bar Point at night.

Ultimately Lederer struck a deal with the Bar Point's owner: He would run errands and mop the floors in exchange for being able to sleep in the club. Each day he'd buy the groceries for the spread the club put out and then hang around through the night on the chance that he could make tip money by fetching smokes or snacks from the nearby Korean deli. He usually accumulated the minimum buy-in of $10 by 2 or 3 in the morning, then busted out before the game broke up around 7 a.m., at which point he borrowed $2 from one of the players. "Two bucks would get me a pack of cigarettes and a souvlaki sandwich at the deli," he says. "I borrowed two dollars perhaps more than anyone ever."

Lederer enjoyed the camaraderie of the older players and the rush from occasionally flopping the nuts, but paid little attention to how certain people managed to win almost every session. It took him more than two years to start winning at even the Bar Point's micro limits. The turnaround occurred after he noticed that the game degenerated on weekends when the cocaine-fueled regulars played straight through from Friday to Sunday. He started leaving the game on Saturday morning and returning after a nap, then doing the same thing on Sunday. He'd come back to find his adversaries so bleary-eyed they couldn't read their hands correctly, much less make reasoned decisions. "Sunday was the day that you could really make some money," he says. "That was the first time I formulated a plan and executed it. The first two years, I was just gambling. I didn't understand about skill or that things outside the table could influence your results." Lederer slowly put together a bankroll of about $5,000 and moved out of the Bar Point.

In 1984, during one of his late shifts at the Bar Point, Lederer struck up a friendship with Steve Zolotow, a failed actor-turned-sports bettor with a bald head and a Fu Manchu moustache. As it turned out, Lederer liked to bet on sports and Zolotow needed someone to covertly place bets with various bookies who wouldn't allow him to bet as high as he wished. Lederer eventually rose to full partner in what became one of the largest sports betting teams in the country. The brains behind the operation was a secretive handicapper out of Nebraska who established his own line on pro football and basketball games. Lederer and Zolotow then compared the lines with those offered by casinos and bookies around the country and, if there was a discrepancy, they took advantage of it. It was fundamentally no different than a Wall Street analyst who determines, based on his research, that a stock should be trading at $5 instead of $2 and therefore instructs his clients to buy the stock. In this case, the handicapper was Lederer and Zolotow's private sports-betting analyst, and the magnitude of the inefficiencies he found dictated the size of their bets.

"If our guy thought the line was four, and we could get it at seven, then that was a great bet," Lederer says. "If he thought it should have been four and it was at five and a half, it was a small bet. We just went out there and shopped around to find the best prices."

Their wagers were tens of thousands per game, enough that bookmakers frequently adjusted their lines once Lederer and Zolotow weighed in. Lederer's role was primarily to move the money—that is, get bets down at the most advantageous level. This is not nearly as easy as it sounds, since it often required him to play cat-and-mouse with the bookmakers who tried to anticipate his plays.

"I devised all sorts of plans," he says. "I would bet the wrong side for five minutes with everyone I could, get the whole world heading in one direction, and then come back at them when they were headed in full flight the wrong direction. It was certainly my right when I was out there betting. If people are going to take advantage of my patterns, I am going to have to take advantage of my patterns too. In that way, it is very much like poker."

Sports betting occupied most of Lederer's days, but poker consumed the nights. Having discovered that success was more than a function of luck, he applied himself to understanding the correct strategies, most notably by reading David Sklansky's *The Theory of Poker*. The book, originally published in 1978 and targeted specifically to professionals, establishes rational guidelines for poker decision-making that appealed to Lederer's logical mind. Sklansky isn't concerned with how to play certain situations as much as identifying all of the factors to consider before making a decision, and then acting on that decision in a way that keeps your opponents guessing. He even developed what he calls, "The Fundamental Theorem of Poker":

> Every time you play a hand differently from the way you
> would have played it if you could see all your opponents'
> cards, they gain; and every time you play your hand the
> same way you would have played it if you could see all their
> cards, they lose. Conversely, every time opponents play their
> hands differently from the way they would have if they
> could see all your cards, you gain; and every time they play
> their hands the same way they would have played if they
> could see all your cards, you lose.

Reading Sklansky was a revelation for Lederer. He realized that his job was not just to play his hands optimally but to find ways to keep his opponents from playing their hands optimally. For the first time, he had an intellectual skeleton around which he could build his game. "Sklansky gave me the analytic framework to understand poker situations," Lederer says. "It allowed me to get in my head and start thinking about hands in a proper way."

Lederer explored abstract concepts such as the reasoning behind popular gambits such as check-raising (trapping your opponents by declining the opportunity to bet and then raising when one of them does so) and slow-playing (betting conservatively with a strong hand in the hopes of luring other players into the pot). He also learned the basics of how to apply math through factors like pot odds, which is the ratio of money in the pot versus the amount of money it would cost to stay in the hand. If there is $100 in the pot and it costs you only $10 to call the last bet, for example, the pot is laying 10-to-1 odds. Players weigh pot odds against another kind of odds: the likelihood of making a winning hand (which they determine based on which cards they've seen and which they haven't). So if your odds of drawing a flush on the last card are roughly 5-to-1, and the pot is laying you 10-to-1, it makes mathematical sense to call.

By 1986, Lederer was playing $50/$100 at the Mayfair Club, home to the top players in New York. Only 21, he was an average player at best but was slowly developing his own deliberate, technically sound style. In a purposeful effort to supplement his book knowledge, he also tapped into what he calls "the power of the collective"—another way of saying he purposefully surrounded himself with bright poker minds.

In stark contrast to the degenerates from the Bar Point, the Mayfair boasted a collection of brilliant men who applied their intellect to poker: Jay Heimowitz, Dan Harrington, and Billy Horan, to name a few. Through observation or casual conversations around the Mayfair, or during beery nights at Streets, a bar around the corner from the club, Lederer slowly absorbed the poker wisdom of these more seasoned players.

"Howard was clearly a precocious talent," says Horan. "You could just tell by his concentration and his focus at the table that he really wanted to get good. He would remember a hand five hours after it was played and want to know, 'Why did you play this hand this way?' Or, 'How did you manage to get off that hand?' Most people play a hand and when they lose, they say, 'Oh, well, I got unlucky,' and then go on and play the next hand. Howard would try to figure out where he screwed it up."

In 1987, Lederer joined some of the Mayfair gang on their annual trip to Las Vegas for the World Series. Remarkably, he and Harrington both made the final table of the main event. Lederer ultimately finished in fifth place, but it was a move by Harrington that made the biggest impression.

The chip leader at the start of the day was Jim Spain, a relatively unknown player out of Alabama, and Spain lost a big pot right after play began. Soon thereafter, Harrington opened with a small raise before the flop and Spain countered by moving all-in. Harrington, who was ironically nicknamed "Action Dan" because he played so tightly, almost beat Spain into the pot with his chips. Lederer was not involved in the hand but watched the action closely. He assumed from Harrington's confident call that his friend had a monster hand, either a pair of Aces or at least Kings. But Harrington turned over Ace-Queen off-suit, a strong hand, to be sure, but one that is not likely to be a favorite over many hands Spain was apt to play so strongly. Harrington's instincts were correct: Spain turned over Ace-6.

As it happened, Harrington was knocked out of the tournament when Spain hit two 6s on the flop. But Lederer was amazed by Harrington's call, and later asked Harrington how he was so certain he held the best hand.

"The guy wanted to go home," Harrington said.

As Harrington explained it, there is always at least one player who cannot handle the pressure as it steadily builds during a tournament. He's nervous and uncomfortable and, although he would never admit it consciously, he really wants it all to be over with. "That had a profound affect on my tournament career," Lederer says. "Everybody has their breaking point and you've got to keep looking for the guy who wants to go home. He's playing worse and worse because the pressure is getting to him."

To this day, Lederer believes surrounding himself with other top players improves his game immeasurably. Healthier, but still not slim, he now works out with Gus Hansen, the unpredictable and dashing young Dane whose gun-slinging table image is the polar opposite of Lederer's deliberate style. "We are in the gym three or four times a week for two and a half or three hours. Maybe an hour and a half of that we are working out, but the rest of that time we are talking poker,"

Lederer says. As a result, "I actually think my style is heading a little bit more in his direction and maybe his is heading in my direction."

As he developed his own repertoire and established himself as a winning player, Lederer became known around the Mayfair for being uncommonly generous in dispensing his own advice to other players. When he returned from Las Vegas, he counseled Erik Seidel, who was then a relative newcomer to the Mayfair game, that he was good enough to compete at the highest levels. Seidel heeded the advice and subsequently took second place in the 1988 world championship.

Not long after that, Seidel resolved to broaden his game to include other variations of poker besides no-limit Hold 'Em. He offered Lederer 25 percent of his winnings in the near future if Lederer would teach him to play limit Hold 'Em, and Lederer agreed. Armed with Lederer's advice, Seidel went on to win two World Series bracelets in limit. "I would say I may have learned more from him about poker than I have from anyone else," Seidel says.

Seidel knows first-hand that most players guard their secrets zealously. When Seidel offered Heimowitz the same deal if he would teach him the intricacies of pot-limit Omaha, Heimowitz declined. In explaining his decision, Heimowitz echoes the mindset of most top pros: "I don't like to teach anybody anything."

LEDERER MOVED TO Las Vegas in 1993. His sports-betting business with Zolotow was thriving and the proximity to the city's legal sports books was certainly a draw, but he primarily sought the opportunity to expand his "power of the collective" beyond New York's clubby poker scene. He worked his way up to the $800/$1,600 limits, where he learned from greats such as Doyle Brunson, until the raid in 1996 brought his life to a screeching halt.

Lederer spent the better part of the next year dealing with its fallout. He was forced to borrow money from friends to pay his mortgage and take an extended sabbatical from poker. The Brooklyn district attorney who spearheaded the investigation argued that Lederer and Zolotow's hordes of cash stemmed from their collaboration with the mob-connected bookmakers in New York.

The prosecution was similar to the one employed by the FBI in the 1980s against the legendary Computer Group, a nebulous consortium of Las Vegas gamblers that for a time included Chip Reese (though he was never indicted). The Computer Group, in much the same way Lederer and Zolotow relied on their Nebraska handicapper, used the forecasts of a computer programmer to make millions betting sports. Gambling laws are geared toward stopping those that accept bets— i.e. bookmakers—and not actual bettors, because bettors typically lose over the long run. As a result, the government was unable to prove the Computer Group constituted an illegal gambling operation.

Lederer and Zolotow used a similar defense—they were placing bets, not accepting them—but the district attorney "couldn't understand how someone could be betting that kind of money and winning," says Lederer.

Lederer's attorney believed the case would not stand up in court, but Lederer opted to pay a substantial fine in order to settle—less than the $1.2 million seized during the raid, he says, and roughly the same amount it would have cost him to mount a vigorous defense. He sees the fact that he received some of his money back as vindication of sorts, but still chose to close down the operation. "Whether or not it was legal, there were people that didn't want me to do it, people in positions of power who could make my life miserable," he says.

Sklansky, who was so beneficial to Lederer early in his career, has said that poker strategy books are like cookbooks—they can teach someone to be competent in the kitchen but they can't teach the artistry required to be a four-star chef. Now with more time on his hands, Lederer wanted to take that next step. He felt he was already a strong technical player but recognized that some players— the so-called "feel" players—were able to occasionally outmaneuver him because they were so skilled at the psychological aspects of the game. He made a conscious effort after 1997 to stunt his development as a technical player in order to concentrate on the people side of the game.

He focused his efforts on learning to read other players at the table. Before long, he became known for his long, piercing stare, a tactic so disconcerting that, in a moment captured on the ESPN telecast of the 2003 World Series, Lederer forced his opponent to zip his windbreaker over his head until Lederer reached his decision.

"I am looking for the oversell, in either direction," Lederer explains. "Basically, every time someone takes an action at the poker table, they are telling me something with that action—they are making a statement. If someone checks, they are saying, 'I am weak.' If someone makes a big bet, they are saying, 'I am strong.' If someone makes a small bet, they are saying, 'I'm okay.' And once they make the statement, I need to decide whether they are telling the truth or not. That's what it's all about. How did they act when they put their chips in the pot? How did they act after they put their chips in the pot? Certainly a person with a good hand wouldn't throw his chips in the pot, sit up tall in his chair and stare down his opponent. It's just like a homicide detective is looking for the oversell. If you are a murderer and you are being interrogated, it is very hard to deny in a way that is believable. It's a hard thing to do at the poker table too."

His development paid dividends: In 2000, Lederer won his first World Series bracelet after more than a dozen years of trying. The next year, he won another. And in 2003, he joined his workout partner Gus Hansen as the only two-time winner on the *World Poker Tour*.

For the first time, Lederer was unquestionably among the best poker players in the world. But he was convinced he could still get better, and searched for a final breakthrough in the pages of yet another book, *Zen in the Art of Archery*. The book, by German philosopher Eugen Herrigel, details Herrigel's quest to achieve a Zen state through, as the title suggests, the study of archery. In the introduction, Daisetz Suzuki, Japan's foremost authority on Zen, seems to be speaking directly to Lederer: "If one really wishes to be master of an art, technical knowledge of it is not enough," Suzuki wrote. "One has to transcend technique so that the art becomes an 'artless art' growing out of the Unconscious."

Lederer's goal is to achieve a state of relaxation that allows him to be fully "in the moment" so that he is acting almost without thinking. It is something of a counter-intuitive notion at the poker table; conventional wisdom holds that the most successful players are constantly drawing from an internal database of past situations that inform the way they should respond to the situation in front of them. But Lederer believes it is the perfect antidote in this era of televised poker tournaments, when he is performing under stage lights and in front of hidden cameras with millions of dollars in prize money in the balance. If he can reach a Zen state of almost perfect concentration, he is able to block out all distractions and subconsciously draw on all his years of study.

"If I think to myself, I'm going to concentrate really hard right now, it can't happen," he says. "That's the whole point of it—you can't do something that you are trying to do. It just happens when you are in the moment and you realize, I just had an amazing half-hour in which I wasn't thinking about anything except what was going on at the table."

As Herrigel wrote, "The master archer hits his target without having aimed."

IN MAY 2004, Lederer squared off at the Bellagio against another uncommonly bright student of the game, a billionaire Dallas banker by the name of Andy Beal. The match took place during the World Series of Poker and, among those in the know, it briefly overshadowed the game's premiere event. After all, Beal and Lederer were playing in arguably the richest contest in the history of poker—and Beal presented a surprisingly formidable challenge.

A certified math geek, Beal started his eponymous financial institution, Beal Bank, with a $3 million investment. By employing mathematical modeling and game theory to quantify risks in commercial lending and financing, he turned his little boutique into a national powerhouse in less than 10 years. His fortune assured, Beal then tackled a series of other intellectual challenges: In 1993, he proclaimed a breakthrough related to an obscure math problem known as Fermat's Last Theorem, and eventually offered a $100,000 prize to anyone who could prove or disprove what became known as "Beal's Conjecture." (Despite much interest from the world's leading numbers theorists, nobody has done so.) In 1997, he set his sights even higher: With no background in aviation or science of any kind, he pledged tens of millions of his own money to design and build a fleet of the largest privately owned rockets in history, with the goal of blasting commercial satellites into space. (The rockets worked, but the business ultimately failed.)

In 2001, Beal turned his attention to poker. Never one to do things by half measure, he wanted to play for stakes higher than anyone in Vegas could afford. Further, he didn't want to sit in the Big Game, for fear that the local boys would effectively isolate him and slowly bleed him of his cash. After negotiating with a poker dream team including Doyle Brunson, Chip Reese, Johnny Chan, Lederer and a handful of others—dubbed "The Corporation"—he agreed that they could pool their money and play limit Hold 'Em heads-up against him, in shifts. The blinds started at $10,000 and $20,000 and, during subsequent games, grew to an astronomical $100,000 and $200,000, which is believed to be higher than anyone has ever played.

The pros initially clobbered Beal for more than $10 million, but, everyone agreed, by 2004 he was getting much better. When it was Lederer's turn to face him that year, Beal was already ahead of the pros by several million dollars on the session.

Set up at a sequestered private table in the back right corner of the Bellagio poker room, it was an incongruous match—the math wizard against the Zen master. Beal was dressed in a crisp white shirt, khaki pants, and loafers, and wore enormous headphones that looked like they belonged on a shooting range. Lederer went without headphones and looked as disheveled as always in jeans and an untucked long-sleeved shirt. In his characteristic style, Beal aggressively pushed the action, rarely conceding a pot until he was clearly beaten. Lederer laid back, pressing his edges only when he had them. As the hours ticked by and millions of dollars got pushed back and forth across the table, the men barely spoke. Gradually, though, the chips migrated from Beal's see-through carrying-case to Lederer's side of the table.

In four hours, Lederer won more than $5 million, and when the session ended, the men cordially shook hands. Lederer offered a tight-lipped smile as his assembled teammates patted him on the back.

Beal went on to capture more than $10 million from the others in the next two days—a feat he likens to climbing Mount Everest. Most of the pros, of course, scoff at the suggestion that Beal conquered them, noting that heads-up limit Hold 'Em is often more about catching cards than skillfully outwitting your opponent—especially against someone with a bottomless bankroll like Beal's. "Let me put it this way," says Chan, assessing Beal's play. "You can't bluff a sucker."

To Chan and the others, Beal is yet another in a long line of wealthy amateurs with the resources and the moxie to venture out to Vegas for the privilege of taking on the world's best. From cocaine kingpin Jimmy Chagra in the 1970s to George Paravoliasakis, the Greek shipping magnate who dropped tens of millions in the late 1990s, it rarely amounts to more than a very expensive story for their pals back home. While Beal enjoyed a spectacularly successful run, he is still a loser overall in the game. And even though his win in 2004 cost each member of the Corporation a few hundred thousand dollars, the sting amounts to no more than what most of them would blow on a couple of miscalculated sports bets or an unlucky afternoon in the craps pit. If Beal wants to prove a point, the pros say, he needs to do it over the long haul, or else they'll consider him a fluke.

Lederer, however, is more charitable. He sees Beal doing the same thing he did: attacking the game intellectually until he finds a way to beat it.

"I appreciate that spirit and that energy. He really likes the challenge and I give him a lot of credit," Lederer says. "Poker is a fascinating game. It's got so many life skills to teach you. You have to recognize your limitations while at the same time going beyond yourself. You have to admit your failings in order to get better. You have to be willing to take the worst of it in order to get better. If you find a game that you can beat, and beat it every day, then at some point you need to go beyond that game and find a game that you can't beat and figure out how to beat it. That's how you get better at poker."

David "Devilfish" Ulliott, 2003, at Binion's Horseshoe, Las Vegas

Ten

DAVID "DEVILFISH" ULLIOTT

The Bully at the Table

Armed with naked aggression and a sharp

tongue, a British tough guy lights up

the European circuit—and then

takes on the world.

TWO PLAYERS OCCUPIED A HARD-ANGLED soundstage dominated by a set worthy of *Who Wants to Be a Millionaire?* Blazing TV lights illuminated the contestants, smoke machines created the requisite bit of backroom ambience, and custom-made spy cams captured every glimpse at their hole cards. Eventually more than 5 million Texas Hold 'Em fanatics would tune in to this installment of *World Poker Tour*, the cable TV show that has helped transform the game into a national obsession. But, for the time being, on this high-pressure evening in

January, 2003, it was all about these two guys and the big pile of money between them.

David "Devilfish" Ulliott, 49 at the time, sat at the head of the table. Dressed in a midnight-blue Hugo Boss suit, white shirt, and a tightly knotted navy necktie, he resembled a dapper gangster convening a meeting of underworld bosses. Reddish brown hair was slicked back across his scalp and a trim goatee hugged his lips. When Devilfish retrieved two freshly dealt hole cards, he revealed a pair of knuckle-dusting rings, stretched between the joints of each fist. Diamonds drizzled up and down the rings' shiny gold letters that spelled out *Devil* across one hand and *Fish* across the other: slang for fugu, the raw Japanese delicacy that can lethally poison you if it is not properly prepared.

In the brave new world of televised poker games, where charismatic stars boast *Batman*-worthy nicknames, Devilfish is a natural-born badass, full of hard-guy swagger and black-and-blue humor. Oozing intimidation, he inspected his cards through brown tinted shades riding low on the bridge of his tapered nose. He had been competing for three days, against 160 players (each of whom put up $10,000), at the World Poker Open, in Tunica, Mississippi. Now it was down to just him and Phil Ivey, the deftly aggressive poker champ who's so hard-wired to gamble that he's been known to casually drop a million dollars in the craps pit before winning it back in the card room.

Already the most famous poker player in Europe, British-born Devilfish personifies the degree to which poker has become a global game without borders. The Internet, televised tournaments, and ever-increasing jackpots have conspired to draw international rosters of competitors to wherever the action is sweetest. Instead of chasing white lines behind the wheel of a DeSoto, going from Elks lodge to firehouse to sketchy home game, top tournament players spend nine months out of each year flying business-class around the world, tracking games from one casino to the next. Devilfish and a passel of European players—modern-age crossroaders such as Erik Sagstrom (a Swede who's reportedly snagged more than $3 million in two years of playing online), Spain-based World Series champ Carlos Mortenson, and a young Brit named Julian Gardner who won the European Omaha championship at 21—routinely crisscross the continent, going from the Concord in Vienna (where the big winners in the mid 1990s were Hungarian chess masters), to the Merrion Club in Dublin (home of Europe's first poker tournaments), and back across to the Holland Casino in Amsterdam. "I won $20,000 playing heads-up there," boasts Devilfish, "and I can't even remember the name of the guy I beat."

As with most European players, Devilfish was raised on pot-limit and no-limit poker, making him all the more deadly on the tournament circuit (where no-limit stakes are the stakes of choice). Fittingly, for a 21st-century poker stud, he made his bones by winning the United Kingdom's *Late Night Poker*, a less flashy antecedent of *World Poker Tour*. Beyond bringing him notoriety, televised poker has helped make Devilfish far wealthier than he otherwise would be. Like Phil Hellmuth and Annie Duke, he has cut a lucrative deal with ultimatebet.com. And, in line with those players, he recognizes the importance of maintaining a distinct persona while looking good on the tube.

And that brings us back to the heads-up showdown in Tunica. Devilfish led with about $1.39 million in chips to Phil Ivey's $198,000 or so, and a hand was dealt with the potential to revive Ivey. Both players limped in preflop. The board came 8-7-3. Devilfish checked, Ivey bet a modest $20,000, and with nary a moment of consideration, Devilfish declared, "I'm going all in."

Naturally subdued, Ivey replied by silently pushing his chips to the table's center as well. He rolled his cards to show King-8, giving him two 8s. Devilfish had 5-6, adding up to an open-ended straight draw. It made Ivey a slight favorite. But before the turn card even hit the table, Devilfish stolidly raised his right fist into the air. It was a 4, giving him his straight, and the tournament.

Upon becoming $589,900 richer, Devilfish shook Ivey's hand and patted him on the back, practically dispatching him to some losers' circle. Then, speaking in a muddy British accent, Devilfish told an interviewer, "I will happily wear a bloody pork chop around my neck, while swimming across a sea filled with man-eating sharks, to play the Americans in poker." What he meant, of course, was that it's worth risking your life when you can come up against such easy action. He failed to mention that he had shut down Ivey by getting lucky on that last card. He could just as easily have not drawn out, and Ivey would have doubled-up, leaving the two players' chip stacks much closer to even.

But humility has never been the Devil's strong suit.

SIXTEEN MONTHS AFTER Tunica, in a snug corner of the Binion's Horseshoe poker room, Devilfish's situation seemed markedly different. Here the game was all cash, there were no TV cameras, not a bit of fanfare, and getting a decent cup of coffee was an iffy proposition. It was old-fashioned poker, in a stripped-down setting, complete with 34 years worth of World Series winners, photographed, framed, and hanging against the room's red flock wallpaper.

Outwardly oblivious to all that, Devilfish was being eaten alive by a table full of pros and sharp amateurs in a game of pot-limit Omaha. A perversion of Hold 'Em, Omaha has five community cards, but the players are dealt four in the hole. They must use two of those hole cards in making a hand—which turns it into a heartbreakingly unpredictable game where the stone-cold nuts can be sliced up with the turn of a single card. Though betting is limited to however much is in the pot, aggressive players make it very expensive, very quickly.

For about an hour, Devilfish had rained thousands onto the table, and passed many of his seemingly endless supply of Benjamins into the happy hands of Phil "Unabomber" Laak, a San Francisco–based pro nicknamed for a tendency to shade his eyes with a sweatshirt hood, à la Ted Kaczynski. During one hand, Devilfish dropped several grand with a busted straight. Reaching into the right hip-pocket of his Wranglers, he extracted a thin wad of hundreds and slipped it down behind a diminishing chip stack in front of him. Between hands, Unabomber—slender, boyish, fair-haired—chatted away with a nerdy-looking poker player called Larry the Lock and a couple of blondes who stood behind him with vacant stares. "Hey, Bomber," said Devilfish. "What are you doing tonight?"

"Going to the O.G."—the Olympic Garden, a well-known topless bar near the Strip—"drinking Dewar's, seeing some old friends," said Unabomber. "You're welcome to join us."

Devilfish hesitated for a beat and inspected the blondes. "Hey, Bomber," he said, eyeing the blonder of the two females. "Send one of them down here."

Unabomber let the request hang in the air. An olive-skinned man in a blue sweater playing next to Devilfish leaned over and softly told him, "Dev, I think that's his girlfriend."

"Then," said Devilfish, "I like his girlfriend."

Unabomber ignored the comment and Devilfish kept throwing hundreds into the pot, seemingly content with the results, even as he consistently lost. The impression he gave was that it was all part of some grand scheme. A few hands later, Unabomber, who by now had skyscraping chip stacks, stared across the table at Devilfish, the only other player still in the hand. His eyes briefly looked down to scan a pot that contained about $20,000, built up from various bets that had been made on the first six cards. "Let's gamble," he casually suggested. "How much do you have in front of you?"

"Nothing," said Devilfish, one red card away from hitting a flush. "Only about $1,800."

"Put it in," said Bomber, shoving black chips to the felt's center.

With so much in the pot, it would be impossible for Devilfish not to call the bet. But when a 4 of hearts hit on the board, it proved to be the wrong red suit, he failed to make the flush, and his cards lost to Unabomber's three 5s. Bomber raked in the bills and jammed them inside his pants pocket. He laid his chips in a plastic rack, then walked off with Larry and the girls, leaving Devilfish and seven others behind at the table. Apparently, the O.G. invite had been rescinded.

After glancing at their disappearing forms, Devilfish cursed his luck and made eye contact with the olive-skinned man playing to his right. They exchanged no words, and the mystery man handed him $10,000 in banded hundreds. Devilfish set the money on the table and continued playing without a glimmer of concern.

Within a half-dozen hands, however, the tenor of the game changed. Devilfish went on operating with the same apparent recklessness that had seemed to be destroying him—but now everything wrong was suddenly right. He got plenty of calls from players with made, but inferior, hands, and he scared out card chasers who had the potential to beat him. "I've never seen you like this," said a bald guy at the opposite end of the table as Devilfish pulled down his third pot in a row. "You're playing like a maniac."

Devilfish furrowed his brow and stacked his chips.

Next hand Devilfish's straight to the Queen sent the bald guy packing. "You're lucky he went in against you," said a chubby man playing to the left of Devilfish, the implication being that a better player would have quickly folded.

"You've got to give action to get action," Devilfish tersely replied.

Then he eyed the dealer, who was carefully inspecting both up-turned hands, insuring that Devilfish did indeed have the superior cards. After a second, the Devil impatiently snapped, "Dealer, pass me my money."

An hour later, he got up from the table and walked away with $60,000 or so in profit.

Such a stunning turnaround is more than mere luck, of course. Losing to Unabomber was essentially a cost of doing business. It advertised him as a loose player. So, while Devilfish would have greatly preferred winning Unabomber's money, being beaten by him came with an upside. Because Devilfish specializes in an aggressive form of play, in which he bullies the game and controls the table, the primary way he can generate action is by appearing to be a wild player. Precisely the opposite of guys like the meticulous and ever-changing Erik Seidel, Devilfish brings a big personality to poker and capitalizes on his negative swings by making opponents think twice about folding—and run the risk of being bluffed out. "He wants you to think he's crazy; that way you get into tons of hands with him," says Diego Cordovez, who's tangled with Devilfish in heads-up situations. "It's constant aggression without stupidity. He makes tons of plays, and they look way more random than they actually are. In reality, he's making them at the right time"—either when he wants opponents to fold, lest they beat him with superior hands, or when he wants to fatten a pot that he's favored to win. "Then he complements his aggressive play with how he acts at the table. He talks a lot and criticizes people's moves. He aims to make people wonder if they will look stupid by doing something unconventional against him—never mind that you must be unconventional in order to consistently win at poker."

Beyond that, explains Cordovez, Devilfish's endless hectoring and chattering combine to have a more insidious effect. He is, essentially, a modern-day British version of Amarillo Slim (complete with macho posturing and a quick wit): "One time we were playing heads-up at a World Series event; he knew nothing about me, and he said to me, as a joke, 'I'll give you the bracelet [and, essentially, throw the tournament], and you give me an extra $25,000.' He knew there was zero-percent chance that I'd agree to do it, but how I responded would help him to figure out my motivations and the kind of person I am. Maybe he thought I'd be intimidated by there being a $150,000 difference between first place and second. Or maybe he thought I was a rich amateur who wouldn't care about the money but wanted the glory."

Cordovez never accepted the offer—and he wound up winning the tournament—but he grudgingly respects Devilfish and his aggressive ways. He recognizes Devilfish as a big-gunning player who may go down in flames, but, more often than not, will head-butt his way to the jackpot—with or without winning cards. "Players know that if I bet before the flop, I will also bet on the flop, on the turn, and at the end," brags Devilfish. "I will be betting or raising throughout the hand. They know there will be a war, and they don't want to take me on. I have a profile that gets a lot of players scared." He smirks and adds, "I make a bet and they make shepherd's pie in their trousers."

DEVILFISH CAME BY his tough, hard-quipping exterior honestly. If he sometimes seems straight out of a Guy Ritchie film, it's because his early years could easily provide the bedrock for one of Ritchie's guns-and-goons scripts. The son of a truck driver, Devilfish grew up in the working class city of Hull, 200 miles north of London.

As a young boy, he played penny-ante poker against his parents and developed an early fascination with cards. During primary school he was clearly good at math, but could never figure out a real-world application that would make the subject interesting. Then, at age 15, while laboring in a factory that produced trophies, he met Jack Gardner, a semiretired 60-year-old with a sharp fashion sense and a penchant for gambling. Gardner exposed Devilfish to a three-card poker variation called Brag. It was the game of choice at Hull's main casino, a subterranean joint called the 51 Club. The 51 attracted hard-working men who came in after long days on the nearby docks, looking to blow off steam and risk a little bit of money.

On first exposure, Brag, a game in which you bet without looking at your cards, seems like a total crap shoot. But a 51 Club regular told Devilfish that he would be able to find an advantage by tracking and counting the cards as they were dealt, then capitalizing on lazy dealers who hardly shuffled—thus allowing him to accurately predict the order of cards as they came. "I made fortunes," remembers Devilfish, adding that gambling, and the money that flowed from it (which, really, was a fortune only in relative terms), didn't exactly sit well with his father. "He threw me out of the house when I was 16. The old man didn't like me coming home in the morning, just as he was leaving for work, and earning 200 quid a night while he made only 60 or 70 all week."

With nowhere else to go, Devilfish hit the road, traveling around the U.K. playing Brag and Strip-Deck Stud (you got one card up, four down, and all cards below 7 were removed). Both games were easy enough to beat, but the profits never translated into a steady bankroll. Wildly undisciplined, Devilfish blew his poker winnings by betting on horse races at the storefront bookmaking parlors that are ubiquitous throughout the UK. "I would lose so much," he remembers, "that the bookies sent taxi cabs to bring me to them."

Between rounds as a poker player, Devilfish had a number of day jobs for which toughness was a prerequisite. He was a boxer, a roofer, a nightclub bouncer. Eventually he did a 12-month prison stretch for assault—"I broke the guy's nose, blackened his eyes, shattered his cheekbones," he says—after an incident that took place at a Hull nightclub. While serving time, Devilfish befriended a career criminal whose sentence was about to end. Impressed by the way the young thug handled himself behind bars, the veteran thief offered to take Devilfish under his wing when he got out. Among the inmates, this man was known for living large on the outside, with a big house, a Jaguar, and closets full of nicely tailored suits. Immediately upon his release, Devilfish, 29 and reckless, was contacted by the seasoned crook. "He asked me to work with him on a job," remembers Devilfish. The next day he was supposed to come by and get me in his car."

Devilfish waited. He kept waiting. Finally, he called the robber's home. His wife answered. "The police picked up my husband this morning," she said.

The close call gave Devilfish a moment of pause. It made him consider the vicissitudes of luck and gambles. A week later he met a local girl named Amanda in a pub near Hull, fell in love, got married, and put his criminal ambitions behind him. "I think about it sometimes and realize that if this guy hadn't gotten nabbed that day, I'd probably be running around with a gun"—or worse.

Instead, he and his betrothed scraped together about 10,000 pounds, bought a storefront with living quarters upstairs, and opened a pawn shop in Hull. It was probably the biggest long shot of the Devil's life. Because of his criminal record he couldn't get licensed, but, after hitting the law books, he found a loophole that allowed him to pawn merchandise for minimal amounts—no more than 30 pounds at a time—without any kind of certification. "I got tickets printed up for 30 pounds apiece, and I lent out 30 pounds at a time," he remembers. "My arm ached from writing all those 30 pound tickets. But I managed to build up the business until my wife got licensed."

That was in 1984, a good dozen years before Devilfish became a serious, full-time poker player. But his gambling skills frequently came in handy. He hosted games, after hours, in the back of his shop, and when business slowed down, he used poker winnings to maintain a cash flow. "My wife would put on spreads of food like you couldn't believe—just to keep people coming and playing," he says. "I once had this alcoholic, a nice guy, come over. He got to winning. Then he started putting away his money and told me that he needed to get going. I said, 'Why are you doing that?' He said, 'There's nothing left to drink.' I turned to the wife and asked if we had any alcohol. She told me that there was a magnum of champagne that we had gotten as an anniversary gift. I said, 'Get it!'" The guy guzzled Moët and Devilfish turned things around, sending him home with a fuzzy head and empty pockets.

Devilfish terrorized the home games in and around Hull. By using instinctive mathematical skills and betting with a degree of calculated fearlessness that few opponents could defend against, he rose beyond the typical players around town. At best, they were instinctive gamblers who required winning cards in order to take down pots; Devilfish, on the other hand, was creative and manipulative enough to push them off their top hands through crafty betting strategies and bullying at the table. Two decades later, he continues to prey on passive players, whom he derisively refers to as "calling stations." "They aren't aggressive at all, they don't bet before the flop, they don't bet on the flop unless they've got the nuts, and they don't bet on the turn unless they've got the nuts," says Devilfish. "They're people who can't win a fucking hand—and they are lovely to play against."

But even the most passive suckers eventually get tired of losing to a braggart. This point was driven home during the early 1990s. In an attempt to shake Devilfish—who clearly lacks the naturally ingratiating ways of a Chip Reese—the big game around Hull moved from one player's house to another. Though Devilfish stopped being informed of the new locations, he'd suss them out anyway and show up uninvited. Players could have asked him to leave, but, for propriety's sake, they never really did. One night, he appeared at the home of a Turkish guy named Chef, where the game was scheduled to be played. Devastated by recent losses at the racetrack, Devilfish arrived early and ready to gamble. He and Chef sat in the living room, made small talk, and waited for the others. The phone kept ringing. After answering it each time, Chef would engage in a muffled conversation. After one such call, he hung up and turned to Devilfish. "The guys saw your car outside and none of them want to play here," Chef said in a grim tone. "They've moved the game."

Cursing himself for showing up so early, before the card-playing was well underway, Devilfish had no choice but to accept the ousting. He now acknowledges, "I felt sick about that. But it turned out to be good thing." In casting around for fresh opportunities, Devilfish heard about a game in nearby Leeds. The poker being played there was Omaha and Texas Hold 'Em, two variations that would become the cornerstone of his livelihood. "Initially I went broke in Leeds," he says. "But, over time, I learned those games and eventually beat them."

ONE OF THE marks of a great gambler is an ability to avoid thinking of your bets at the table in terms of dollars and cents. Nor can you worry too much about going broke. Either of those thoughts will hobble you as a player. Even before he made his way to the high-stakes poker circuit, Devilfish had mastered the issue of mind over money. "I've always gambled to the absolute maximum," he says. "I remember playing snooker with a guy who was better than me. For 100 pounds a game, he beat me. For 500 pounds a game, he beat me. But once we got it up to 1,000 I won. The money made him choke. It had the opposite effect on me. The more I play for—in poker or snooker or anything else—the better I play."

Devilfish's personal development as a poker player dovetailed with the game's evolution in Europe. For most of the 20th century, Stud and Draw poker were fairly common in casinos throughout the U.K. and across the continent. But it wasn't until the early 1980s, after a well-known Irish bookmaker by the name of Terry Rogers happened to stop in Las Vegas on a trip home from the West Coast, that Hold 'Em was introduced. In 1983 Rogers hosted a tournament called the Irish Open, flew a planeload of top American pros (Doyle Brunson, Chip Reese, and Cyndy Violette among them) to the Isle of Man, and the game caught fire among gentleman gamblers who then typified the local pool of players. "In Europe, where gambling began as a hobby for royalty, the attitude was that you played a game because you could afford to lose," explains Jesse May, a poker pro turned author who relocated from the U.S. to Scandinavia. "In America, though, it's always been about playing to win." Over the last 15 years, however, the scene in Europe has become increasingly money-driven as well—and that suits Devilfish just fine.

The Grosvener Victoria Club, home of London's most venerable poker room, jumped on the Hold 'Em bandwagon and became a stomping ground for Devilfish in the mid 1990s. He won a couple of tournaments there in '96, netting a total of $50,000, as well as a good deal of side-game cash. And it was in one of those side games, against a Chinese player named Stevie Young, that Devilfish was christened with his nickname. Frustrated by his opponent's seemingly miraculous suck-outs, Young threw down a losing hand of cards and blurted, "You just like a devilfish!" The name stuck, and in 1997, when Devilfish won $90,000 by defeating Men "The Master" Nguyen in a tournament at Las Vegas's Four Queens casino, the day's press release was headlined DEVILFISH DEVOURS THE MASTER.

That tournament marked Devilfish's first big exposure to stateside poker pros, and he wanted to make sure they remembered him. So, after Men the Master failed to pull off a couple of high-flying maneuvers, and left himself with maybe 10 chips, just as the players were slated for a break, Devilfish showily told him, "I'm going to take a piss while you sit here and work out your next strategy."

ONE OF EUROPE'S favored poker haunts is the Aviation Club. In the heart of Paris, right on the Champs Elysées, it is a de facto private casino with the biggest action in town—almost all of it pot-limit and no-limit. Wood-paneled and austere, it opened just after World War I, as a refuge for French flyboys. After World War II, it grew into an elite baccarat club, attracting the elegant likes of Omar Sharif, before spreading poker games in the 1990s—much to the chagrin of the club's oldest members. Poker didn't seem very French or very elegant, but it brought new blood into the Aviation and probably saved the place from extinction.

The Aviation is a regular stopping point for Devilfish. In November, 2002, he came to town for a tournament and spent the lead-up nights playing cash games against raucous Frenchmen with wads of Euros. Between rounds of poker, in the Aviation's formal but clubby dining room, Devilfish sliced into a well-done steak and sipped red wine. "The difference between the French players and those in the rest of the world is that the French are more likely to win a little and leave the table," he said. "They like to hit and run. Then they come back later and try again."

For someone like Devilfish who endures big swings—during a session in Vegas he once went from being down $70,000 at dinnertime to up $50,000 by lunch the next day—quick-hit players can generate extra levels of stress. Never mind that the approach runs counter to one of poker's main precepts: minimize your losses (by quitting early in an unwinnable situation) and maximize your wins (by playing long and hard when things turn positive). "The good thing is that if they lose, the French can go down for any amount imaginable," Devilfish continued. "But they'll win 5,000 Euros and leave. Then they come back in for the bare minimum, 1,000 Euros, and you need to break them five times if you want to get your money back."

He shrugged it off as an inconvenience, since cash flow doesn't seem to be much of a problem for him. Devilfish lives a in a sprawling house in Hull, with a pond in his backyard. He parks a brand new Lexus convertible in the driveway, hangs a bunch of designer suits in his closet, and keeps enough fancy guitars in his home music-studio to outfit a touring rock group (Devilfish is big on AC/DC and the Stones). "If I were Tom Cruise I would not have a better life," he said. "Nobody tells me what to do, I travel the world, stay at the nice hotels everywhere, ride around in limos." He hesitated for a beat, then soberly added, "But all of that is only good as long as you keep winning."

Devilfish got up from the Aviation Club dinner table, signed a chit for his meal, and headed back to the poker room, walking past a dim cocktail lounge, through a leather sofa–ed library, and down a corridor lined with portraits of young aviators. Entering the card room, which was blue with smoke from Cuban cigars and Gitane cigarettes, he strode up to the club's manager and asked a single question: "Where's a cash game with an empty seat?"

The only availability was at a tight and short-handed table, which presented limited opportunities for profits. While waiting for an opening at the adjacent table—where every seat was taken and the action looked heavy—Devilfish bided his time here and tried to liven things up. "You bully these players," he said, making a bet that doubled the pot. "You push them around and always keep the pressure on."

After winning a big hand, he stacked chips, needled a loser, and began a pattern of referring to himself in the third person: "Double the Fish up," he said.

Defeated, the casino player looked back at him and grumbled in broken English, "If I had your luck, I could fly."

Sitting alongside Devilfish was the suave French pop star Patrick Bruel, a talented poker player and an Aviation Club fixture. The two guys bantered. "If you beat me this time, I'll slice off my nuts on the Champs Elysées," said Devilfish.

"Get a knife," Bruel replied as he turned over a winning hand that stung Devilfish but completely busted a too-tight player at the opposite end of the table.

Dawn encroached and Bruel said he was tired and thinking of going home to get some sleep. What kept him playing thus far was an impending seat at the busier table, where the action would be alluringly juicy. Devilfish, a place or two behind Bruel on the wait list, wanted nothing more than to sit down there before daybreak. He offered a proposition: "When your seat comes up, let me take it, and you go get your beauty rest. Then you invest 5,000 Euros in me, I'll put up 5,000, and we'll split the winnings." Considering the hour, Bruel was not sure how much table time 5,000 Euros would buy him. Clearly he didn't want to give Devilfish the money, have him play his standard superaggressive style for an hour, then leave after it was blown. "You'll play till 9 a.m.?" asked Bruel. "Guaranteed?"

Eyeing the lustier game, Devilfish said what could be his poker career motto: "I'll play till I'm too goddamned tired to play anymore." Bruel laughed, then raised his future partner. Devilfish, of course, raised him back.

Annie Duke, 2004, in Las Vegas

Eleven

THE WOMEN OF POKER

Aces and Queens

Annie Duke, Jennifer Harman, and Cyndy

Violette head up a gender revolution at

the table by turning stereotypes

upside down.

BACK IN THE MID-1980S, PRODUCERS of the tabloid TV show *PM Magazine* stumbled upon what they believed to be a bizarre story: Woman Wins $74,000 in a Stud Poker Tournament. It seemed like a natural for the program's largely female viewership, and a camera crew was promptly dispatched to downtown Las Vegas.

But before focusing on the woman, producers snagged a sound bite from Amarillo Slim. Slim wore a cowboy hat with an open-mouthed rattlesnake coiled around the brim and sat across from a chipmunk-cheeked blonde single mom who had just become $74,000 richer. As the segment opened, Slim and the blonde were in the midst of playing a mock game of Seven-Card Stud—put on purely for *PM Magazine*'s cameras. Each player sat behind a medium-size stacks of chips and looked dead earnest.

Between hands, a deadpan Slim stared into the lens. "If a woman ever beats me ..." he began, and made a throat-slitting motion by dragging a thumb across his Adam's apple. "With a dull knife," he emphasized. Slim stared down the gal across from him, vowed to "eat her up like a ginger cake," and blithely turned back to the game, as if simply being part of the male species was, in and of itself, the stone cold nuts.

Lucky for Slim, nobody's ever pressed him to make good on his suicidal vow. In the years since *PM Magazine* aired its segment, women have not only stepped up to the forefront of poker but have managed to beat plenty of the very best men (including the irascible Slim). To be sure, men still greatly outnumber women on the pro circuit, but a woman at a high-stakes poker table no longer attracts so much as a raised eyebrow from anyone else.

Cards, everyone knows, are ignorant of gender, and women are perfectly capable of pulling off balls-to-the-wall bluffs when they fail to fill their inside straights. The game's most talented females— "chicks with decks," as author James McManus once dubbed them— have turned poker into the ultimate occupation without a glass ceiling. En route to the top, women have found their unique comfort zones while devising strategies for overcoming stress, snagging pots, and confounding perceptions that the game's most hidebound competitors hang onto at their own risk. Poker's best female players all recognize that they're up against longstanding stereotypes—say, that women aren't aggressive enough or are weak at bluffing—and have been known to exploit them by pushing in the opposite direction.

It works. Annie Duke, who might as well be named Annie Oakley, outshot the likes of Doyle Brunson, Chip Reese, and Phil Hellmuth to ace 2004's $2 million single-table Tournament of Champions on ESPN. Former pool hustler Evelyn Ng, Patty "Ball Buster" Gallagher, and one-time Junior League member Clonie Gowen are all rising to be respected forces on the tournament circuit. Petite and fearless Jennifer Harman is a cash-game queen who's talented enough to play for the world's highest stakes against billionaire banker Andy Beal.

And what of that chipmunk-cheeked blonde being dissed by Slim? Her name is Cyndy Violette, and she has since evolved into a top-flight poker pro who clears six figures a year, flies first class to tournaments, and drives a gold Lexus to her regular game at the Taj Mahal in Atlantic City.

SOME TWO DECADES after appearing on *PM Magazine*, Cyndy Violette found herself well positioned at the final table in the 2004 World Series of Poker's Seven-Card Stud Hi/Lo Split tournament. Still girlish, her face slimmed down, her blond hair cut and styled into a choppy 'do, 44-year-old Violette wore a black warmup suit, with a thick purple stripe running down each arm. She was locked in battle against gray-haired and grizzled Pete Kaufman, 36 years her senior and a fixture on the local tournament circuit.

Between them, Violette and Kaufman had outlasted 222 opponents over the past two days. Now they fought, heads-up, for a first prize of $135,900. A former blackjack dealer who took up poker while on pregnancy leave, Violette had clearly come a long way from being the punchline to Amarillo Slim's sexist posturing.

In the Series showdown she held the taller stack of chips, but Kaufman, who was enjoying what could well have been his last shot at big-time poker glory, proved to be an intractable opponent. He would not be put down. In fact, after four hours of poker, on this final day of the tournament, Kaufman seemed poised to mount a comeback. Sporting a Jolly Roger smile and boundless resilience, he scooped a pot with two Kings in the hole—after Violette gambled on flush and low draws that never materialized.

Then, as she lost the hand, and momentum shifted to favor Kaufman, something strange happened: Violette sensed herself becoming embroiled in a second battle. But this one took place in her head—and it felt like nothing less than a death match between good and evil. *Good* was ending the tournament, winning the money, and taking home her first World Series bracelet. *Evil* was losing focus, blowing her lead, and walking away with second place and a relatively meager $69,100.

Unfortunately for Violette, the internal battle was nothing new. She literally believed that some emotional block had recently clicked on in her psyche and was preventing her from mustering the final bursts of brilliance required for winning major tournaments. She could finish second or third or fourth, but simply could not close the deal.

She struggled to commit herself to the job at hand, focusing every bit of energy—psychic and otherwise—on slipping back into her comfort zone and beating the old man across the felt. Between hands she silently chanted: *I want to win. Stay centered. I deserve to win.* She tried to slay the beast in her brain. But, like Pete himself, it would not go down. And she could not find her bearings.

Parallel battles—one at the poker table, one in Violette's head—raged as Nolan Dalla, the bearish media director of the World Series, who happened to be helping out in the management of this particular tournament, leaned in and broke up both fights with a few words of distraction. "Would you like to take a dinner break?" he asked the players between hands. "Or should we just stop for 15 minutes and come back to finish up?"

Violette responded to Dalla without hesitation: "Dinner break. Let's do it now."

It gave her a 75-minute retreat. While Pete Kaufman enjoyed a greasy dinner at the Horseshoe buffet, Violette ran across Fremont Street to her room at the Golden Nugget, which she had transformed into a temple of tranquility, complete with scented candles, cones of incense, a portrait of serene-looking Brighid, Celtic goddess of the sun, and a fridge full of health food.

Violette luxuriated in the positive vibes, listened to a self-help CD, and meditated on a yoga mat. She ate a bowl of spaghetti and broccoli cooked on her hot plate, and took a warm bath. Then she slipped back into the black and purple warmup suit, fearing that fresh clothing would defuse all the good fortune that had already gotten her this close to the gold. "I went to the '04 Series with the very specific goal of winning a bracelet," says Violette. "Normally I focus on the cash games and do really well. But this year was different. I stayed right across from the Horseshoe—instead of at the Bellagio, where the big cash games tend to be—and wanted to give myself the best opportunity. Poker's about having a clear head and finding your comfort zone."

For all of its history, the culture of high-stakes poker has centered on men, and that has made it harder for women to find their "comfort zones." What Violette did, in effect (and what many of the most successful female players have done), was, rather than struggle to find a comfort zone within the existing culture, make a concerted effort to import her own culture. "I needed to reclaim my power," Violette says. "If my head gets screwed up, I get lost and do badly."

Strolling back across Fremont, heading past the slot machines and craps tables that front the Horseshoe, she felt like a warrior with an edge. Recharged and refocused, she returned to the tournament and played with renewed vigor. Over two more hours, working around a couple of never-say-die winning streaks for Kaufman, she chiseled away at his chip stack.

He had only a minimal number of bets remaining in his arsenal when she caught pocket 4s and picked up a third one on Fifth Street. It was a perfectly invisible hand—made even better by an Ace on board, which created the impression that Violette had at best two pair.

Kaufman showed Deuces. He hesitated, then made a bet. Violette put him on a set of 2s and knew she had him beat. She raised, he looked sick, but with hardly any chips left he had little choice but to go all in. Sure enough, he turned over a third 2 when she called, and Violette won her first World Series bracelet—becoming the eighth woman to snag one of poker's ultimate accessories—and $135,900.

BECAUSE THERE ARE so few women competing in poker's top echelon, their progress is closely monitored by male competitors, and taking sides has become something of a parlor game. Barry Greenstein, for instance, insists that his protégé, press-shy cash-game specialist Thithi "Mimi" Tran, plays better than any other female on earth.

Daniel Negreanu votes for Jennifer Harman. And those firmly in the camp of Annie Duke (who won her first World Series bracelet in 2004) include her brother Howard Lederer and his good friend Erik Seidel.

Greenstein stands firmly by his belief, and he has backed it up with a couple of bets. One, for $100,000, is with Negreanu, and centers around who will be the first to make a televised World Poker Tour final table—Mimi Tran (who happens to be a former girlfriend of Greenstein's) or Negreanu's bud Jennifer Harman. Greenstein has a similar bet, for $10,000, with cash-game specialist David Oppenheim. This one pits Tran against Annie Duke *and* Oppenheim himself.

Such a hothouse environment makes the prospect of being a poker champ acutely stressful for women. No wonder, then, that most of the females who played when Violette was coming up—including hairdresser Jackie Jean, Chip Reese's old girlfriend Terry King, and the great no-limit Hold 'Em diva Betty Carey (who mysteriously took off in the 1990s and only just recently surfaced for a low-profile appearance at the '04 Series)—have split from the scene. "Mostly, they quit," says Violette. "Often they couldn't handle the pressure."

Kathy Liebert, the first woman to win $1 million in a single tournament (2002's partypoker.com Texas Hold 'Em event) has no problem with pressure, but she figures that men and women often play poker differently—that many women have a harder time summoning the requisite aggression. She's found her comfort zone, she says, by capitalizing on those differences. "Men tend to bluff more, and they underestimate women," Liebert says. "That can be made to work in a woman's favor, particularly when a guy mistakenly believes that you are incapable of bluffing"—and, of course, you straighten him out by bluffing like crazy.

Annie Duke says she's only recently overcome an inability to represent more than she has when playing tournaments. "It took a long time before I was able to force myself to make truly big bluffs, the ones that put an entire tournament on the line," says Duke. "You need total faith in your read. And I did not have enough faith to pull off those big money plays."

As Liebert discovered, when somebody bluffs into you but you lack the confidence to represent back, there is but one recourse. "You need to be *more* combative," Liebert says. "You need to call *more*. Normally, calling is not the best play, but in that kind of a situation, it is what's required." Show the best hand enough times, her logic goes, and the other players will think twice about betting into you with nothing. By overcoming, or at least working around, the perceived gender differences, Liebert and Duke have actually turned them into advantages. They play off of stereotypes and generalizations—in this case, that women are less adept at bluffing—to add levels of unpredictability to their games.

Thirty-seven-year-old Liebert grew up on Long Island and used to be a business analyst for Dun & Bradstreet. In 1991, after a year on the job, she got sick of it and quit without a next move in mind. Liebert wound up in Denver, where poker had just been legalized, and she tore up the $5/$10 tables. She won her first two poker tournaments and found herself to be a natural.

Because she had such immediate success on the tournament circuit, Liebert continued to focus there. It brought her decent amounts of money and a fair bit of fame, but her area of concentration also came with a downside: "Tournaments are more volatile than cash games. There's a heavier luck element in the short run, though skill makes you a winner in the end. But one key hand can break you in a tournament, so you need to play well, even when you're running badly."

For Cyndy Violette the trick to overcoming those bad streaks is meditation and positive thinking. For Annie Duke—recently buffed up and taken to favoring designer jeans and tight-fitting jerseys—the secret is relentless concentration. Duke has the ability to get so locked in to a game that whatever may be going on around her ceases to exist. "You can't talk to me when I play a hand of poker because I won't hear you," says Duke, who won her first World Series of Poker bracelet in the 2004 Omaha Hi/Lo event. "I have very good hand recall"—which allows her to remember the ways in which opponents previously played certain situations in other games—"I move into the flow of the hand, watch everything, and process the information. I can be on Sixth Street in a hand of Stud and recognize that somebody else has a single card out of order."

Duke has a background in statistics and was a Ph.D. candidate in psycholinguistics at the University of Pennsylvania before chucking it all for a career in cards. "[Annie was] incredibly creative and very charming," Duke's co-advisor Henry Gleitman told a reporter from the *Philadelphia Daily News*. His student's departure, he added, "was a loss to psychology but clearly a gain for poker."

In spite of being highly educated, Duke eschews the mathematical and intellectualized aspects of the game for something closer to brute force. She describes herself as a "feel" player, having more in common with vintage Puggy Pearson than with the endlessly calculating computer geeks who infiltrated the game in the '90s.

Recalling a hand in which she laid down top pair, with an Ace kicker, Duke says she simply sensed something vaguely fishy in an opponent's hesitant style of betting; in fact, he was slow-playing his flush. "Someone asked me how I could not have gone broke on that hand"—meaning, how could she have not gotten all her chips into the pot with such seemingly strong cards. "I said that I *just knew*. So much of this game is that you've played these situations so often, and you know how people act. You go with what you feel. It's a reflex, like when you are skidding on ice in a car. That's not the time to sit there and figure out what to do. You just do it."

After Annie left Penn's graduate program, she and her new husband, Ben Duke, (from whom she's now divorced) wound up living near Billings, Montana. He had family there, but the economy was depressed and the couple couldn't find any suitable money-making opportunities. Take-charge Annie became determined to figure something out. Legal, low-stakes poker games in which pots were capped at $300, held in the back rooms of rustic bars near Billings, caught her attention. She asked her big brother, Howard "The Professor" Lederer, for pointers and a bankroll. He sent $2,400 and she found a seat at the Crystal Lounge's nightly game.

As each session of play concluded, Annie routinely called her brother for a read on what she had done and advice on what she could do better. The long-distance clinics served their purpose, and within a month Duke more than doubled her $2,400 bankroll.

Duke's less quantifiable level of poker skill went on a growth spurt as well. Initially the questions she asked Lederer were basic, centering on how to play certain cards in specific situations. He patiently answered them while reading the *New York Times*. Three months later, however, he had to put away the newspaper and focus. "Suddenly we started talking about subtle, stylistic issues," remembers Lederer. "I found myself telling her that I would have had to be there to fully understand the circumstances. That happened very quickly. I taught her to be a good player, but she taught herself to be a world-class player."

Despite her skill level, and the respect that it should engender, Duke seems to be a magnet for controversy. One woman on the poker circuit maintains that she's a cocky winner who displays bad form by razzing losers ("The mere act of enjoying myself pisses people off like you wouldn't believe," admits Duke), and several prominent male players insist that her success rate has been exaggerated. They can snipe all they want. The fact is, Duke has become a star, and has helped to ignite a big new poker market composed of females playing in casinos and at home. On TV Annie Duke comes across as strong, smart, and impossible to intimidate. What woman wouldn't want to be like her? She even managed to parlay poker into a friendship with one of Hollywood's biggest heart-throbs. "The first time I played against Ben Affleck, I beat him out of $20,000," says Duke. "He was playing in a game, I walked over, it was full, and he made somebody get up for me. He thought it would be funny to go up against the girl poker pro."

After winning Affleck's 20 grand, Duke wound up as his poker instructor. It got her photographed in the tabloids and brought a level of exposure that made poker-world scrutiny pale in comparison. The association also coincided with interest from Tinseltown's producers, bookers, and packagers. There've been speaking engagements for Duke, a pair of book contracts, a movie deal, and a TV pilot based on her life as a divorced mother of four on the high-stakes poker circuit.

When the *National Enquirer* called for details about their relationship, Duke insisted that she and Affleck were nothing more than student and teacher. She also warned the reporter that he'd get sued if he wrote anything more salacious. Duke was not bluffing—about her and Affleck being platonic, that is. But her tutelage did pay off. In June

2004, Affleck won the California State Poker Championship at the Commerce Casino in Los Angeles and raked in $356,400.

Despite Affleck's success, Duke makes it clear that she has little interest in becoming a star teacher. "Coaching Ben was really time intensive," she says. "Beyond that, I took someone who was the worst player I had ever seen and turned him into someone really good. That is not financially sensible."

THE ULTIMATE GOAL for many of the women in poker is to reach a point where there are no "women in poker"—where it's just people playing against one another for money. Jennifer Harman has come closest to getting there, by winning the respect that comes to anyone with the guts and talent to play for pots that exceed a relatively wealthy person's life savings. On a Friday night in May, 2004, she stood outside the Bellagio's poker room, sweating a game in which she had a six-figure investment at stake. Despite a lifelong kidney ailment, which would soon be resolved through a transplant, she puffed deeply and tensely on a cigarette. ("I know I shouldn't be doing this," she said.) Occasionally, she glanced up toward the high-limit area and caught glimpses of her player raking in chips. Nevertheless edgy, Harman remained all too aware that a brief run of bad hands could decimate their winnings.

Her slender body floated inside a baggy white Juicy Couture warmup suit (a change from her usual garb: punky black leather jacket and skintight jeans). She had shaggy blond tresses, dipping down to her shoulders and groomed by her hair-stylist husband Marco. He loomed nearby and admitted that, upon first meeting Harman, he found it impossible to imagine how someone as sweet as she seemed could be a fabled poker-table assassin. But Jennifer Harman is a dangerous woman. She's won two World Series of Poker bracelets and is the only female to play in the legendary Big Game with Doyle Brunson and Chip Reese—two of her poker-playing role models. Harman maneuvers in their world by maintaining the very same kind of low-key strength that they personify. She exudes little attitude at the table, plays her cards with brilliant aggression, and, like Reese and Brunson, skirts the limelight.

For instance—in a world characterized by players who happily dissect the moves that make them great—Harman is less than eager to discuss what happened when she squared off in a heads-up match against billionaire banker Andy Beal. Never mind that their show-down, in 2003, resulted in her winning what then stood as the single biggest cash pot ever. With a bit of coaxing, though, Harman allows that the history-making hand began with her being dealt King-Queen. After the flop came Ace-Jack-10, she and Beal entered into a series of bets and raises. Harman appeared to be a made woman. She had drawn a straight to the Ace, and nothing at that point could have beaten her.

Against the billionaire banker, it was an especially sweet situation, as he'd be liable to go off for hundreds of thousands—and he seemed poised to do just that, making eight raises on the flop while Harman kept her composure and booted him right back. Beal has no fear at the table and no altitude sickness where money is concerned. But it sometimes turns him into a high-risk underdog who can afford to lose a lot more than his opponents can. Of course, in this particular situation, it made him the perfect opponent for Harman to be up against.

After a rag came on the turn, Harman bet, Beal raised, she raised back, and 13 more raises ensued. Then, on the river, the board paired Jacks. Harman's stomach suddenly felt queasy. She feared that he might have pulled a superior hand. Looking for information, she checked. "If he bets at that point, he's supposed to have drawn a full house," she says. Beal bet $60,000 with no hesitation. Harman stared at a $1.7 million pot full of the Bellagio's $25,000 chips. "My heart jumped out of my chest, went out the door of the casino, and got run over at valet parking," says Harman.

She hated the thought of throwing good money after bad, but now, with nearly $1 million of her stack already invested, she had lit-tle choice but to call. She tossed in the chips and held her breath, fig-uring that Beal had to have made his full house. Unblinking, she stared at Beal's cards, waiting what seemed like an eternity for him to show them. The billionaire turned over and revealed King-10. It was virtually a bluff; he had nothing more than two pair. Harman played it totally cool on the outside, but she was doing a victory dance on the inside, elated to have won all that money.

The rush didn't last. "Since then," she says, "I've won bigger pots playing $100,000/$200,000 with the guy."

Like Annie Duke and other top female players, Harman approaches poker as a game of feel rather than of mathematics—playing in a style that is often more artful and less predictable than that of her opponents. "If you have a player crushed"—especially mathematically inclined players like Chris Ferguson—"you make a small bet and he calls because he knows it is the mathematically correct thing to do. If I have a strong hand and he thinks I am weak, I'll play it weak—and then I strike."

It's a strategy that Harman began perfecting when she was 13 years old and occasionally sitting in on her father's home game. Harman grew up in Reno, the granddaughter of a wealthy entrepreneur who founded a successful waste-removal company, and, much to her relatives' chagrin, she had zero interest in entering the family business. Instead, she became a cocktail waitress in a Reno poker room. She learned about the game by serving players during the day and going after their money at night.

In the late 1980s she moved to L.A., where Texas Hold 'Em and Seven-Card Stud had just been legalized. One night she happened into the Bicycle Casino's poker room. Offering the most no-limit games in town, it was as sprawling as a bus station and filled with action junkies who ate dinner, played poker, and got shoulder rubs simultaneously. She looked around, took in the scene, and said to herself, "I'm home."

Four years later, Harman made her way to Vegas, where she fell in with top players, dated Todd Brunson, and now regards Doyle as a second father. She quickly ascended poker's heights in a way that's indicative of her general aggressiveness. "I just kept moving up," she says. "I went from $20/$40 to $30/$60 and from $200/$400 to $300/$600. I'd lose some, then I'd drop back down and grind my money up to the point where I got back what I lost. Then I'd take another shot."

Slowly but surely, the approach worked. And when Harman rose to where she had nowhere else to go, the Big Game (with its $4,000/$8,000 stakes) beckoned. "What I've learned is that every time you move up, the play gets that much better," says Harman. "And when you get to the point where you are playing really, really high, you can throw out the cards because you are just playing the person's mind. Sometimes, in the lower-stakes games, there are no decisions. It's so easy and the game just kind of flows. But you play with Doyle and Chip and every pot is a major decision. It can be scary."

The Big Game imparted her with a degree of humility that's key for anyone who wants to play well. Annie Duke calls it "having no ego," and she offers tips for reaching such a state. Speaking in the kind of mystical, self-help terms that Cyndy Violette would surely appreciate, Duke says, "You need to be willing to say that some people are better than you, know who they are, and pay attention so you can improve your game by watching them. You also need to know that even players who are worse than you can teach you things. And you have to admit that the biggest game is not necessarily the best game for you." She hesitates, draws a breath, and says something that any mother would understand: "You need a weird combination of confidence and self-effacement."

Chris "Jesus" Ferguson, 2004, at Binion's Horseshoe, Las Vegas

Twelve

CHRIS "JESUS" FERGUSON

The Human Cyborg

Going from college to the card room,

a computer programmer finds the

winning formula for bluffing opponents,

snagging bracelets, and becoming

a World Series icon.

THE YEAR WAS 1988, THE computer revolution was in its awkward adolescence, and gawky 25-year-old Chris Ferguson was one of the geeks at the center of it all. He kept his hair so short that it involuntarily tufted up in unruly spikes. His skin was pale as paper. He wore baggy dress pants, collared golf shirts, and white sneakers. Fueled by tap water and pizza, he toiled at writing code in a small, windowed office at UCLA. En route to earning a doctorate in computer science/artificial intelligence, he worked in furious spurts and recharged his brain by taking lost-in-thought strolls around the campus—an activity that earned him a nickname: Christopher Walker.

Ferguson lived with his parents and drove a 22-year-old, Bondo-flecked Mustang, commuting from their ranch-style home, in the posh Los Angeles community of Pacific Palisades, to UCLA's Westwood campus. Always a late riser, he generally made it to school by noon, fired up his Macintosh II, and focused his energy on devising a piece of software that would beat humans at the game of Othello. For a campus-bound programmer, far away from the nascent big-bucks boom in Silicon Valley, this seemed like a perfectly reasonable thing to do with his time.

Back then, PCs had yet to completely infiltrate the mainstream, Macs still seemed newfangled and odd, and the World Wide Web was more frontierland than superhighway. But a Finnish programmer by the name of Jarkko Oikarinen had just invented Internet Relay Chat (IRC), a groundbreaking protocol that allowed dozens of people to simultaneously communicate with one another, in real time, over telephone lines, via computer. IRC was embraced by techno tastemakers— they quickly got into online socializing, conferencing, and networking—but, like a prototype Model T, unable to do anything but circle the block, it was a cool invention without a compelling argument for existing. That came one year later, when Todd Mummert, a dark haired, pasty-skinned senior researcher at Carnegie Mellon University, introduced a piece of software programmed to deal hands of cards and manage poker games. Mummert quietly merged his poker-bot with Oikarinen's IRC technology, and the world's first online card room, dubbed IRC Poker, was born. (This was nine years prior to the explosion of online gambling—now a multibillion-dollar industry dominated by slick Web operations such as pokerstars.com and partypoker.com.)

News of IRC Poker's existence spread like a virus through communities of game-inclined programmers. Twenty-four hours a day, the site attracted a motley assortment of players ranging from computer-savvy poker neophytes to accomplished gamblers looking to refine a move or two. Toward the end of '89, Ferguson, who had some experience as a winning novice, having dominated a quarter/50 cent game in high school and low-stakes Seven-Card Stud in Las Vegas, logged on and evolved into a regular presence at the virtual tables. Though some people played for cash and settled up offline, actual gambling was not Ferguson's thing. He was more jazzed by the intellectual possibilities of the game itself, the challenge of trying to outmaneuver other participants.

During long sessions of no-limit Texas Hold 'Em and Omaha—his black-lit screen illuminated with flashing green characters signifying flops and hole cards, bets and chip stacks—he developed sophisticated game strategies and betting parameters. He formulated an analytical approach to poker that had everything to do with the way he tackled Othello and little in common with the manner in which poker's reigning experts viewed the game. On an instinctive level, Ferguson knew that poker could be reconfigured as a series of equations, complete with codified strategies that would make the game beatable. Computer-powered mathematics guided him through most everything else in life. Why should poker be any different? And so he sat at his computer, stared at the screen, punched at the keyboard, and started solving 52-card math problems.

Although, win or lose, Ferguson had no financial stake in any of his poker playing, his obsession with the game remained laser sharp. "It meant a lot to be at the top of the IRC list of money winners; it was important," he remembers. "And it took a ton of discipline to stay there. If you went broke, you automatically received a fresh $1,000 in chips, but in order to play the no-limit games, which were where everyone always wanted to play, you needed $2,000. So you had to double-up, and it took a lot of time, as long as a week, to do that. Then, once you bought into the no-limit game, the IRC rule was that you had to play with your entire bankroll"—thus upping the level of competition and increasing the risk of being kicked back down to a lowly limit game. "There was a ton at stake—even if it wasn't real money—when you had $100,000 and you were playing against somebody with $200,000. You always ran the risk of going broke. And that was a wonderful thing."

As darkness enveloped the UCLA campus, Ferguson kept the office lights burning and worked away at his projects. He had fun and gave no thought to where it would all end up. Lost in a supercharged world of zeros and ones, he really didn't care.

FAST FORWARD 16 years, to the 2004 World Series of Poker. Up in the utilitarian tournament room, on the second floor of Binion's Horseshoe in downtown Las Vegas, an ESPN camera panned across an expanse of green felt, then skittered up to the blank-slate face of a man wearing a black cowboy hat and a matching jacket. Impenetrable Oakley wraparounds covered his eyes, a full beard masked any facial tics, and chestnut-colored hair cascaded past his shoulders. He had $100,000 in tournament chips on the table in front of him.

Rail-thin and six-foot-one, no longer the anonymous computer nerd with a dorky wardrobe, 41-year-old Chris Ferguson looked like he ought to be punching cattle or running drugs. Now nicknamed Jesus, the former math geek ranked among professional poker's biggest stars. He oozed intensity and a kind of physical gravitas that worked like a radiation shield to keep opponents from cuddling up and table-talking between hands. Whenever a player asked about anything more involving than the weather, Ferguson buried his mouth inside praying fingers and refused to answer.

His reticence was right on. Against astute players—who read voices as casually as most people read the Sunday funnies—responding to even the most innocuous question can be the equivalent of turning up your cards for an opponent's enlightenment. "Somebody wants to know how much I bet, let the dealer tell him," Ferguson says.

It was about two in the morning, and Ferguson was one of three players remaining in this tournament, which began with 46, all of whom had put up a $5,000 buy-in (and sweetened the prize pool with rebuys). Set aside for the lone survivor was a first-place prize of $294,000, with diminishing sums going to the top six finishers behind him. The game was no-limit Deuce-to-7, a variation of poker in which the object is to get the lowest possible hand without making a straight (hence the name: 2-3-4-5-7 is unbeatable). The dealer shuffled his cards and slid five to each player.

Extending long, tapered fingers, Ferguson picked up his cards, cupped them, considered the possibilities. Across from him, Barry Greenstein, the slight but intense former Silicon Valley programmer, moved in his big stack of about $500,000 in chips, telegraphing that he had a monster hand. Anyone who wanted to call would have to risk the whole tournament. Ferguson took some time to consider the situation, gave away nothing in the way of slumped posture or an errant tap of the foot, and pushed in all of *his* chips—a considerably smaller stack that equaled about $100,000. Both men revealed their hands. Ferguson's top cards were 10-8; Greenstein's were 10-9. Still wearing his shades, Ferguson betrayed no emotion as the dealer pushed piles of chips in his direction.

An hour or so later, when the tournament concluded, Ferguson finished second to Greenstein, winning $169,200. Not bad, considering that he had never before played Deuce-to-7 heads-up. "Barry is an expert in this game," says Ferguson, "so I played more aggressively, bet more frequently, and folded less frequently than I ordinarily would have. Because he was more skilled than me, I wanted to turn our contest into a game of chance."

Despite his Vegas-cowboy facade, Ferguson remains every bit the computer geek he was at UCLA. His programming long ago told him what to expect when he's low on chips against a highly experienced opponent and, more importantly, what to do. A player who is outskilled needs to employ high-risk strategies—not unlike a football coach resorting to trick plays when he knows his team is overmatched. By running numbers, analyzing scenarios, and using computer calculations to figure out the hands that a perfectly playing opponent will call with, Ferguson discovered that sometimes dumb luck is better than minimal skill.

For example, according to Ferguson's calculations, a person with 50 times more money than the amount of the big blind, who bets all of his chips, every single hand, regardless of his cards, in a heads-up situation against an opponent with an equal number of chips, will have around a 40 percent chance of winning the tournament. That, he says, is a stunning mathematical reality. On the other hand, if that same inferior player tries to outplay his opponent through skill—an arena in which he is all but beaten before he starts—his odds of emerging victorious can go down to 10 percent or less. In other words, sometimes leaving it to luck is the best possible gambit.

Implementing a seemingly off-the-grid defense such as that one is a scary proposition—if you don't understand the strategy's underpinnings. For Ferguson, lack of understanding is rarely a problem. "Mathematics," he says, "gives me a certain degree of confidence that I am doing the right thing when other people might not see it as clearly."

So, no doubt, does his tournament-poker track record. By the close of the 2004 World Series, Ferguson had won a total of $2.7 million in five years of Series events. He's taken home five gold bracelets, and between 1999 and 2004 he's had more in-the-money finishes than any other World Series player.

FERGUSON STANDS AT the forefront of poker's high-tech revolution. In ever-growing numbers, players have been leaping from university labs and technology firms to poker rooms and the tournament circuit. By using computers to write software for learning and analyzing card games, they've created mathematically sound strategies that run counter to the instinctive approaches employed by veteran poker pros. "When you turn poker into a math problem, you don't need the guts and heart that people think this game requires," says Andy Bloch, an MIT graduate and former card counter, who, along with Ferguson, is a leading analyst of poker. "Instead, you rely on the math."

Those who've taken poker's high-tech plunge include Internet millionaire Paul Phillips, quantitative analyst Bill Chen, Stanford graduate Patri Friedman (25-year-old grandson of Nobel Prize–winning economist Milton Friedman), and an Arizona-based Scrabble champ named Jim Geary. "I will always raise if I am the first one in the pot," says Geary. He echoes one of Ferguson's baseline strategies, though both reached that conclusion through independent computer analyses. "[Poker theorist] David Sklansky recommends that there are certain hands you should limp into when you're first in. But that's completely wrong. It is based on his brain. He believes that the millions of hands he's played over the past 20 years have made him a sort of oracle on the mountain. He believes that his experience at the table has taught him what to do in just about any given situation. That's nice. But my computer can play a million hands in a minute and use mathematics to tell me the likelihood of a particular starting hand beating other starting hands. Computers don't forget, they don't have their judgment altered by the times they got lucky. They are cold, superior analysts of poker."

But what about the countless winning players who subscribe to Sklansky's thinking? Plenty of people limp in when they want to test the water with medium hands that might be improved upon, and they still manage to win. How do they do it? "They're good enough at other things to compensate for misplaying before the flop," Geary dryly states. "Think of them like Shaquille O'Neal. He's a great basketball player. But wouldn't he be a lot better if he learned to make free throws?"

Relying on mathematical analyses not only helps these players to win, but it cushions their inevitable losing streaks as well. This lesson became painfully clear, between early 2002 and mid-2003, when Ferguson went on a seemingly endless bender of bad beats and failed bluffs. Things hit a nadir during the Legends of Poker, a monthlong series of tournaments at the Bicycle Casino in Los Angeles. Ferguson not only found it impossible to win a tournament there, but he made a final table only once—despite playing in nearly 25 events. It was a disastrous showing.

At that point, a typical poker player would have stepped back, reevaluated his game, and altered his strategies. Not Ferguson. He recognized a statistical deviation when he saw one. "I made a conscious decision not to change my game at all," he says. "I knew the math and knew why I was losing. It all made sense. I think I experienced a run of bad luck"—which, Ferguson knows better than anyone, is an inevitable component of the game.

While Ferguson built his game around math, it goes way beyond simply figuring odds and playing each hand based on his likelihood of winning—which is something that most serious poker players do, to varying degrees, and in various ways. "It's a putdown to call someone a mathematical player," he admits. "People think of mathematical play as simply knowing the odds of one hand beating another, and that is such a small part of what I do." The more critical, more artful element is what is known as game theory, a mathematical decision-making process originally developed for chess but now used for strategizing in military conflicts, economics, business, and many other competitive environments, including poker. As employed by Ferguson, game theory tells him when to attack, when to retreat, when to confuse other players. "If I have only a vague notion of the odds, but I know exactly how to play against those odds, then I am head and shoulders above a guy who knows odds perfectly but doesn't know what to do."

Ferguson maintains large black binders full of papers that document game-theory-based calculations for specific scenarios. They include instructions on when and how to pressure stronger players during tournaments (when you are close to the money or in the money, but not heads up); when to bet for value (only with the very best hands); when to check (with mid-range hands); and when to bluff (only with the very worst hands). This last is key: Many players tend to bluff with medium-strength hands, but, as Ferguson explains, that's needlessly risky. When you have the worst of it, bluffing is your only chance to win. When you have a middling hand, there's still a chance of winning on the merit of your cards.

In 1995 Ferguson began keeping a folded sheet of paper in his wallet. It contains a matrix of hundreds of tiny numbers that tell him, based on the size of his chip stack and the cards he's been dealt, whether or not to wager everything from the big blind. Often, that all-in play is what wins or loses a tournament. If ignored, the move can leave you short-stacked; if miscalculated, it can get you eliminated. On occasion, during breaks in play, Ferguson has retreated to the men's room and studied his sheet. Quickly reconstructing past hands, he's considered how they could have been played differently, and mulled the ways in which similar situations should be handled in the future.

Back in the mid-1990s he figured he was alone in analyzing poker so intently and thought that other players would find his raw data to be interesting. Early on, he showed Mike Sexton one of his big black books. Sexton looked at it, chuckled, and wondered if this was a good use of Ferguson's time. He walked away, thinking, *Chris is going to lose all his money.*

Like many others, Sexton simply did not comprehend the extent to which math could be deployed in a game as bluff-intensive as Texas Hold 'Em. Breaking through Sexton's dogmatism was like trying to convince a 15th-century mariner that the earth was anything but flat. And, like a latter-day Columbus, Ferguson was so secure in his beliefs that he shrugged off the doubters and continued toward a possible abyss.

Then, in 1996, during a tournament break, he nipped out to the Golden Nugget coffee shop for a quick bite. He spotted bookish Andy Bloch, sitting alone at a table, eating dinner while immersed in a tiny, wallet-size spreadsheet that looked amazingly familiar—even though Ferguson had never shown anyone his secret weapon. "I was pissed off to see that somebody else had done the very same computer work," says Ferguson. "I had spent six months on that analysis and was inordinately proud of it. I remember being very upset that someone else knew this stuff."

Quickly, though, the emotion passed. Now, Ferguson and Bloch are buddies, partnered in a firm called TiltWare, which created the client/server software for the online poker site fulltiltpoker.com.

CHRIS FERGUSON GOT his first exposure to the theorizing of poker as a third-grader in Pacific Palisades. His father, Thomas Ferguson, a professor emeritus of mathematics at UCLA, had been commissioned to analyze a poker variation called Lowball (you get dealt five cards and try to make the lowest possible hand, with Ace to 5 being unbeatable). "I remember him showing me the charts on which he worked out probabilities," says Ferguson. "I thought to myself, Get paid to analyze games? Cool."

The Ferguson home was a hotbed of game playing and strategizing—all for the sake of intellectual dominance, not gambling. His mother, Beatriz, who has a doctorate in mathematics, played bridge and canasta with Chris when he was only nine years old; Thomas brought him obscure numbers-related games like Reversi (which later evolved into Othello) and Nim. Chris and his brother Marc, four years older and now a computer programmer, played intensely strategic mail-order war games such as Panzer Blitz and Tactics II. "We received a new game each month," recounts Marc. "They were created by war historians, and had pages and pages of very complex rules. Sometimes it would take days to complete a single game. But Chris, at age 10, was as good as any of my 14-year-old friends."

Shortly after his 17th birthday, in 1980, hard on the heels of an obsession with Dungeons and Dragons and nearly a decade before he'd be challenged by IRC's no-limit games online, Ferguson turned his sights to Las Vegas. He had already played poker with friends—and won—but this was something far more serious. He viewed low-limit poker as his equivalent of wandering into the Alaskan wilderness with nothing more than a bowie knife. "I saw Las Vegas as a hostile environment where people try to take advantage of you," Ferguson says. "I wanted to prove that I could survive there."

One-to-four-dollar Seven-Card Stud is the cheapest, most basic game in any poker room. It served as Ferguson's poker primer. He would drive his hand-me-down Mustang from L.A. to Vegas, play supertight against tourists, bet only with the biggest hands, and make enough money to pay for the weekend. He took comfort from having the patience and discipline to do it. Years later, after making his millions at high-stakes tournament poker, Ferguson would create a similar challenge for himself by putting $1 into an online poker account. Never risking more than 10 percent of his bankroll—which necessitated long stretches of time playing one-cent/two-cent poker—he meticulously ran it up to $20,000 over a six-month period.

Through the 1980s, Ferguson worked as a research assistant for Leonard Kleinrock (an early father of the Internet), developing various types of game-playing software and harboring vague ambitions to write and use a stock-trading program that would find undervalued securities. Along those lines, he astutely invested in burgeoning high-tech companies and did well with shares of AOL, Apple, and 3-Com. Though Ferguson made some money through card counting and continued to sporadically play low-limit Seven-Card Stud, his earliest exposure to poker for considerable sums came one evening in 1991. That's when, while wandering through the Commerce Casino, a sprawling poker club near Los Angeles, Ferguson stumbled across a table full of Korean men gambling at something called Asian Stud.

Elements of the game immediately appealed to him. For starters, he liked that the lowest limit game of Asian Stud was relatively high-stakes—players were allowed to bet anywhere from $10 to $50 (as compared, for example, with $2 and $4 in Texas Hold 'Em). Experiences in Las Vegas showed Ferguson that the cheapest games attracted the worst players. And at these stakes, there would be lots of weak players risking as much as $50 per bet. Additionally, the structure of Asian Stud—one card down, four up, with 2s through 6s removed from the deck—made for a game with limited variables, and that kept it easy to analyze on his computer.

Back at UCLA, Ferguson embarked on a mission to crack Asian Stud. "I created programs that go through the hand combinations and the chances of every hand beating every other hand," he says. Following that initial step—which Ferguson still uses in the dissection of poker—is a trickier one, which employs game theory: "Next I need to analyze different situations and how to actually play them. I found out, for example, that if you don't strip a deck [take out the 2s through 6s] it is very hard to catch a guy with a pair when you don't have one yourself. But with the stripped deck, it's easier to catch up. The later cards, in that game, are much more important than the early ones."

Asian Stud was rife with collusion, and Ferguson, usually the only Caucasian at the table, had to become more street smart than the average mathematician. "I incorporated very specific rules," he says. "For instance, if I had, say, a Queen showing, and two other Queens were visible, I would never represent having a pair of Queens. Asian Stud players who were about to fold had a habit of flashing hole cards to their friends"—and, if one of those folding players happened to have a Queen in the hole, he would foil Ferguson's bluff.

Over the course of a few months, Ferguson, who'd by now grown out his choppy hair and developed an interest in playing poker for real money, reached the point where he was able to steadily make $75 per hour at Asian Stud. He enjoyed it immensely, and still describes that game as the "purest form of poker, thanks to its heavy emphasis on bluffing." Despite the decent and sure revenue, though, he had little interest in spending his life grinding it out at the Commerce. "I decided that I wanted to get really good at all forms of poker," Ferguson recalls. "But I knew that the only way to do this was to play against the best players."

FERGUSON FELT FORTIFIED by his success at Asian Stud. IRC poker had taught him the rudiments of no-limit play. And there was little question in his mind that game theory could be used to help beat Texas Hold 'Em in the casinos. He spent the years between 1992 and 1995 running analyses on Macs at home and at UCLA.

He began by breaking Hold 'Em up into manageable nuggets, isolating very specific tournament situations and analyzing them as if they were their own games rather than part of a bigger game. "For example," he says, "I spent six months working on nothing but short-stack play; I not only learned to be aggressive with more hands than most people would be, but I learned exactly how aggressive I need to be in a range of very specific situations. If I'm low on chips—with, let's say, four times the big blind in my stack—I move all-in from the small blind and call all-in from the big blind about 75 percent of the time." More specifically, game theory has told him that short-stacked players (with, again, four times the big blind) who are dealt 10-5 off-suit and better or 9-3 suited and better, before the flop, should *not*, as common wisdom would seem to dictate, fold and preserve their chips for better opportunities. Ferguson says that those low-chipped players, with relatively weak cards, should *raise*. Though his advice might seem reckless, Ferguson's mathematical models have proved to him that, under short-stacked conditions, precisely this high level of aggression is called for.

Ferguson even found that bluffing, which would seem like a seat-of-the-pants move, can be tightly predetermined. "For Lowball, I worked on a single situation: what hands to bluff with when I draw one card and my opponent draws one," he says. "It turns out that you should bluff when you pair 7s, 6s, or 5s. This is because you bluff with your worst hands"—particularly after you've already represented strength by drawing only a single card.

When the time came for a real-world test of his stringent computer work, Ferguson immediately turned to the highly competitive tournament circuit, where losses are limited by entry fees. "Playing against the best players in cash games would have been too expensive," says Ferguson. "But I found that I could spend $300 to enter a tournament and some of the best would be in there."

But before hitting the tournament circuit, Ferguson decided it was imperative that he not appear overtly brainy. Thus the louche western-style get-up. It was as calculated a move as some of his seemingly audacious raises. "Usually academics are the ones who can get away with having long hair; and I wanted to hide the fact that I was an academic," says Ferguson. "Plus I liked that the hat and sunglasses made me look tough."

Operating with a low-six-figure bankroll, which grew out of his smart stock investing, he entered tournaments and expected to experience early losses. He didn't disappoint himself. During 1993, Ferguson dropped $13,000; he gave up $20,000 the next year. He figures that the beatings stemmed from a combination of bad luck and lack of tournament savvy. But during those 24 months he learned how to handle himself in no-limit situations, refined his analyses, and has never again had a losing season. Even the 15 months in 2002–2003 without tournament wins was salvaged by a handful of hard-fought second- and third-place finishes.

Ferguson's ongoing success is rooted in his ability to follow his set of mathematically derived rules. "Let's say, for example, you're playing Hold 'Em, the pot is $100, and your bluffing bet is $10," says Ferguson, "Well, according to my calculations, in that particular circumstance, you are supposed to bluff one time for every 11 value bets. And if you win one out of 11 bluffs, you'll come out ahead. That's the baseline and I adjust it accordingly; I bluff more often against passive players and less often against aggressive players. Win one out of eight bluffs and you will be *way* ahead. But it is very hard for most players to think of it that way. You lose eight bluffs in a row and it will be humiliating. It's difficult to take that pain." And because Ferguson employs a coldly calculated math game—"playing like a computer," it's been called—he can tolerate the sting of having a bluff exposed: It is nothing personal; it's just numbers.

Perhaps no tournament better illustrates the success of his strategy than the 2000 World Series, when Ferguson worked his way to the final table of the world championship, competing for $1.5 million—laid across the felt in piles of banded hundreds. Ultimately, the series came down to Ferguson and former football pro and Texas road gambler T.J. Cloutier. It was the classic showdown of new technologist vs. old-school Luddite. "I put a lot of pressure on T.J. during the World Series," Ferguson remembers. "I didn't think he was willing to gamble as much as he should. I thought he would fold too often because he didn't understand how valuable certain hands could be in a heads-up tournament. I believed it would give me a very small edge."

Though the two-man showdown began with Ferguson leading—$4.6 million in chips to Cloutier's $500,000—that margin was soon eclipsed. In one particularly damaging instance, Ferguson got lured into calling with Kings and Jacks to Cloutier's three Kings. Suddenly the chip-stacks were virtually equal. Then, on the 93rd hand of the day, with Ferguson a slight chip leader, Cloutier raised the opening bet to $175,000. Ferguson, with Ace-9, was convinced he had a superior hand and believed Cloutier would fold, so he raised him back, making it $600,000. Then, without a second of hesitation, Cloutier pushed all his chips into the pot. Minutes passed as Ferguson considered his options. The crowd, jammed into three sets of bleachers, remained silent. ESPN cameras focused on Ferguson's unreadable face.

Behind the mask, though, Ferguson was running calculations and thinking more like a game theorist and less like a poker pro. Playing aggressively had already gotten him very far in the Series. He knew that *aggressive* was the way to play. And though he didn't think Cloutier would bluff off his entire stack, Ferguson didn't see himself as too much of an underdog, either. Considering his cards, factoring in the way Cloutier's game was going, Ferguson figured he had about a 35 percent shot at winning the pot, which would give him the tournament. If he were to fold, Ferguson would absolutely lose the $600,000 he had already put in.

After six long minutes of agonizing, Ferguson dramatically slipped off his hat and shades. Looking emotionally frail and physically wiped out, he pushed his chips toward Cloutier's. *Call.* Ferguson turned over his Ace-9. Cloutier's Ace-Queen made him a heavy favorite (in fact, Ferguson's 35 percent estimate of his own chances overshot the true odds by only several points). The crowd roared with approval. Fans believed they were about to see Cloutier get to within a few baby steps of winning his first, and long overdue, World Series championship bracelet. The flop came 4-2-King, helping neither player. A second King came on the turn. If a 4 or a 2 showed up on the river, the pot would be chopped (because both players would be tied with two pair and an Ace high). The only card that could help Ferguson was a 9. Anything else, and Cloutier would be poised to win the 2000 World Series of Poker championship.

The crowd held its collective breath—as, no doubt, did Cloutier and Ferguson. The dealer burned a card. He turned the next one, and Ferguson jumped from his seat victoriously as a 9 dropped to the felt. It was pure luck that he caught his card, but the very fact that he remained in the hand and left himself open to getting lucky had everything to do with game theory. While most players would be loathe to risk an entire tournament on Ace-9, Ferguson saw it differently. According to the precepts of game theory, it's a bigger mistake to fold a potentially winning hand than it is to stay in with a potentially losing hand. With that in mind, Ferguson really had little choice but to call Cloutier's bet.

Ferguson bear-hugged Cloutier as the tournament room erupted. Family and friends poured down to embrace Ferguson, who, in turn, embraced the piles of money, a look of uncharacteristic, unmitigated glee overtaking his poker face.

By all appearances, the moment was overloaded with joy. Four years later, though, Ferguson insists that his display was as calculated as any of the bluffs he made during the Series. "I kind of decided, ahead of time, that showing emotion after winning the World Series of Poker would be appropriate," he says. "Bizarre as it sounds, that was actually a conscious decision. If there were no TV cameras and no audience, I would have displayed no emotion whatsoever. If it was just me and T.J. in a back room, my normal reaction would have been to shake his hand, to tell him he played a good game, and to walk out."

Then, as if wanting to emphasize his lack of feeling where poker and money are concerned, Ferguson adds, "As it was, my friend drove me home to L.A. that night, and I slept the whole way."

ON THE SECOND to last day of the 2004 World Series of Poker championship, Ferguson had a decent shot at making the final table and possibly winning the big one for a second time.

He had been enjoying a good overall showing at that year's Series and had executed some remarkable plays, including one against a seasoned sports bettor/poker pro named Alan Boston. "People in the Seven-Card Stud tournament thought I had been playing overly tight," says Ferguson. "Actually, I just wasn't getting cards. So it forced me to fold more than usual, and that conveyed an artificially tight table image." Ferguson capitalized on the inadvertent perception by stealing pots from players who figured he'd only go in with superstrong hands. Such was the case against Boston. When Ferguson found himself showing Ace-3 suited on Fourth Street, he raised and induced Boston to fold a pair of Kings. "He figured I had him beat," says Ferguson, shrugging. "But I was sure he'd go all in with that hand."

Sweet and simple as this sounds, the very same assumptions and strategies that allowed Ferguson to bluff out Boston can sometimes backfire brutally. On that penultimate afternoon of the Series, evening encroached and Ferguson had around $700,000 in chips. It was a decent amount for the moment, but, with blinds and antes rapidly escalating, he needed to keep building in order to survive for the next and final day.

A few seats to Ferguson's left sat a baby-faced Brit named Gary Jones, who had been raising more aggressively than appeared optimal. Ferguson, who again had been running cold, was waiting for an opportunity to straighten him out—maybe thinking about how he had pushed Boston away from a pot days earlier. Holding two 4s, Ferguson faced a $100,000 bet from Jones—who went so far as to announce that it was his fifth raise in a row. Figuring him for a less than premium hand, Ferguson moved all in, pushing $643,000 toward the center of the felt.

Jones spent a long time considering his options. "Then," says Ferguson, "he called me with Kings."

The Kings held up, and Ferguson was left with a measly $4,000, which he promptly tossed into the pot on the next hand. And won. He proceeded to move all his chips in, five more times, in close succession. Miraculously, he ran the $4,000 up to $137,000 and seemed to be back in contention. Not long afterward, Ferguson was dealt Ace-10. In a risky attempt to double up, he pushed his chips in once again. This time he was called by Mattias Andersson, a wiry and high-strung 24-year-old Swede. Andersson showed a pair of 5s, Ferguson caught no cards, and he went out in 26th place, out of 2,600 entrants, with a prize of $120,000.

Though, naturally, Ferguson would have loved to win a sixth World Series of Poker bracelet (and the $5 million that went with it), he nevertheless insists that his five weeks of poker playing at the Horseshoe was anything but a bust. Beyond his $343,435 in prize money, he took home something with potentially more value: a recognition that poker has changed. "Game theory is based on the assumption that your opponent plays perfectly and is better than you, and for the last nine years I had been playing poker in precisely that way," Ferguson says. "But partly because my game has improved and partly because the popularity of poker on TV and the Internet has brought in a lot of new, weak players, the average level of poker playing is actually down." Therefore his game-theory assumptions have become less valid. "As a result," continues Ferguson, "I should go out on a limb more, I should play possum more, I should spend more time calling behind players."

After the World Series, Ferguson repaired to his poker lab, now situated in TiltWare's Los Angeles office, and he worked on making fresh adjustments in a totally scientific way. Like a programmer updating software to accommodate a change in the marketplace, Ferguson tweaked his game to reflect the shift of poker and its practitioners. Upon returning to the tables, he will know exactly what he's doing and why. Competing in a game famous for its instinctive players and psych-out artists, Chris Ferguson will make surprising plays as plotted and precise as mathematical equations on a UCLA chalkboard.

Chris Moneymaker, 2003, at Binion's Horseshoe, Las Vegas

Thirteen

THE WEB KIDS

Doing the Digital Hustle

A new generation of Net-surfing rounders

makes the leap from playing online Hold

'Em to storming—and winning—

the World Series.

INSIDE A CRAMPED, WINDOWLESS OFFICE, just a 20-minute drive from the honky-tonks and pool halls that once drew Puggy Pearson to downtown Nashville, the hour crept toward noon. Freshly arrived from home, still bleary-eyed from last night's poker marathon, a thickly built, squinty-eyed accountant with a dark blond mustache and goatee sat down on a padded swivel chair. He removed his wraparound sunglasses, booted up his computer, and clicked his way to the on-line gaming site pokerstars.com.

From neighboring cubicles, his colleagues could be heard discussing business matters, but, on this afternoon in January 2004, the accountant remained oblivious. Phone calls went unanswered, e-mails ignored. He relentlessly bullied his way to a pot on one of the site's $30/$60 games of Texas Hold 'Em. "This guy's either got a diamond-flush draw or 8s," he said, after an 8 of diamonds came on the flop and the opposing player made a raise. "He hasn't done anything in these few hands to show that he can bluff worth a flying flip."

After powering in a couple of additional bets and raises, the accountant pressed his opponent to fold. Within seconds, more than $300 changed hands electronically and fresh cards were dealt. The accountant continued to abuse his hapless opponent, who almost certainly would have cashed out and quit had he known who he was going up against: Chris Moneymaker, Nashville-based accountant and 2003 World Series of Poker champion.

Not only did Moneymaker craftily steal the 2003 World Series, but he also got into the championship by winning a flight of online pokerstars.com tournaments with a measly $40 buy-in. So, in addition to being a major league poker talent, he's particularly adept at the digital variety. In fact, Moneymaker represents a new breed of card player: battle-tested on the Internet and operating with the fast-firing style that is the hallmark of nearly every World Series champion.

A magnet for would-be Moneymakers, online poker rooms are not just convenient places to play; they are the proving grounds for a whole new game and the next generation of Goliaths. Open 24/7 and spreading dozens of poker variations at any given time, operations like ultimatebet.com and pokerstars.com foster the deployment of new strategies, styles, and skills. A blustery table presence—as perfected by Puggy Pearson, Amarillo Slim, and Devilfish Ulliott—is virtually worthless online, as Internet players are judged almost exclusively by how they bet their hands. Online play removes the people component from poker and reduces it down to a pure card game. Consider this: You're playing online, you make a huge raise, and your opponent sits for 15 seconds without acting. Is he thinking? Consulting a poker strategy book? Or did he just get up and go to the bathroom? You have no idea. And, really, it doesn't matter.

For professionals, the anonymity of the Web turns online poker into a gold mine. After all, few amateurs would knowingly sit down to gamble against Chris Moneymaker in a brick-and-mortar card room and risk hundreds, or even thousands, of dollars—but they blindly do it all the time on the Internet. And while members of poker-centric bulletin boards, such as rec.gambling.poker, make a parlor game out of matching online handles with the names of well-known professionals, absolute detection is impossible. Then there are the downright corrupt players who team up and confer via telephone or instant-messaging to collude against the rest of the table. But even their edge pales in comparison with that of the so-called poker-bots—computers programmed to play the game perfectly—that are said to be rampant on the Internet.

None of these drawbacks was much of a turnoff for the thousands of players who wagered nearly $110 million online during a typical 24-hour cycle in August 2004. The Internet's most popular site, party-poker.com, has more than 28,000 gamblers logged in during peak hours. Those numbers become all the more impressive if you consider that commercial poker did not exist online before 1998, when planet-poker.com kicked off the phenomenon. Competing sites quickly sprang up, and competition for new blood became fierce. In order to attract neophytes, just about every site allows customers to join without charge and use play-money to get acclimated or enter the occasional free-roll tournaments, in which the card room puts up small cash prizes. Meanwhile, real-money games (from which sites take a rake out of every pot, same as in a casino) are, tantalizingly, just a mouse-click away.

Among serious players, though, online poker serves as the most efficient learning tool in the game's history. For example, almost all sites offer the chance to request hand histories—which can chronicle an entire game. These can be invaluable resources for identifying patterns in yourself, as well as in your opponents.

Additionally, you can keep databases of notes on other players: "John Smith always checks after the flop when it helps his hand," or, "Jane Doe chases straights and flushes." The sites even inform you when weaker opponents you've identified are logged on, so they can be tracked down and battered. Best of all, hands are dealt two to three times faster than in a land-based casino—as many as 200 an hour—and it's possible to play multiple games at once. As a result, diligent newcomers can accrue the equivalent of six years of poker experience in as little as 12 months online.

For evidence of the technology's effectiveness as a learning tool, look no further than the 2004 World Series, where more than 800 players qualified via the Internet—nearly one-third of all entrants. Four of those players made the final table of nine, and one of them, Greg Raymer, actually won the tournament's first prize of $5 million when he drew a higher full house than 23-year-old college student David Anthony Williams, the runner-up, who also qualified on pokerstars.com.

Raymer became online poker's second World Series champion in two years, and further stoked the dreams of desktop Hold 'Em fanatics around the world. He also caught the attention of poker's top pros, who were initially dismissive of the online interlopers. "Many of these Internet guys believe that they can outplay the name players," says Erik Seidel. "And maybe some of them can. Out of this huge group, a handful will come through and be very successful. They may not play better than Phil Ivey"—a highly accomplished young player in both cash games and tournaments—"but they will be good."

THE ONLINE WORLD has already grown large enough to boast its own stars, with well-known handles and fearsome reputations. Obsessively private Prahlad Friedman has had months in which he's earned as much as $200,000 playing on ultimatebet.com. A group of young Scandinavians, headed up by 21-year-old Erik Sagstrom, turned a Linkoping, Sweden, Internet café into a virtual casino and made their bones online before biting into the European tournament circuit in 2002. Thomas "Thunder" Keller, who developed a name for himself as a college kid playing the Internet's biggest cash games in the late '90s, transferred his online skills to the live world and snagged a first prize of $382,020 at the 2004 World Series of Poker's $5,000 buy-in no-limit Hold 'Em tournament. And Jim "Krazy Kanuck" Worth found online poker to be so lucrative that he sold his successful coffee distrbuting company in Calgary, moved to Toronto, and logged onto the virtual poker world fulltime. He plays for three to 10 hours every day, often winning more than $1,000—sometimes much more—and enduring an average of only about three losing sessions every couple of months.

During the 2004 World Series, Worth skipped many of the Horseshoe's preliminary tournaments and didn't bother testing out the Bellagio's cash games. Instead he spent his days in the swank three-bedroom house he had rented across town, lounging on a recliner and playing on the Internet while watching movies on the bigscreen and occasionally looking up to check out his statuesque girlfriend sunbathing outside. The decision was a no-brainer: Ultimatebet.com gave Worth a higher expected profit than he could have gotten at either of the casinos, and the view was unbeatable.

At the core of Worth's success is disciplined money management. First thing every morning, he plays a series of $100 heads-up matches, using those games to build his bankroll for the coming evening (when the competition is softer than it is during the day). If he wins, he's set to play after dark; if he loses, he spends hours trying to grind himself into a profitable position. What he doesn't do is chase money or move up to higher levels in order to make back his losses from the lowerstakes tables.

Several times a week, Worth also enters online tournaments, where hundreds, sometimes thousands, of players compete for prizes that regularly reach into five figures. Because Internet players are used to going up against such large fields, Worth believes they bring an advantage to massively attended events such as the 2004 World Series. "With that big a field, I play more hands early on and chip up quickly," he says. "It helps me to do the most important thing you can do in a tournament: survive."

Like other hardcore Net-heads, Worth worked out the kinks in his tournament strategy by trial and error online. For starters, he had to get over the recurrent problem of making it to the bubble but often finishing out of the big money. "I learned how to steal blinds and antes," says Worth. "You don't pick on the big stacks and small stacks, because they're likely to call"—since neither has much to lose by taking a shot against you. "The middle stacks are the ones you pick on because they see themselves as having the most at stake once they're on the bubble, and they stop taking chances because they want to walk away with *some* money. For me, though, breaking even, or winning a little, is a joke. Nearing the money in a tournament, I increase the aggression and can easily move from 18th place to 11th or 12th"—if he doesn't go bust. "Then I keep moving up and try to win."

Worth applied a similar self-improvement regimen to every aspect of his online game. He sometimes played with the sole purpose of experimenting rather than winning money. He learned how to trap players, betting equally big with Ace-King and with 9-2 off-suit, in order to keep opponents guessing. "I got comfortable with making big bets and big bluffs," he continues. "It gave me the ability to put decision-making on other people. Then, by making everyone sick of my constant raises, I controlled the table. People feared me. Good players realized I was dangerous because they couldn't put me on a hand; bad players thought I was lucky. Now when Krazy Kanuck sits down to play, people start chattering, wishing they weren't at the same table as him."

During the summer of 2003, Worth had an opportunity to put his lessons to a real-world test. He found himself heads-up against T.J. Cloutier in a pot-limit Hold 'Em tournament at the Bellagio. Gazing through aviator glasses, Cloutier, the astute, road-hardened gambler from Richardson, Texas, immediately identified Worth as an online guy, with limited live-game experience, and he quickly took advantage: chatting Worth up, hunting for tells, critiquing his play. Though it was all done with a smile, Cloutier's subtle psych-job freaked out Worth, causing him to second-guess good decisions and make inappropriate moves.

During a break, by which point Cloutier was a 10-to-1 chip leader, a stranger tapped Worth on the shoulder. He introduced himself with his Internet-poker moniker, Txbandit, and said, "I've watched you play online for six months. You're one of the best heads-up players I've ever seen. I try to model my game after yours. Right now, if you're interested, my advice to you is that you should forget who you're playing against. Make believe you're online."

Returning to his signature style, Worth stole one small pot after another with aggressive moves and eventually grabbed the chip lead. "T.J.'s demeanor completely changed," he remembers. "T.J. was frustrated and slouching over. He got real quiet and began concentrating on the game." The title was within Worth's reach—but then he got sloppy and made an amateur's mistake of becoming overly aggressive with top pair. He bet most of his chip stack, lost to T.J. Cloutier's two pair and was crippled for the rest of the tournament.

The loss was disappointing, but came with its own reward. "I was up against one of the great pot-limit players," says Worth. "And I played with him for more than an hour. How could I not feel good about that?"

WORTH'S DIFFICULTY TRANSLATING online success into beating a big live game is not uncommon. Greg Raymer, 2004 World Series champ, qualified for the tournament online but also boasts a wealth of off line experience. He notices several frequent mistakes that online players make when they get into live situations.

Most destructive of all is that, when they're playing in casino card rooms, they tend to telegraph whether they will raise or fold before the action comes to them. This is obviously because nobody in cyberspace can see your tells—or know that you're playing in your skivvies. But it's also indicative of a certain restlessness that comes from gambling at your keyboard and tapping your mouse as you wait for slow players to make their moves. "The other thing," says Raymer, "is that during no-limit Hold 'Em tournaments, I see poorly calculated bet sizes from the online players. That's probably because online you can click a button for a minimum bet rather than adjusting a sliding scale or typing in a number for a larger bet." It's easier to make the minimum bet, and, slowly, right or wrong, that becomes ingrained in a player's gambling psyche.

So, conversely, does over-betting. "They also go all-in way more than they should," continues Raymer. "They get used to doing it during the low buy-in tournaments online, where they can bust out of one and immediately sign on for another. But it doesn't work like that in live play."

Thunder Keller, who calls himself Gummybear on the Internet, learned this lesson the hard way. As a 17-year-old freshman at Stanford (he and his twin brother, Shawn, hopped right from junior year of high school in Phoenix to the Stanford economics program), he routinely snuck onto the tables at the slick and tournament-intensive Bay 101 Casino in nearby San Jose, where the over-aggressive style he developed on the Internet got his clock cleaned. "Any two face cards, Shawn and I would go in," Keller remembers. "During a terrible week at Bay 101 we were playing $30/$60 limit Hold 'Em, and we lost around $12,000. It just about killed us."

Like lots of mathematically inclined teenagers, the Keller brothers refined their gambling chops through a combination of online poker and a strategic fantasy-based card game called Magic: The Gathering. Sometimes referred to as "geek poker," Magic combines elements of chess and bridge. Thomas, a huge guy with a shock of bright yellow hair and a perpetually blissed-out smile on his face, turned from Magic to Hold 'Em after being inspired by *Rounders*. And, in the style of the movie's protagonist, played by Matt Damon, he had a habit of blowing off class if he was in the midst of winning or losing big; yet, very much unlike Damon's character, he still managed to finish with a GPA of 3.1. "I pride myself on having the highest grade-to-attendance ratio in my class," he says.

Not surprisingly, Keller was besieged by Stanford students wanting to know how they too could win hundreds of thousands of dollars messing around in the online poker rooms, and his advice was simple: "Don't focus on how good your own game is. Focus on how bad the other players are. At $20/$40 or less, 90 percent of what you have to do is be patient and wait for strong hands to come your way."

Once he learned to keep his aggression in check, Keller became an unstoppable force, both online and in the card rooms of his native Phoenix. At one point, he corralled nearly all of one Indian casino's $100 chips and carried them with him in a messenger bag. "When people in the game needed chips, they bought them from me," he says. "The casino wanted me to sell the chips back, and I did—but only after they lowered the poker limits, which made me stop playing there. Why bother if I can play $200/$400 online?"

ALTHOUGH OTHER ONLINE stars, like Worth and Keller, are arguably more consistently successful, Chris Moneymaker remains the face of Internet poker—and enduringly popular to poker's throngs of newcomers. A week prior to 2004's World Series of Poker championship, in which he would defend his crown, Moneymaker tuned up by playing a no-limit cash game downstairs at the Horseshoe. He situated himself cowboy-style on a chair, leaning his chest into its back as a silky haired Asian masseuse pounded, kneaded, and stretched his muscles. He had been dealt two down cards but couldn't reach them because the masseuse happened to be pulling back his arms at that very moment. Moneymaker relaxed the sneer he generally maintains at poker tables, smiled, and told her that he needed his arms back.

This got a big laugh from the dozen or so people pressed in on the table and scrutinizing his every move. By playing online, he said, "I've learned to intimidate people out of pots." He pushed in a big raise and illustrated his point by scaring away opponents before the flop. Then he smirked and added, "But that comes natural for me. I'm an action junkie."

Of course, there is a fine line between being an action junkie and being a compulsive gambler. Moneymaker walks it precariously. He was close to broke before being saved by online fortune and fancy playing at the 2003 Series. During the early months of that year, seemingly a lifetime ago, he was bogged down with $7,000 in credit card debt, he'd endured numerous losing sessions at the nearby riverboat casinos (often dropping $1,000 at a time, which he couldn't afford), and his sports betting was a disaster. It had gotten so bad that, as Moneymaker came close to winning the qualifying tournament that catapulted him into the Series, he actually hoped to finish fourth. He figured that the consolation prize of $8,000 would be more useful than a seat in a tournament where he'd pretty much have zero chance of finishing with a profit.

In need of money, he sold 50 percent of his potential winnings, for $5,000, to his father and his friend Dave Gamble (yes, these names are real). "I would have sold 100 percent of myself," he says, "if anybody had wanted to buy it."

Then Moneymaker shocked the world by reaching the final table and improbably bluffing his way past the suave veteran Sam Farha to claim the title and $2.5 million. Overnight, he became a star. "People treat me like a celebrity just because I play poker," he says. "Maybe I give everybody hope that they can do this, that you don't need to be a professional in order to come out here and win the series. I don't know. I have to tell you, it's baffling to me."

Perhaps. But the adulation and money, a promotional deal with pokerstars.com, the TV exposure, and endless high-stakes challenges, are all having an impact. Despite efforts to seem unaffected by his notoriety, Moneymaker is a changed man—even from January 2004, just months before his Series appearance, in that claustrophobic accountant's office. He's lost weight, upgraded his wardrobe from jeans and sweatshirts (at the 2004 World Series he generally wore pressed slacks, flashy pullovers, soft leather shoes), quit his day job, and made a couple of final tables in high-profile tournaments that preceded the Binion's classic. This last factor was critical, as it helped erase the widely held belief that Moneymaker was a fluke, nothing more than a casual online player who happened to get lucky at the 2003 World Series. "I like when people say I'm lucky or crazy or whatever," says Moneymaker. "You make your own luck."

Although Moneymaker is the first to acknowledge that everybody has to get at least a little lucky in order to win a World Series, he also insists that a great poker player always lived inside him but needed a bit of reshaping before it could come out. Now, he says, that player is in action: "I'm 10 times the player I was last year. You play with better people, you get better. You play in bigger games, you learn more. Now I don't mind getting tangled up with Johnny Chan. Since I knocked him out [of the 2003 series] I know I can play with him."

That confidence showed in Tunica, Mississippi, in the early months of 2004, when a rich, unknown amateur wanted to take on Moneymaker in a game of no-limit Hold 'Em with $50/$100 blinds. "We were both drinking heavily," Moneymaker remembers. "Those were pretty big stakes, and he wore me out for four hours."

It got to the point where the other guy had $15,000 in front of him—$10,000 of which had once been Moneymaker's. But the former champ didn't sweat it. He just pulled another wad of $100 bills out of his pocket. This not only kept his opponent interested in playing, but it had the potential side benefit of getting the guy to focus on the cash rather than on his cards. From Moneymaker's perspective, a stack of hundreds on the table kept him prepared to capitalize on promising situations. The last thing he wanted was strong cards and too little dough—casino rules dictate that money in your pocket can't be used in the middle of a hand. Meanwhile, between sips of whiskey, the other guy raked in pots and crowed about beating a world champ.

Sucking up the abuse, Moneymaker maintained a stolid facade, just as if he were sitting at home and playing online. He remained intent on winning back his 10 grand and then some. After getting 8-Jack, he called a $200 preflop bet. Then the flop came 9-10-Queen, which gave Moneymaker a straight—the nuts. Playing into the other guy's aggression, he issued a small bet of $500 and hoped for a raise. His opponent came over the top, pushing all $15,000 into the pot and trapping himself. "I called, he had Kings, and I got all the money in a single hand," says Moneymaker. "My style now is that I will get my chips in there with the worst of it, but, in the end, I will catch you. You need to realize that sitting down with a big bankroll makes all the difference. If I couldn't support that style of play, I'd go broke."

Though Moneymaker is a natural live-game player—he's got a big personality and obviously enjoys the limelight—he is quick to acknowledge that the aggressive aspect of his game, which he uses to great advantage in casino situations, developed through online play. "I sit back and raise more frequently online," he says, acknowledging that he tones down his Internet approach for live action. "Generally, online you encounter two types of players: the one who plays real tight and waits for hands and the one who will play crazy insane. By playing aggressive, I can counteract both of those players: I steal blinds from the tight guy and outplay the crazy guy. In a live game, you pick up a 3 of hearts for your first card, and the chances are very good that you are about to give up your hand, no matter what you get dealt next. Online you'll probably play that hand if your second card is high enough—say, a King."

Like Moneymaker, Thunder Keller and Krazy Kanuck Worth also

know the importance of honing one's game at the virtual tables. Even Keller, who sometimes seems to have scaled poker's heights solely on natural-born instinct, developed his sense of gamble and an all-important financial-disconnect by playing on the Internet. It taught him to view his chips as tools that can be used for winning more chips—not as plastic discs with monetary value. That mindset quickly got him going in the high-stakes arenas around Stanford, and currently sustains him in tournaments where the prizes can be dizzying. "Poker to me is a game," Keller says, echoing the sentiments of countless online players. "I'm in it to have fun. I get more nervous driving down a highway. The only thing at stake here is money."

Barry Greensten, 2004, in Tunica, Mississippi

Fourteen

BARRY GREENSTEIN

Taking Care of Business

A math wunderkind abandons Silicon

Valley and amasses a poker fortune

through cold-blooded tactics worthy of a

corporate CEO—and then reveals a

surprising soft side.

IN THE TWILIGHT OF A flawless Friday afternoon on the Palos Verdes peninsula, an hour south of the city of Los Angeles, a secluded beach cove slowly filled with jet-skiers and surfers. On the shore, at a distance safely removed from the crashing waves, two teenagers settled in for a romantic picnic while, farther down, a young dad taught his son the rudiments of building a sand castle. Perched on the cliff above, in an 11,500-square-foot pink stucco behemoth of a house, Barry Greenstein had just rolled out of bed. He peered down at the pleasure seekers and contemplated his own plan for the weekend: Try to win more than a million dollars in cash at the poker tables—"a nice thing to be able to do," he says.

Greenstein, 49, slipped a pair of silver slacks and a canary-yellow button-down over his five-foot-eight, 150-pound frame, ran a comb through his bristly black hair, and ignored the perpetual five o'clock shadow that covered his long and narrow face. He strolled to the kitchen in the other wing of the house, where his girlfriend, Alexandra Vuong, handed him an energy drink, told him where to find his favorite Gucci belt—the one with a gold "G" buckle that his kids teased actually stood for Greenstein—then pushed him out the door with a kiss. Save for the unusual hour of departure, Greenstein acted like any other successful businessman preparing for his daily commute—and that's not exactly an accident.

To Greenstein, poker is purely a business. He is one of the world's wealthiest, shrewdest, and most fearsome card sharks, but all things being equal, he'd rather return to his old job as a computer programmer or maybe pursue his dream of becoming a math professor. All things are not equal, of course, and math professors don't live in mansions overlooking the Pacific Ocean. "There are a lot of people who feel that they would play poker regardless of how they do, because they love cards," he says. "The reason I play is strictly to make money."

In the first five years of the new millennium, Greenstein earned more money playing poker than anyone alive—by some estimates in excess of $20 million, a figure he does not dispute. His prosperity is on copious display in his massive home, which overlooks not only the ocean but a seaside golf course being built by Donald Trump. Greenstein recently added an indoor pool, and his girlfriend is planning to gut their immense kitchen, mainly because she doesn't care for its austere black-and-white color scheme. The one blight in all of this domestic luxury is an interrupted view from one of his balconies: It ought to look down upon the adjacent course's clubhouse; instead, it offers a view of his neighbor's Spanish-style roof.

Until four years ago, that property was vacant, and Greenstein planned on purchasing it to preserve his view. But then he lost $1.5 million in a monthlong game of Chinese poker with high-stakes gam-

bler Ted Forrest and fell into a brief cash-crunch—which allowed another buyer to swoop in and snatch the property out from under him.
The neighboring house, he says, "is a reminder not to do foolish
things."

AS HE STEERED his silver Jaguar out of a private cul-de-sac and toward the night's game, Greenstein confronted a glut of voicemail mes-
sages on his cell phone. Because he has been on such a tear—through
both tournaments and cash games—he is a sought-after commodity
for the TV producers and reporters who feed the public fascination
with the game's stars. "Poker has just gotten too huge," Greenstein
muttered under his breath.

On his better days, he admits that he doesn't really mind the attention as long as it adds to the game's ever-growing popularity. Because, ultimately, that boosts his bottom line. "There are a lot of
wealthy people who have not been able to play poker because of the
stigma associated with it," he says. "But it is becoming more socially
acceptable. That means you are going to have more of those people
dumping money to people like me."

Alternately dialing and talking, Greenstein maneuvered the sports
car through the mountains that buffer his swanky community from
the L.A. smog and, going against rush-hour traffic, descended into the
depths of gritty suburban decay: block after block of liquor stores and
pawn shops, their steel gates sprayed with gang graffiti. In the heart
of downtrodden Gardena, he reached the incongruous art deco facade
of the Hustler Casino, owned by porn magnate Larry Flynt. He zipped
into the parking lot and over to a private parking space near the entrance. A security guard greeted him at the front door: "Good evening,
Mr. Greenstein."

Greenstein nodded and strode confidently into the casino, ignor-
ing double-takes from low-limit grinders shocked to catch a poker lu-
minary in their midst. Ever since 1987, when the state Supreme Court
ruled that poker was a game of skill—and not a form of gambling—
California has boasted a handful of reputable, no-frills card rooms,
most notably the Bicycle and Commerce casinos, both near downtown

Los Angeles. But Flynt raised the bar in 2000 when he opened his $40 million venture. The décor is less tawdry than you might expect from the man who built his fortune on the "beaver shot" in *Hustler* magazine—all dealers and waitresses are fully dressed—but the maroon-velvet walls and deep-red-and-black checkerboard carpet exude the vibe of an upscale brothel.

In a quiet back-left corner of the main room, beneath a gaudy chandelier that makes it seem as if the roof is leaking costume jewelry, Greenstein joined poker pros Phil Ivey, Johnny "World" Hennigan, and Danny Robison, who were all waiting for Flynt to arrive before they started playing. Flynt, after all, was the draw—not only because he owns the casino but, more significantly, because he doesn't mind dropping several hundred thousand, or more, in a few hours of poker. He is a serious player, and a good one, but he's smart enough to know that the pros compete to get their greedy hands inside his deep pockets.

"I've been supporting these guys and their families for five years," Flynt says. "I like to play with the best. Otherwise what fun is it?"

It was hardly a put-down to be the weakest player in this lineup. Ivey, the lanky 27-year-old African-American out of Atlantic City, is considered one of the game's top young professionals. Robison, until he was derailed by a cocaine addiction in the 1980s, had been one of the premiere Seven-Card Stud specialists in Las Vegas for more than 10 years. Now born-again, he splits his time between running a Bible study for poker players—God's Winner's Circle, he calls it—and playing high-stakes poker himself. (To those who question the apparent contradiction between his faith and his profession, Robison counters with Scripture: "I am the God who gives you power to obtain wealth that you may establish my covenant on the earth.") Hennigan is a hard-charging natural gambler and an unabashed sinner. The chrome-domed former pool hustler from Philadelphia once won a million dollars in a day of poker, and then blew it all that night at the blackjack table. His self-destructive tendencies include a propensity to drink at the table, but they're more than matched by his awe-inspiring talent. "When he's at the top of his game, Johnny may be the best Seven-Card Stud player in the world," Greenstein says. "When he's not, he may be one of the worst." On this night, Hennigan was drinking coffee, and everybody knew to take this as a sign that he would be a formidable threat.

As Robison sat quietly and Hennigan monitored a notepad with a long list of his sports bets for the day, a poker-room manager brought Greenstein a tray stacked with maroon-and-pink $5,000 chips and yellow-and-blue $500 chips. Without a signal from anyone, a dealer instinctively divvied out 13 cards to him and an equal amount to Ivey, Greenstein's good friend and frequent gambling companion. Two of the most successful players in the game—and arguably the most dominant pros of 2004—they are too restless to be out of action for very long, so they regularly occupy their down time by playing Chinese poker for $2,000 per point (serious stakes that quickly and routinely end up with six figures flowing one way or the other). Yet, because it's a fairly mindless form of poker in which luck generally trumps skill, watching Ivey and Greenstein screw around at this is akin to witnessing Tiger Woods and Phil Mickelson playing a million-dollar round of miniature golf.

On first blush, Greenstein appeared to be repeating the mistake he made against Ted Forrest: risking a sizable chunk of his bankroll at a frivolous activity in which he lacked a distinct advantage. But he insisted this situation was different. For one thing, Greenstein was much richer than he had been in 2000. On top of that, he and Ivey gambled together so often, with neither owning a distinct competitive advantage, that they figured it would simply even out in the end. Still, he said, if he ever dug himself into a deep hole against Ivey, he would quit playing before his losses began to seriously hurt.

In the course of the next hour, Greenstein took Ivey for close to $200,000—all before the real action started.

WHILE OTHER MEN of his financial stature might hire expensive interior decorators for their homes, Greenstein made most of the design choices for his palatial digs himself, drawing inspiration from the casinos where he spends most of his time. In terms of understated elegance, his place ranks closer to Flynt's club than to the typical spread in *Town & Country*. A rainbow collage of blown-glass flowers, modeled on the installation in the lobby of the Bellagio, hangs over the foyer; an 1,100-gallon curved aquarium, similar to the shark tank at the Mirage—and built by the same company—forms the base of the staircase in the entryway; and the marble tile in Greenstein's bathroom floor matches the pattern in the Venetian's suites. He went so far as to take a cue from casino mogul Steve Wynn and create his own miniature museum. Even the most art-deprived visitors recognize—if not by name, then at least by sight—the works that dominate Greenstein's collection: Van Gogh's *Starry Night*, Picasso's *The Dream*, Rembrandt's *Night Watch*. But, then, as one looks closer, it all starts to feel a bit suspicious. Even Greenstein couldn't afford these priceless works of art, could he? A section of the Sistine Chapel? The Mona Lisa? Greenstein chuckles and admits that he paid an artist to create reproductions of the world's most famous paintings so that his friends and family could enjoy seeing them up close. "Who wants to look at a painting they've never heard of?" he asks.

It's ironic that the house is an unabashed paean to Vegas opulence, because Greenstein's career is a testament to the healthy state of poker *outside* Las Vegas. Consumed with slaughtering games throughout the Midwest and California for more than 30 years—he once broke a home game in Illinois within five minutes—Greenstein was virtually unknown in the poker capital of the world until he first challenged the Big Game in 2001.

To Vegas locals at the time, he appeared to be one more rich guy who would blow into town, drop a bundle to Doyle Brunson and company, and promptly disappear, making room for the next fish. "I always say it's impossible to come from out of nowhere and play at the highest levels," says Eric Drache, the veteran poker pro and card room manager who organizes the Flynt matches and had a hand in bringing the Big Game to the Golden Nugget in 2004. "It would be like trying to become the heavyweight champion of the world if you'd never fought anybody any good. But that's just what Barry did. He came into the Big Game and started winning every day. Barry got a lot of heads shaking."

If they had known a little more about who they were dealing with, the poker cognoscenti might not have been so surprised.

When he was a young boy, growing up in the Scottsdale neighborhood on the west side of Chicago, Greenstein scored so high on his IQ test that his father, a grammar-school principal, complained to the school board that the test had to have been flawed. It seemed impossible that his son was a certified genius.

By junior high, Greenstein spent much of his time in math class at the chalkboard explaining logarithms and complex integers to his peers and, not infrequently, to his teachers. He never studied, and still managed straight A's and a perfect score on the math portion of the SAT. During senior year, his calculus teacher gave him some computer terminals and a manual and suggested he tinker around with them over the weekend. On the following Monday, Greenstein returned with a program he had written that made it possible to play 18 holes of golf on the computer. After that, the teacher allowed Greenstein to spend class-time writing code, but still rewarded him an A in calculus.

"If anybody ever heard I gave Barry Greenstein anything less than an A in math class, they would put me in jail," the teacher explained to the *Chicago Sun-Times* in a profile that appeared after Greenstein made a name for himself.

Supremely confident—he told classmates he planned to be president of the United States—Greenstein sought avenues outside academics where he could test his capabilities. With his scrawny build and thick glasses, he was not exactly the prototype jock, but he threw himself into sports anyway. He became a scratch golfer, a star on the baseball diamond, and a varsity wrestler by his sophomore year. Though his natural weight was about 105 pounds, he competed in the 98-pound weight class because his team needed to fill that slot. He fasted and ran seven miles a day to make weight, and by the time each match came around, he would be weak, dehydrated, and barely able to perform. According to the *Sun-Times* story, his futile record prompted one teacher to comment, "Greenstein's lost eight matches in a row. Doesn't he know when to quit?"

"Don't you understand," another teacher replied. "He's the only kid in the school who can lose eight matches and not quit."

Scottsdale was a tough, working-class neighborhood, where brawn was valued above brains. It was the kind of urban area where the kids—mostly sons and daughters of cops and plumbers—didn't have allowances, but jobs. Greenstein first capitalized on this at age 12, when he began making money from cards while caddying at a local golf course. His highly profitable gaming escalated during the later years of high school, when weeknight tutoring sessions devolved into blasts of Five-Card Draw and Seven-Card Stud. Greenstein and his classmates first played for quarters, but the stakes quickly rose to dollars. In college, at the University of Illinois at Urbana-Champaign, he found soft games with local businessmen and was able to cover a semester's tuition in a good night at the table.

With his combination of math skills, an unshakable work ethic, and a dogged determination to succeed, Greenstein was well-suited for high-stakes poker. He recognized early on that even the most talented players were unable to control the wild ups and downs that are inevitable in a long game. He found that he usually made most of his money toward the end of a session, when other players were tired or steaming. One of his favorite games took place above a bar in a rough section of Decatur, where the action commenced around sundown and raged till dawn because the parking lot below was too dangerous to traverse at night. Greenstein fortified himself with bologna sandwiches, then pounced on his worn-down opponents as daylight approached.

By the late 1970s, as he neared 30, Greenstein was conflicted. He had been working toward a doctorate in math, which was his passion, but he was making more than $100,000 a year playing poker on the side. He started traveling more, taking trips to places like Houston, Aruba, and London in order to play against well-heeled suckers as well as some professionals, including Jack "Treetop" Strauss and a young Johnny Chan. He bought his first Jaguar, moved into an expensive, house and married a woman named Donna Doss, who shared his taste for the good life. Donna had three kids from a previous marriage, and Greenstein fought to gain custody. His lawyer, however, warned that his chances were slim. "You're never going to get custody as a professional gambler," the lawyer said, "and you don't make any money as a graduate student."

Faced with the prospect of losing Donna's kids, Greenstein flew to California and looked for work in Silicon Valley's burgeoning software industry. In 1984, he signed on as the fifth employee at a company that would later be named Symantec. His salary was a measly $40,000—a sum that didn't come close to covering his standard of living—but he knew he could always supplement his income through poker.

"It was like a gift," he says. "When I wasn't making big money, poker was there. There is always going to be a poker game, around the country or around the world, and I'll always be able to beat it."

While working at Symantec, now best known for its Norton antivirus software, Greenstein developed a broad range of personal-computing products. He worked on one of the first search engines and almost single-handedly developed a word-processing program called Q&A that, upon its release, in 1986, with Greenstein and family pictured on the box, was named *PC* magazine's top word-processing program of the year.

By 1991, though, Symantec had grown from five employees to more than 1,000, its corporate culture had changed, and Greenstein had grown weary of the stifling bureaucracy. After seven years and countless round-the-clock work crunches at Symantec, he left the company—but not for another job. He was faced with piles of debt from living beyond his means in Silicon Valley, so he sold all his remaining stock options and paid off creditors. All told, during his seven years at Symantec, Greenstein, amazingly, earned less than a million dollars. He had packed up and moved to California in order to keep his family together, and now he needed to provide them with the financial security and comfort he felt they deserved. So he returned to poker full time, where $1 million would soon look like chump change.

GREENSTEIN IS AMONG a small elite of top-ranked professional poker players with corporate experience, which helps explain why he manages his career a bit differently from other high-stakes specialists. For starters, he doesn't endlessly hang around card rooms sharing bad beat stories and bull sessions with other poker denizens. He's not there for the camaraderie: If he doesn't like the games, he goes home. His self-professed strength is what could best be described as game management. Like any good businessman, he identifies markets where he possesses an advantage and then moves aggressively to capitalize. To him, success at the poker table is determined less by how you play than *when* you play.

"The way you earn the most is to play against weak players who have a lot of money—that's how you really do well," he says. "I don't go out and say, 'Let me see who the best players in the world are, and I want to beat them just to prove I am better.' My thought is, What is the most lucrative situation I can get into and how can I exploit it?"

It's initially surprising, then, that Greenstein has become a regular in the Big Game, as it's literally impossible to find tougher competition (imagine a successful little microbrewery deciding to slug it out with Budweiser and Miller). Yet unlike a lot of players who have popped into the Big Game over the years just to say they did, Greenstein saw it as a legitimate money-making opportunity. He insists that if he had gotten off to a slow start or felt overmatched his first time in the game, back in 2001, he would have had no problem stepping down to a lower-stakes table. But, going in, he felt that he played as well as anyone, and perceived a slight advantage against the game's two most venerable pros. "Doyle is the Arnold Palmer of poker, and Chip is the Jack Nicklaus. I would never say I am better than them," Greenstein says diplomatically. Still, he points out, Brunson is 70 years old and lacking the stamina he once had, while Reese is fabulously wealthy and admittedly not quite as hungry as he used to be.

Greenstein admits that he loses about half the time he plays poker, but he generates huge profits by setting loose boundaries on his wins and losses in much the same way that a stockbroker designs a stop/loss order on a trade. He wants to limit his downside without capping how much he can earn in a given night. This is harder than it sounds, as most players—even very good ones—instinctively ease up once they get comfortably ahead in a game. When Greenstein is winning and faced with tired or inferior opponents, he doesn't relax or head home for a few hours of sleep; he ratchets up the pressure, mercilessly tormenting his outmatched foes until he has squeezed every last $1,000 chip from their stacks.

Reese is among those who admire such tenacity. "I like to play, and I could win a million or lose a million—but if I get sleepy, I'll quit,"

Reese says, acknowledging that these days he's more interested in the challenge of poker than the potential profits. "However, when you are playing your best—and things are going well for you—your opponents are probably playing their worst and feeling unlucky. The right thing to do is to stay as long as it takes and win the money. Barry is good at that."

Greenstein is willing to stick around for hours, even days, until he bleeds his victims of the maximum amount of cash. That requires him to risk his hard-earned profits against desperate—and therefore dangerous—opponents, but it gives him the chance for a really big score.

"So many people are afraid to make money," Greenstein says. "They get ahead and start thinking, I don't want to lose all this back and look stupid. For most people, it becomes a self-fulfilling prophecy. They lose some of their winnings because they are protecting. I *am* going to turn a win into a loss sometimes. But I also know that I may very well take a $300,000 win and turn it into an $800,000 win. I do it often enough that I *have* to stick it out for hours on end when people are playing bad and dumping their money off."

In 2001, when Greenstein first began competing in the Big Game, there was one player—whom Greenstein declines to name on the record—with a reputation for getting stuck and playing wildly for several days straight until he fought back to even. Once this player—Player X, let's say—got down, the game spun into a familiar pattern: Player X stole countless little pots with aggressive raises while the other players sat back and opted not to gamble with their profits unless they held big hands. That was seemingly a prudent strategy for the winners, but it allowed Player X to slowly claw his way out of the hole.

When Greenstein first encountered this situation, he realized that Player X was more vulnerable than ever because he was playing too many hands and being too aggressive. Greenstein chose not to retreat into a conservative mode, as everyone else did, but retaliated with his own aggression. He slightly lowered his own requirements for starting hands, and gambled more frequently with Player X than the rest of the table. More often than not, he still got his money in with the best of it.

"The result was, I destroyed him," Greenstein says. "He lost several million once I started playing on a regular basis. Now he won't play with me when he gets stuck."

Greenstein's tactics were formulated during the all-night games he played in Chicago, Decatur, and throughout the Midwest, and the Vegas pros had never been exposed to his kinds of moves. This wasn't the first time that happened, of course. Puggy Pearson, Doyle Brunson, and Chris Ferguson were also outsiders when they introduced techniques that had previously eluded even the best players. Las Vegas may be the poker capital of the world, but the game's revolutionaries always seem to formulate their strategies far from the glittering lights of the Strip.

WHEN POKER BECAME a national obsession in 2003, it migrated from the backrooms to the living rooms virtually overnight. As recently as '02, high-stakes players had to practically beg poker room managers for dinner comps. By 2004, they were being paid $10,000 to wear logos on TV. This transformation was largely due to the *World Poker Tour*. Suddenly, thanks to scripted commentary and sharp editing, run-of-the-mill grinders came off as superstars. Self-consciously bookish Howard "The Professor" Lederer and backgammon wizard Paul Magriel—known for his confounding tics, such as muttering "quack, quack" before betting—turned into minor celebrities. Bad guys, like the bullying Brit David "Devilfish" Ulliott and bratty Phil Hellmuth, practically became household names.

Around the country, seasoned pros rejiggered their public personas. They hired publicists and managers and shamelessly hammed it up for the cameras. Greenstein, though, was unimpressed by the WWE-style posturing. He disdained tournaments as a distraction. After all, he played for fortune, not fame, and knew that the biggest and most consistent money would always be in cash games. "I looked at tournaments as an ego weakness," he says. "So I intentionally didn't play in them."

But the WPT's ascendance in prestige dovetailed with Greenstein's blistering performance in the Big Game. Long wealthy by most standards, he was now a millionaire many times over and providing a comfortable, some would say extravagant, lifestyle for his family. Yet he was beginning to pay a small price for his success. He felt his kids were overly materialistic (though divorced from Donna, he retained joint custody of the three children from her previous marriage and the two they had together). The kids drove nice cars and palled around with the children of other millionaires in an exclusive neighborhood, and Greenstein believed that they failed to understand how privileged they were in relation to others around the world. He decided to rectify that with a grand plan: Play in tournaments and set an example by donating all of his tournament winnings to charities that help children.

Greenstein did not abandon his bottom-line mentality—he just pledged to direct a portion of his poker riches toward a higher purpose, just as hugely profitable companies establish philanthropic divisions when the corporate coffers are overflowing. The timing was perfect for Greenstein, as playing poker for nothing but his own gain had turned into a soulless and debilitating grind.

"I am allergic to cigarette smoke," he says, "and at times I looked at my life like Christopher Walken's character Michael, in *The Deer Hunter*, where he would play Russian roulette for money and send it back to his crippled friend and his wife. He saw that his life was worthless, but he had a purpose: to make money and send it home. I knew I was slowly killing myself, sitting in these smoky rooms, but I just put my head down and played."

Rejuvenated by his pledge to play for a greater cause, Greenstein captured a Seven-Card Stud tournament at Flynt's casino in March 2003, and thereafter donated more than $400,000 to Children Inc., a nonprofit organization that aids impoverished kids across the globe. Nine months later, he made his first final table on the *World Poker Tour*. He started as the chip leader over a table of less-accomplished players, with the notable exception of his Big Game rival Chip Reese. It was a rare television appearance for Reese, who doesn't often play tournaments, but Greenstein made it impossible for him to showcase his skills. In the process, Greenstein put on a clinic of how to push around opponents with an overwhelming chip lead and isolate the most threatening player at the table.

From the outset, Greenstein viewed Reese as the sole obstacle between him and the title, so he targeted Reese early on by raising almost every pot in the opening rounds of play. Because Greenstein sat on Reese's right—meaning he was usually in position to act first—he was able to play the bully and effectively forced Reese to wait for big hands or else risk his tournament on a ballsy bluff. He never allowed Reese to see a cheap flop, where he could then out-maneuver the other less-experienced players at the table. On the one occasion Reese came back over the top with a reraise, Greenstein simply folded. His goal was not to get in a confrontation with Reese, but to slowly whittle down his chips by stealing blinds and antes.

"I made sure if someone other than me got the money, it wasn't going to be Chip," Greenstein says. "I never let him see a flop. He's a good player and he wanted to get in there and outplay people, but I didn't want that to happen."

After more than an hour of being abused by Greenstein, Reese's chip stack was dwindling down to nothing and he was forced to take a stand to combat yet another raise. Reese held King-5 suited, and moved the rest of his chips in. A car wash owner from Ohio named James Tippin called the bet with a pair of Queens. Greenstein also moved all-in. This time, he held a real hand: Ace-King. After the flop came Ace-King-6, Greenstein was in total control of the tournament and steamrolled to victory.

Greenstein gave the first prize—another $1 million—to Children Inc., raising his total contributions to the organization to $1.4 million. He subsequently used other tournament winnings to fund donations totaling an additional $1.5 million to a variety of charities, including his old high school, a children's hospital, and Guyana Watch, which provides medical assistance to the kids in that South American country. WPT commentators Mike Sexton and Vince Van Patten gushed about Greenstein's philanthropy and dubbed him "the Robin Hood of Poker." That moniker, and resulting publicity, catapulted Greenstein out of the shadows and into the spotlight. Most surprisingly, at least to him, was the indescribable joy he felt in giving away his hard-won money.

"I got such a good feeling," Greenstein says. "For the first time, I felt like I did something good for the world."

Greenstein is now semiretired from the lucrative cash games that furnished his fortune. As of early 2005, he expends most of his poker energy on the tournament circuit but, because he gives away 100 percent of his tournament winnings, he needs to play in cash games occasionally just to cover expenses—such as the ongoing renovations to his house. Further, the government allows him to deduct only 25 percent of his income as charitable contributions, so he could conceivably end up paying taxes on money that he actually gave away. As a result, he needs to earn several hundred thousand dollars a year in cash games just to cover his tax burden. Which explains his sporadic appearances in Gardena to play with Flynt and the others.

AT 5 P.M., an hour after the Flynt game was scheduled to kick off, the host rolled up to the table in his gold-plated wheelchair. Sporting a powder-blue V-neck sweater, with his reddish hair combed back neatly, he appeared almost grandfatherly. Flynt has been in a wheelchair since a white supremacist shot him with a deer rifle in 1978 for publishing an interracial-sex photo. Because of his disability, his dexterity is limited and he can't look at his cards without exposing them to the rest of the table. To protect against less-than-honest opponents, a bodyguard positioned two six-inch-high wooden slats in front of Flynt, forming a makeshift barrier behind which he could survey his cards.

Flynt prefers Seven-Card Stud, so that was the brand of poker they played for more than two days, stopping only when Flynt tired. The stakes were $2,000/$4,000. Over the course of the game each player could possibly win or lose more than $1 million.

Greenstein started playing in this game seven years ago, when it was held in Flynt's Hollywood Hills home. For reasons unknown, Flynt keeps his house cold as a meat locker, and players would have to bundle up in thermal underwear before arriving. (One player who didn't use the necessary precautions was even treated for a minor case of frostbite.) As always, Greenstein felt like his determination gave him an advantage in adverse conditions—in this case, the freezing cold—and he needed a psychological edge because he knew almost nothing about Seven-Card Stud at the time.

Early on, Greenstein stayed afloat just through his poker smarts, but he is a quick study and is currently regarded as one of the top Seven-Card Stud players in the world. To him, the key in learning any poker game is recognizing mistakes—your own as well as others'—and not repeating them. "You are not analyzing it correctly when you believe you played it right when you won and you played it wrong when you lost," he says. On almost every hand, there is a way you could have made it more profitable. Maybe you could have saved money by folding earlier or kept more opponents on the hook by slow-playing a disguised full house. "If you get too caught up in how good you are, you start missing your mistakes."

Greenstein and Flynt are now close friends—Flynt half-jokingly tapped Greenstein to be his lieutenant when he ran for governor of California in 2003—but Greenstein is necessarily deferential toward his host. It's all part of the gamesmanship that comes with being a winner in another man's game.

On this night, after a few opening hands, Robison launched into a catalog of old stories about Puggy Pearson on the golf course, but, because Flynt cannot play golf, Greenstein redirected the conversation by asking Flynt to tell about his experiences playing poker against Pearson. When Flynt won a pot, Greenstein made a point to lavishly compliment his host.

"Larry built this place with his poker winnings," Greenstein said, an obvious lie that Flynt indulged with a wry smile.

On one occasion, Flynt mucked his hand when Greenstein showed a straight, but another player pointed out that Flynt actually had four Queens—not three. It's highly questionable for someone not involved in the action to call another player's hand, but Greenstein stayed silent and Flynt got to rake the $40,000 pot. "As a winning player, I can't say anything," Greenstein later explained.

So the mood turned slightly awkward when Flynt, in his trade-mark croaky drawl, complained that he had never been invited to Greenstein's opulent home.

"Larry, I've got a 16-year-old daughter!" Greenstein protested. "They would arrest me for child endangerment if I brought you to my house!"

The table was silent, as players nervously waited to see if Flynt would take offense.

"I'd bring her a lollipop," Flynt croaked, deadpan. The moment defused, everyone laughed heartily, including Robison, who was wearing a matching T-shirt and hat that read JESUS PAID IT ALL.

The game gradually gathered momentum and the banter subsided. The action moved rapidly, with each player giving less than a second's thought to folding, calling, or raising. There were none of the drawn-out, anguished decisions that mark televised poker: Greenstein was dealt a Jack for his one up card, and Hennigan, with an Ace showing, led out with a $2,000 bet. Greenstein called. The next round brought Hennigan a King and Greenstein a Queen. Hennigan bet another $2,000, and Greenstein silently stacked eight $500 chips in front of him—a raise to $4,000. Hennigan, whose Ace-King was the best hand showing, turned over his cards and tossed them in the muck. Greenstein raked the pot without comment—making a nifty $12,000 in less than two minutes. If Greenstein was bluffing, he didn't boast about his brilliant play. If he was sitting on a monster hand, he didn't give any indication of that either. Like all high-stakes cash games, this one promised to be a marathon, not a sprint, and Greenstein refused to give anything away during an early leg of the race.

Greenstein won two more five-figure pots in rapid succession, further inflating his already disproportionately large chip stack. He appeared to be in perfect control of the table, even though he was falling behind Ivey in a series of so-called "prop bets," in which the players bet on which three-card combinations will appear face-up. Each bet, according to the skyscraping stakes they had established, was $5,000—though the payouts doubled and tripled in certain situations.

After a Queen came up—a good card for Ivey—Greenstein casually tossed his friend a $5,000 chip. With a flip of his hand, Ivey indicated that Greenstein owed even more. (One of the main tenets of playing props is that you have to pay only if your opponent demands to be paid; that is, if a player is not paying attention, he can't win.

Which is one of the reasons Greenstein and Ivey play props. It forces them to stay actively engaged in the game even if they are not involved in the hand.)

"How much is it?" Greenstein asked.

"Fifteen thousand."

"Oh," Greenstein said, tossing two additional $5,000 chips. "I thought it was $25,000."

"You thought you owed me $25,000 and you paid me $5,000?" Ivey asked, incredulous. He knew Greenstein was merely testing him to make sure he was paying attention, but he couldn't resist the chance to jab at the man's rosy public image. "Okay, Mr. Robin Hood."

The dealer slid out the next round of cards and the game marched on. Greenstein folded his hand, leaned back in his chair, and shook his head. He smiled broadly. It almost looked as if he was having fun.

Daniel Negreanu, 2004, at Foxwoods Casino, Connecticut

Fifteen

THE NEW SUPERSTARS

Heirs to a Poker Empire

Young Guns Daniel Negreanu, Phil Ivey,

and Erick Lindgren revive old-school

tactics to become the envy of a

poker-crazed generation.

ON A CLOUDLESS MAY AFTERNOON, Daniel Negreanu darted through the streets of downtown Las Vegas in a new white Lexus SC 430 convertible. With his high-lighted blond mop-top and two hoop earrings blowing in the breeze, he looked straight out of a car commercial, the picture of 21st-century stylish prosperity. He showed off the global-positioning system, which gave him an alternate route when construction blocked the entrance to Highway 95, and toyed with the bumping stereo. Sporting his perpetual cat-that-ate-the-canary grin, it was impossible to tell that Negreanu had busted out of a 2004 World Series of Poker event minutes earlier.

The 29-year-old high school dropout, whose only real job was a three-week stint at a Subway sandwich shop, was utterly content—and why not? He pals around with ubercelebrities Tobey Maguire and Leonardo DiCaprio, splashes $100,000 in poker chips on his desk like loose change, and paid for the Lexus in cash. He plans to upgrade from his three-bedroom house in the posh Las Vegas suburb of Summerlin to one that includes basketball and tennis courts, similar to the setup of his close friend Erick Lindgren. Lindgren's straight-out-of-*MTV Cribs* bachelor pad is furnished with six flatscreen TVs, a Galaga arcade game, a pool table, a swimming pool, and a framed picture of *Seinfeld*'s Kramer over the living-room mantle. But even Lindgren's 4,000-square-foot manse doesn't match the massive spread Phil Ivey has overlooking the lush Tournament Players Club golf course.

The heirs to a burgeoning empire built on the shoulders of road-weary gamblers like Puggy Pearson and Doyle Brunson, Negreanu, Ivey, and Lindgren are the embodiment of the dream that has taken hold of thousands of teens and 20-somethings across the country. They are each under 30 and sitting on piles of cash earned playing a game that requires them to perform no task more strenuous than chasing straights and flushes.

Yeah, it's good to be one of the hot young stars of poker.

To say that the face of poker is changing is as obvious as raising with pocket Aces from early position. At the 2004 World Series, there were as many oversize throwback jerseys as cowboy hats, more earrings than cigars. A record eight championship bracelets went to players under the age of 32, including four to players younger than 24.

These poker whiz kids emerged from a different culture than their forebears, one in which legalized gambling is prominent across the country, bookstores are loaded with an overabundance of strategy books, and it's possible, by playing multiple games online at once, to compress years of experience into a few months. And, of course, they came to the game at a time when becoming a successful professional didn't just ensure a good living. It meant you could become something more than rich—you could become a star.

But as Negreanu emerged from downtown and pointed the Lexus west toward his home nestled in the shadow of the Red Rock Mountains, he offered this advice to the kids coming up behind him: Don't quit your day job.

"Everybody likes to say the poker world is this glamorous lifestyle, living in mansions with four Rolls-Royces in the garage," he said. "Of a thousand people who attempt to become successful doing this, maybe one makes it. And when I say successful, I don't mean playing 50 hours a week and grinding it out. I mean having a beautiful home, a car, and some money in the bank. You would be better off randomly going to Hollywood and trying to become movie star."

What to make of this? It's undoubtedly good advice, as the number of pros struggling to scrape together a bankroll far exceeds the handful who inhabit Negreanu's rarified tax bracket. Then again, in the weeks following his admonition, Negreanu captured the best overall player award at the World Series, and then bested a world-class field in a subsequent tournament at the Plaza. His take for roughly six weeks of work: more than $600,000. This is a man who lies for a living, and it suddenly seems entirely possible that he's trying to bluff an entire generation out of a pot he'd just as soon keep for himself.

IF NEGREANU IS bluffing, the Toronto native with a passing resemblance to *Rounders* star Edward Norton is simply living up to his reputation as a loose cannon willing to win by even the most unconventional means. During the 2004 World Series, for example, he entered a $1,000 no-limit event that allowed players to buy back in as many times as they wanted within the first two hours—a structure that generates fairly loose play in the opening rounds. Negreanu took that approach to the extreme: He played almost every two cards he was dealt, and usually raised with them, laughing giddily all the while. Every time he busted out, he produced another thick wad of hundreds and reentered the fray. He ultimately bought back in a record 28 times, which meant he needed to finish fifth out of 538 entries just to get his initial investment back.

"People see me acting silly, it adds to my game," he explains. "It's good for my table image for the future. They will know I'm capable of going crazy. Because I will play with those people again, and they'll always wonder when I'm in there playing a lot of pots, 'Is he going crazy again?' "

In this instance, it worked. After the re-buy period ended, Negreanu continued to play aggressively—though he toned it down a tad—and ultimately finished third. His prize money was more than $100,940, a profit on the day of more than $70,000.

Negreanu clearly revels in his wild-card reputation, but he says there is a definite method to his madness. He believes it's becoming increasingly difficult to win with a traditional tight-aggressive style, in which you wait for big hands and play them forcefully. As a result, he enters more pots than almost anyone at poker's highest levels. While most players get involved in at most two or three hands out of 10, Negreanu doesn't mind playing five or six.

"It's the correct strategy," he says. "In the old days, there was this myth that you have to play tight and only play certain hands. Poker has evolved. The mathematics behind what everybody thought was correct—the 'book play'—is absolutely not correct anymore [because there are so many less experienced and often reckless players coming to poker]. It's way too conservative. The way the game was played in 1980, if somebody raised and then there was a reraise, that meant a premium hand. [David] Sklansky even wrote that you should lay down pocket Jacks in that situation. Well, the way the game is played now, the first raise could be 10-8 suited and the next raise Ace-8."

Although he's played professionally since he was 17, Negreanu didn't begin to develop his signature style until he was 23. It was 1998 and, as a newcomer to Las Vegas, he was playing with world champion Stu Ungar and Erik Seidel in a no-limit game at the Bellagio. Negreanu sat to Ungar's immediate left, which meant he was always forced to react to Ungar's play. Ungar was only months away from his drug-induced death, but managed to bully the table relentlessly even on autopilot. "He was in complete control of every hand," Negreanu says. "Every hand went through Stuey. Everybody had to be completely aware of him at all times."

Negreanu calls the evening "the biggest revelation of my poker life." The lesson: By dictating the action, you can knock other players out of their comfort zones.

"The majority of players are looking for reasons to fold. I am looking for reasons to play," Negreanu continues. "Even before I look at the hand, I am trying to map out the table and figure out where the strength is and where the weakness is based on the chip stacks and personalities of each player. Like in chess, I usually have my move already decided based on a range of hands that I might be dealt. As soon as I look at the hand, I am deciding whether this is ridiculous to play or not. If it's not, then I usually play it."

It's worth noting that Negreanu's method of dealing with poker's new landscape is the direct opposite of that of Phil Hellmuth, who advocates playing supertight in the face of reckless opponents. Negreanu's strategy is a dangerous one, of course, because its risks equal the rewards—it's a mathematical certainty that if he plays more hands than anyone else, he starts without the best hand on a regular basis. It's a strategy that's viable only for the best players, those who are able to capitalize on weakness in other players while also recognizing when a good hand might not be the best one. It takes a lifetime of card sense to pull it off, and Negreanu has it.

The oldest son of recent Romanian immigrants, Negreanu was valedictorian of his junior high and a promising student when he discovered poker in the Toronto pool halls where he spent his free time. By his junior year of high school, he had abandoned all pretense of being a student. He left his books at home and arrived each morning with just a deck of cards and a stack of poker chips. He ran two games out of the school cafeteria, which typically earned him at least $100 a day, but he finally got expelled when one of his players paid him off with a check the boy had stolen from his mother. Soon he was playing professionally in home games and underground clubs.

In 1995, at age 21, he traveled to Las Vegas for his first World Series. Two years later, he became the youngest player ever to win a bracelet when he captured the $2,000 pot-limit Hold 'Em title.

In 1998, he moved to Vegas full-time. By his own admission, Negreanu was a talented but wildly undisciplined player in his early years. He played the way he played back home: like it was a game, not a job. He made consistent money at the middle limits, but stretched to play higher even when his bankroll couldn't sustain him. He was frequently broke. He also sometimes drank heavily at the table, especially during what he dubbed "party day," when he would get drunk and play foolishly on purpose (not unlike the way he played in the World Series re-buy event, except with no brake). His rationale was that he needed those nights to keep poker fun, and not let the grind of constant playing wear him down, but it took a toll on his funds. The morning after his 26th birthday, he awoke unable to remember a single hand he'd played the night before—an embarrassing episode made worse by the fact that he had blown $70,000.

In the tight-lipped world of high-stakes poker, he developed a reputation as a bigmouth, writing a candid monthly column in *Card Player* magazine and posting frequently to the popular online bulletin board rec.gambling.poker. To the public, he was an approachable everyman, writing openly about "party day" and his troubles with alcohol, but he occasionally stepped on toes when he voiced strong opinions about other pros.

In one notorious example, Negreanu posted a blistering takedown of Annie Duke, commenting on everything from her table behavior to her personal hygiene. The diatribe stemmed from Negreanu's close friendship with Jennifer Harman, who he believed was the best female player in the world, despite persistent media reports awarding that title to Duke. In his post, Negreanu didn't name Duke, but the target was clear to everyone in the poker community. Howard Lederer, Duke's older brother, posted a lengthy response defending his sister. He closed by writing: "I will, from now on, ignore your entire existence, unless, of course, I am trying to bust you at the poker table. You have crossed the line, and I don't really care if you ever come back."

The exchange was a rare public rift between top players. Worse, at least for Negreanu, was that Lederer staked out the high ground (for the most part, anyway; he did accuse Negreanu of getting drunk and snatching the toupee off a player's head).

The episode was something of a wake-up call for Negreanu. In recent years, he has matured noticeably and become one of the more respected, although still outspoken, members of the poker community. "The thing about Daniel is that he made mistakes when he was younger, but he grew up before our eyes," says tournament veteran Adam Schoenfeld. "Unlike someone like Phil Hellmuth, who simply never grew up."

Negreanu's results started to reflect his newfound maturity. In 2003 he won more than $900,000 in tournaments alone, not counting the hundreds of thousands he won in cash games.

Negreanu uses his garrulous persona in much the same way Amarillo Slim did a generation earlier. Both men like to create a flood of information at the table, confident that they can employ it more effectively than their opponents. In Slim's case, he picked up tells from the way his opponents responded to his badgering. Negreanu talks more than most players, but he also resorts to other layers of gamesmanship, like forecasting a player's hand before it's been turned over or showing his own cards even if he wins the hand without a call.

Negreanu "is going to give you information, but he is going to know what he gave you," Lindgren says. "You may lay down a hand if it looks like Daniel may have made a straight, and he'll show you his cards to show he had it. When a similar situation comes up later, he is going to play the hand the exact same way, except he won't have anything."

At the Plaza tournament he won in June, Negreanu put on an impressive display of his table-management skills. When the tournament got down to three players, Negreanu got involved in a pot with the chip leader, Freddy Deeb, an accomplished Lebanese pro. On the river, Deeb made a straight that gave him the best hand—Negreanu held a pair of 10s. Deeb bet at the pot, which caused Negreanu to rub his goatee and audibly walk through the range of hands that he thought Deeb might hold.

"I think you've got Ace-9," Negreanu concluded. "But I've got to see it."

He called the bet, forcing Deeb to reveal his cards. On cue, Deeb showed an Ace and a 9 and took the pot, but the message was unmistakable: Negreanu had a rock-solid read on his man.

Later in the match, when the two players got heads-up, Deeb was dealt Ace-King and Negreanu Ace-7. The flop came King-6-2, with two hearts. Deeb bet $16,000 and Negreanu simply called with no pair and no straight or flush draws. The turn was a 4, and Deeb, who was leading the hand with a pair of Kings, checked. This gave Negreanu an opening, and he bet $30,000. It was a stone-cold bluff, and Deeb called it. But, to Negreanu, the fact that Deeb merely called, instead of raising, signified that Deeb was not convinced he held the best hand. A 4 of hearts came on the river, making three hearts on the board, and Deeb led out with a bet of $65,000.

Negreanu drilled through Deeb's possible hands in his mind: He knew Deeb didn't have the nut flush, because Negreanu held the Ace of hearts; Deeb had bet out on the flop, indicating that it improved his hand; and he only called on the turn when it looked as if the small card could have helped Negreanu make a straight.

After thinking it through, Negreanu correctly deduced that Deeb held Ace-King. Once he was confident in his read, he also realized, based on the cards on the board, that there was no way Deeb could call a sizable raise, since Negreanu could conceivably have a full house, a straight, or a flush. Negreanu calmly raised another $100,000—an amount just small enough that Deeb could interpret it as an indication that Negreanu knew he had the best hand and wanted to get called.

"You must have flopped a set," Deeb muttered, convinced that the second 4 on the board gave Negreanu a full house. Deeb folded, and Negreanu took the decisive pot in the tournament.

"The whole hand, I knew that there was no way he could believe I'd be stupid enough or crazy enough to bluff," Negreanu says. "But it was still a question of executing."

Lederer, Negreanu's old nemesis, who was doing commentary on the event for Fox Sports, called it "one of the great bluffs of all time."

ONLY 27 YEARS old and one of the few African-Americans to penetrate poker's top ranks, Phil Ivey is the stylistic opposite of Negreanu. Whereas Negreanu wears his emotions on his sleeve and expresses himself loudly and often, Ivey is practically a cipher. A dominant force in the largest games in the world, Ivey carries himself with a near-sociopathic intensity that astounds even the battle-hardened veterans who make up the $2,000/$4,000 game of Seven-Card Stud at Larry Flynt's Hustler Club outside Los Angeles, where Ivey was among the big winners in 2004.

"We finally saw him slouch the other day," said Johnny "World" Hennigan, sitting next to Ivey at Flynt's game. "He was loser $750,000. He went like this . . ."

Hennigan dipped his left shoulder almost imperceptibly, and the other players chuckled along—all except Ivey, who picked silently from a plate of sushi.

"But he won it back," Barry Greenstein added.

"Oh, yeah, he won it back," Hennigan replied.

Danny Robison, Chip Reese's old running buddy from the 1970s, wanted to hear Ivey explain his performance (and victory) several months earlier in a televised tournament at Turning Stone casino in upstate New York. The final table was the first live broadcast of a poker event, but Ivey had blatantly refused to put on a show for the cameras. After he got heads-up with unknown 21-year-old John D'Agostino—a time when most players would talk each other up in an attempt to feel out their opponents or at least break the tension—Ivey didn't speak for two hours.

"You had this long, sad face the whole time. It was unbelievable," Robison said to Ivey.

Ivey stared back without a word.

Even more amazing, Robison said, was that when Ivey bested D'Agostino for the title, he ignored the announcers standing by with an oversize $500,000 check and instead walked out a side door in search of the nearest bathroom.

Ivey finally spoke up.

"I was sick," he said. "I had diarrhea."

Ivey's blank expression indicated that he saw nothing amusing about the situation.

"Yeah, but he didn't get mentally sick," Hennigan chimed in. "The guy's a rock." With mock seriousness, he turned to Ivey on his right and added: "You should go on *Oprah*." That finally got a brilliant white smile out of Ivey.

The truth is, Ivey is affable and engaging away from the table, but it's just hard to *find* him away from the table. "I play like 70 hours a week, treat it like a job," he says. "I put in a lot of time, a lot of hours, and try to get better every day. The best thing about poker is that you will learn something new every day. If you are really paying attention, whether it's somebody's body movements or the way they bet or how they play the hand, you learn a lot about the people you are playing against—and you learn a lot about yourself."

Ivey's peers say that, if anything, he is downplaying his work ethic. He is known to play all night in the Flynt game, drive to Las Vegas for the biggest game at the Bellagio, then unwind by logging on to the Internet for a few hours of high-stakes virtual action. A former videogame fanatic, he sees poker as a similar challenge—except the high score is measured in money.

"He plays as if poker is going to end in a week and he needs to get all the hours in while he can," says Erik Seidel. "He really wants to win all the money."

Ivey's single-minded approach is reflected in his refusal to indulge in the trappings of being a poker celebrity. He refuses almost all interview requests and eschews endorsement and sponsorship deals. In July, he visited Guyana with Greenstein to spend a couple of days working at one of Greenstein's pet charities there. He set one condition: no publicity.

For almost five years in the late 1990s, when he was first learning the game, Ivey was known around Atlantic City poker rooms as "Jerome"—the name on the fake ID he carried in case anyone asked if he was actually old enough to be there. "Jerome" was known as a good kid, respectful and courteous to other players, but almost foolishly aggressive. His go-for-broke style generated huge swings in his bankroll. He would go on a rush through the lower limits until he could afford to sit down in A.C.'s biggest game, a $400/$800 Seven-Card Stud game that was built around Roger King, who originally produced the *Oprah Winfrey Show*, and Henry Orenstein, the creator of both the Transformer action figures and the hole-card technology that drives televised poker. Even in that game, Ivey refused to put a governor on his aggression.

"He was willing to gamble his whole bankroll at any one time," says Cyndy Violette, the Atlantic City pro considered one of the top female players in the world. "Some days he would look like an idiot, playing every hand, but he was experimenting and getting creative."

Ivey, whose only regular job was a brief stint selling tickets to the policeman's ball over the phone, came at the game from a unique direction. Instead of starting conservative and picking the spots where he held an advantage, as most players do, his default move was ultra-aggressive. With experience, he learned to keep his impulse under control, if just barely.

Ivey's style reminds many of a young Doyle Brunson, who raised so frequently and effectively in no-limit games that he picked up countless small pots when the rest of the table declined to tangle with him. The result was that when a big pot arose, Brunson could afford to gamble with the worst of it because he was merely risking the chips he'd stolen before. Brunson was forced to adapt after he published *Super/System* and other players began calling his bluffs. But Ivey has yet to be reined in.

"I never played with Doyle when he was younger, but I would assume that Phil takes a lot more small pots than Doyle ever did," says Jeff Shulman, a regular on the tournament circuit and editor of *Card Player* magazine.

"He doesn't care that you understand that he bluffs a lot," agrees Negreanu. "He is looking to be the bully and be in our face. He will continue to push you around until you stand up to him. And when you do, he takes it to the next level."

Ivey's debut on poker's biggest stage came in 2000, when he made the final table at the World Series in the $2,500 pot-limit Omaha event at the tender age of 23. He was the chip leader starting the day but found himself surrounded by a formidable collection of talent, including Phil Hellmuth, David "Devilfish" Ulliott, and Amarillo Slim.

Not intimidated, Ivey repeatedly came over the top of Hellmuth and made him lay down big hands.

"Every time I bet, you raise," Hellmuth complained to Ivey at one point.

Seeing that Ivey planned to stay characteristically silent, Slim interjected. "Why shouldn't he? You keep folding."

Eventually Hellmuth busted out along with the rest of the table, leaving Slim and Ivey heads-up. Slim had grabbed an almost 4-to-1 chip lead by this point, and the announcer for the match informed the crowd that Slim had taken first place in his four previous appearances at a World Series final table.

"Very rarely do the sheep slaughter the butcher," Slim explained to the audience.

At 72, Slim had almost 50 years on Ivey. Poker writer Andy Glazer noted that the scene was reminiscent of *The Hustler*, when young, brash "Fast Eddie" Felson faced off with the venerable Minnesota Fats. Except in that case, the kid took down the wily veteran and, here, it seemed that Slim held an insurmountable lead.

The men represented markedly different styles, as well as different eras. Slim repeatedly tried to draw Ivey into conversation, but Ivey remained stone-faced and silent. "That's his game, not mine, and I'm not going to play his game," Ivey said afterward.

In the first major pot, Ivey went all-in with a flush draw, and caught it on the turn. Next he made a straight on the river. Then he check-raised Slim when he made the nut flush on the flop. In a 10-minute run of bold play and lucky breaks, Ivey had stormed into a commanding lead. On the final hand, Slim made a King-high straight on the flop. He immediately moved all in. Ivey pondered his options briefly, and then called. He hit an Ace-high straight on the turn and claimed his first bracelet.

The assembled media gathered around Ivey, hoping for a juicy comment about toppling the game's most famous player. All they got was a meek, "It feels good."

Two years later, Ivey won three gold bracelets at the 2002 World Series and made the final table in two other events, a performance considered among the most dominating in Series history. By 2004, he was in among the elite group of players who coolly avoid the frenzy—and big purses—of the World Series in favor of the Big Game, which is held across the street at the Golden Nugget. By several accounts, Ivey was the big winner in the monthlong game, taking home a sum deep into seven figures.

In his trademark oversize throwback jerseys, Ivey brings a touch of hip-hop to a game so long dominated by Texans and other rural westerners. But he proudly shuns the wraparound shades that have become de rigueur among poker's under-30 crowd.

"I figure if you can't stand someone looking at you, you shouldn't play poker," he once said. "Suck it up. If you have tells, work on them." (His wife once bought him a pair of $1,100 designer sunglasses, but he threw them in the trash after they contributed to his misreading a hand and losing a pot.)

Which isn't to say he's flawless. Like Brunson, his stylistic predecessor, Ivey has plenty of gamble in him—some say a little too much. He's a regular at the high-stakes craps tables and, although he has posted several big wins there, he once dropped more than a million dollars in a session. Brunson is among several established veterans who have warned Ivey to stay away from the pit games, where, unlike poker, the house has an insurmountable advantage. But few doubt his talent.

"The guy who is going to pass me up is Phil Ivey," says Barry Greenstein, who claims to have won more money playing poker than anyone in history. "He is hungrier than any of us. He has the most stamina and he has the killer instinct. Phil doesn't even play the games well right now. That's what's scary about him. He is a great gambler and he is just getting better. Right now, technically, he doesn't have it all down, but just on gambling smarts, he is able to stay even or win at most of these games. He just gets better and better all the time. By next year at the World Series, you're going to have a monster on your hands."

IN MANY WAYS, Negreanu and Ivey are throwbacks to a previous generation. They earned their stripes in home games, underground clubs, and shabby casinos not very different in spirit from the ones that spawned Brunson, Hellmuth, Greenstein, and others. It seems likely, though, that the old-school route will be less popular in coming years, as players turn to role models more like Erick Lindgren.

On the surface, it seems as if the 27-year-old Lindgren came out of nowhere to capture the World Poker Tour's 2003 Player of the Year award, but Lindgren arrived with a wealth of experience playing both online and against live players.

With his blond hair and square jaw, Lindgren is the quintessential California golden boy. He grew up in sleepy Burney (population 3,000), and chased his hoop dreams for one year at tiny Butte Junior College, but quit the team after a disagreement with his coach. Lindgren found a job dealing blackjack at a nearby Indian casino, where he first started playing poker on his days off, and the next year he took a job as a prop at the Casino San Pablo, in the Bay Area. As a prop—a player paid by the casino to keep the tables full—he earned $160 per day, plus benefits, but had to gamble with his own money, which was a problem at the beginning.

Completely broke from betting on sports, he borrowed $500 from a friend just so he could play $6/$12 on his first day. He didn't harbor dreams of fame and fortune; he just hoped to make a living. "Back then, for the middle-of-the-road grinder guys, you were doing damn good if you could make $50,000. That's all I wanted," he says.

Lindgren studied Sklansky's books and Brunson's *Super/System*, but primarily learned from other players in the card room. Because he was there all the time, he knew which players were winners. He studied them intently and applied the lessons to his own game.

"I always wanted to see what the good players were doing," he says. "Any time you can find people who are better than you, you can pick up a few things."

Despite his steady improvement, he was barely surviving—and considering his parents' advice that he take a real job. Then, one evening in 1998, Lindgren logged on to a now-defunct website called poker.com. He deposited $300 through his credit card and found another player willing to play $20/$40 heads-up. Ordinarily, $300 is not nearly enough to play at that level—you can literally go bust in one misplayed hand. But the cards ran lucky for him and he ended the night ahead more than $1,500.

Within weeks, he quit his job as a prop and reconfigured the desk in his bedroom to accommodate three 19-inch monitors. "I had this tiny bedroom. You couldn't even walk in there," he says. "I just had my bed, a desk, and three computers. I would just sit in there and click all day long. Boom, boom, boom."

Lindgren did little besides play poker online and sleep for three years. By playing multiple games on each monitor, he could log on to six or seven games of $20/$40 at once. During those three years, he says, he won as much as $40,000 in a month and never less than $10,000.

Lindgren essentially compressed 10 years of experience into three. He developed an instinctive feel for which starting hands to play, always the most important decision in Hold 'Em—but, perhaps more important, he learned to beat a variety of playing styles. If his opponents were ultra-aggressive, he laid back and set traps when he found a big hand. If they were passive, he controlled the action and manipulated the table with constant aggression.

"You better learn how to play a lot of different styles, because you have to be comfortable at a lot of different types of tables," he says. "People don't experiment enough with their games. They just say, 'This is my game and it's the way I play.' "

Lindgren made a point to continue competing against live players as much as possible. He says that while the Internet is a great training ground, it can't prepare you for the nuances of playing live. "It's a whole lot harder to bluff someone when you have to look at them," he says.

When the World Poker Tour debuted in 2002, Lindgren was perfectly positioned to navigate the large tournament fields populated equally by longtime veterans, online qualifiers, and other amateurs looking to take a shot at the big time. He created a splash right away: He made the final table at a World Poker Tour event in Paris, then claimed his first WPT title in Aruba and a second win several months later on a cruise ship in Mexico (besting Negreanu, who took second). He celebrated his second victory—and the $1 million check that came along with it—the way any fun-loving 27-year-old would: by running up a $22,000 bar tab with Negreanu and other pals.

Lindgren is convinced that he and his good friends Negreanu and Ivey will be dominant for years to come. "We all love poker so much," he says. "There's no way we're quitting, so someone is going to have to come along and knock us off our pedestal."

Of course, poker history is littered with wunderkinds who captured a couple of tournaments or ran lucky for a year or two before fading into oblivion. As Doyle Brunson says, when asked to evaluate the latest crop of young studs, "Come ask me in 20 years and I'll let you know."

Poker Basics

HAND RANKINGS

Royal Flush: The five highest-ranked cards—Ace-King-Queen-Jack-10—in the same suit.

Straight Flush: Five cards of the same suit in sequence.

Four of a Kind: Four cards of the same rank.

Full House: Three cards of the same rank, plus any pair of a different rank.

Flush: Any five cards of the same suit, but not in sequence.

Straight: Any five consecutive cards of mixed suits.

Three of a Kind: Three cards of the same rank.

Two Pair: Two cards of the same rank plus another pair of a different rank.

Pair: Two cards of the same rank.

High Card: If no player holds a pair, the high card wins. The Ace is the highest card possible, followed by a King and so on.

TEXAS HOLD 'EM

It seems unthinkable now, but Texas Hold 'Em was not played in Las Vegas casinos until the mid-1960s, when it was introduced by a Lone Star gambler named Felton "Corky" McCorquodale. Now, of course, it is the featured game at the World Series and the most popular form of poker nationwide. It's a deceptively simple game with endless layers of strategy.

The deal rotates clockwise around the table. The player to the dealer's left posts a mandatory starting bet called the "small blind"; the next player to the left posts the "big blind." (The bets are called "blinds" because they are made before the cards are dealt.) After the blinds are posted, the dealer gives each player two cards facedown. The player to the left of the big blind starts the first betting round, which continues clockwise around the table. Players have the option to bet, check, raise, or fold. After the first round of betting, the dealer places three cards faceup in the center of the table—this is called the "flop"—followed by another betting round. Another card is dealt faceup—the "turn"—followed by a third round of betting. Then comes the final card—the "river"—and the last betting round. The players remaining in the hand show their cards and use any combination of hole cards and community cards to make the best five-card poker hand. The winning hand takes the entire pot.

Perhaps the most misunderstood aspect of the game is the betting structure. The size of the bets depends on the established stakes. In a no-limit game, of course, a player can bet all the chips in front of him (i.e., "go all-in") at any time. In a limit game, the bets are one of two sizes, depending on how far along you are in the hand. For example, in a $4,000/$8,000 game (the stakes of the Big Game, where Doyle Brunson presides), all bets and raises are in $4,000 increments for the first two rounds, and $8,000 increments for the last two. The stakes also dictate the size of the blinds: The small blind is always half a small bet and the big blind is a full small bet. So in the Big Game, the small blind is $2,000 and the big blind is $4,000.

OMAHA

When Doyle Brunson's *Super/System* was published in 1978, it contained a glossary entry for a game similar to Hold 'Em called Omaha, in which each player was forced to play both of his hole cards in combination with the cards on the board. Four years later, in 1982, the Golden Nugget in Las Vegas began spreading a game called Omaha with one important difference: Each player was dealt four cards facedown and could choose any two—and only two—to play in combination with the board. That is today's standard version of Omaha.

The betting structure of Omaha is identical to Hold 'Em. But those relatively minor differences—four hole cards instead of two, plus the requirement that each player use two of his hole cards—make it a radically different game strategically.

Another variation of Omaha is Omaha 8-or-Better. In this version, the player with the best high hand splits the pot with the player who has the best low hand. In order to qualify for the low hand, a player must combine two of his hole cards with three on the board to total five cards with a rank of 8 or smaller. Straights and flushes may still qualify for the low, so one of the best possible hands is an Ace-to-the-5 straight (known as a "wheel"), which guarantees the low and usually takes the high. If no one qualifies for the low hand, the best high hand takes the entire pot.

Omaha 8-or-Better is becoming increasingly popular because the multiple opportunities to build a good hand create lots of action before and after the flop.

SEVEN-CARD STUD

Seven-Card Stud reigned as the most popular poker game in America for most of the 20th century. It served as the game of choice among U.S. troops during World War II—that's where Seven-Card Stud master and navy vet Puggy Pearson made his first fortune—and then became the game of choice in Las Vegas's burgeoning casinos in the 1950s and '60s. In the ensuing decades, Seven-Card Stud ceded its pre-eminent position to Texas Hold 'Em, but it continues to be played in virtually every card room in America and remains a favorite in most home games.

It's an easy form of poker to learn, yet complex enough to challenge savvy veterans, particularly when they are playing other savvy veterans. The pot builds initially with an ante from each player (instead of the blinds, as in Hold 'Em). The dealer gives each player two cards facedown and one card faceup. The player with the low faceup card opens the betting and, moving clockwise around the table, each player must then call, raise, or fold. In all subsequent rounds, the player with the best hand showing opens the betting. The dealer then deals each player three more cards faceup, with a betting round following each card. Similar to Hold 'Em, the smaller betting limit applies to the first two rounds and the larger limit gets imposed for the final three (in a $10/$20 game, all bets and raises would be in $10 increments for the first two rounds, and in $20 increments thereafter). The seventh card is dealt facedown, followed by a final betting round. The best five-card poker hand takes the pot.

SEVEN-CARD STUD HI/LO SPLIT

This game, popular throughout the Midwest for many years, did not become hot in Las Vegas until the mid-1970s. That's when 23-year-old Chip Reese first hit the casinos. He knew the game from back home in Dayton and shocked the poker establishment by playing better than anyone in Vegas.

The rules and betting structure are identical to straight Seven-Card Stud. The only difference is that after the final round of betting, the player with the best high hand splits the pot with the player who has the best low hand. As in Omaha 8-or-Better, a player must have five cards at a rank of 8 or lower to qualify for the low, and it's possible for a player to capture both the low and the high with an Ace-to-the-5 straight. In a memorable hand against Puggy Pearson and Doyle Brunson during his first stint sitting in the Big Game, Reese scooped a massive pot when he hit the best possible two-way hand in Hi/Lo Split, an Ace-to-the-5-straight flush.

RAZZ

The late poker writer Andy Glazer once called Razz "a game for poker masochists." So perhaps it's somewhat surprising that it was the favorite game of notorious mobster Tony Spilotro, who was more accustomed to giving pain than receiving it.

Razz is simply a form of Seven-Card Stud in which the low hand takes the entire pot. Aces are considered low, and the high card showing opens the betting on each round. It's a frustrating game because one bad card—for example, a card that gives you a pair or a high card like a Queen or a King—can kill what previously looked like the best hand. Also, unlike Hi/Lo Split, in which a player must qualify for the low by showing five cards below 8, the lowest five cards takes the pot in Razz regardless of rank. Think of it this way: The worst hand wins.

CHINESE POKER

Chinese poker is not an event in the World Series, and it's not even offered in most casinos. However, if you approach a table of high-stakes players who seem to be casually flipping around cards and exchanging $1,000 chips, there's a decent chance they're playing Chinese poker to kill some downtime. For example, while recently waiting for everyone to arrive for a Seven-Card Stud game at Larry Flynt's Hustler casino in Gardena, Barry Greenstein and Phil Ivey played Chinese poker for $2,000 a point. Greenstein took Ivey for close to $200,000 in less than an hour.

But here's the thing: Chinese poker is mostly a game of luck—much more so than other forms of poker. If two players understand the baseline strategy and don't make glaring mistakes, the winner is essentially determined by who gets better cards. It's a fun, low-intensity form of poker.

The game can be played with two, three, or four players. Each player is dealt 13 cards, which he then sorts into three poker hands: two containing five cards apiece and one containing three cards. The skill in the game comes from choosing the most advantageous arrangement of the cards. Once a player sorts the cards, he places them facedown in front of him until the other players are done as well. He places the best of the five-card hands (called the back hand) directly in front of him. The other five-card hand (the middle hand) goes in front of the back hand. The three-card hand (front hand) is placed in front of the middle hand. When all players have set their hands, each player compares his hands against each other player. Typically, a player gets two points for winning two out of three and four points for winning all three hands. At the end of the match, the winner is paid a predetermined number of dollars for each point he is ahead.

Poker Glossary

Action: Betting, often used to help describe a person who does a lot of gambling. "Doyle Brunson has always got to be in action."

All-in: When a player has all his chips in the pot. He has no money left on the table. If there is only one other player in the hand, there can be no more betting and both players turn up their cards for a showdown. If additional players are in the hand, they can continue to bet among themselves. Regardless, the all-in player can never win more than the amount of his wager from any of the others.

Ante: A compulsory bet that all players make before the cards are dealt.

Bad beat: When a strong hand is beaten by a heavy underdog through a series of unfortunate events. Phil Hellmuth is known for throwing tantrums after suffering bad beats.

Bankroll: The amount of money a poker player has available to play with.

Belly-buster: A straight draw in which only one card will make the hand. If you have 5-6-8-9, you have a belly-buster because you need a 7 to complete the straight. Also known as an *inside straight* or *gut shot*.

Best of it: To "have the best of it" means you got your money into the pot while the odds were in your favor. You might still lose the hand, but that's just a matter of luck. Top players don't worry about winning as much as they do getting their money in with "the best of it" more often than not.

Blind: A forced bet that starts the action before cards are dealt. Similar to an ante, except only two players—the "small blind" and the "big blind"—post blinds, whereas all players must post antes. The small blind is paid by the player immediately to the left of the dealer button. The big blind is the player two over from the dealer button.

Bluff: To make a bet that indicates a stronger hand than you actually have.

Bust out: To get eliminated from a tournament by losing all your chips.

Button: A white disk, the size of a hockey puck, that indicates the player who is currently in the dealer position. It's considered the best position at the table, as the dealer acts last and therefore gets to react to the other players' moves.

Buy-in: The amount of money you need to put up in order to play in a game or enter a tournament.

Calling station: Derisive term for a weak player who often calls other players' bets but rarely raises or initiates action.

Check: Opting not to bet when the action is on you. Also used as an alternative word for *chips*.

Chop: To split money in the pot—or even a tournament's prize pool—between two or more players.

Coffeehousing: Table talk, usually strategically orchestrated to get a read on an opponent or to psych him out.

Come over the top: To make a large reraise.

Dealer button: See *Button*.

Door card: A player's first face-up card in a Stud game.

Draw: A situation in which you need one card in order to make your hand. Generally refers to a player trying to complete either a straight or a flush. If you have four hearts after the flop, for example, you are on a flush draw.

Early, middle, and late positions: Based on your seat at the table, and the position of the dealer's button, when you will bet or check or raise or fold. In an eight-handed game, the first three players to act are considered to be in early position, the next three are in middle position, and the final two are said to be in late position. Late position is the most desirable of the three.

Favorite: The hand that has the best mathematical chance of winning.

Fifth Street: See *River*.

Final table: The culmination of a tournament in which the remaining players compete against one another at a single table.

Fish: A poor player who drops lots of cash.

Flop: The first three community cards in Texas Hold 'Em, all of which are turned up at once.

Fold: To concede the pot either by throwing your cards away or verbally expressing your intention to do so.

Fourth Street: See *Turn*.

Free card: If none of the players bets during a given round, all players get to see the next card without having put any money in the pot. So that card is considered "free."

Freeze-out: A tournament in which each player starts with the same amount of chips and continues until one player holds all the chips. The World Series adopted the freeze-out format in its second year, a move that helped spur its popularity.

Give action: To make bets in which you do not necessarily have an advantage—in the hope of loosening up tight players.

Gut-shot: See *Belly-buster*.

Heads-up: A game between only two players. The term is often used to describe tournament situations in which the field is down to a pair of contenders.

Hi/Lo Split: A game in which the best high hand and the best low hand split the pot. It is a popular variation of Seven-Card Stud and Omaha.

Hole cards: A player's face-down cards that no one else can see.

Inside straight: See *Belly-buster*.

Kicker: Side card of the highest denomination. If you have a pair of Jacks, an Ace, a 10, and a 7, you have two Jacks with an Ace kicker.

Lay down: To fold a strong hand when you think your opponent has a better one. Phil Hellmuth prides himself on making good lay-downs, and it is a cornerstone of his supertight strategy.

Limp: To enter the pot by simply calling the big blind and not raising.

Live one: See *fish*.

Loose: A style in which you play lots of hands. The opposite of *tight*.

Made hand: A strong hand—say, a flush or straight or full house—that is complete and not requiring any additional cards (even though they are still coming).

Money management: Term used to describe how a player handles his or her cash at the table and away from it—often referring to whether or not a successful player gambles away his bankroll at sucker games. "You'll never see Barry Greenstein blowing his winnings at the craps table. He has excellent money management skills."

Move in: When a player goes all in with a raise, moving his entire chip stack into the pot.

Nuts: The highest possible hand based on the visible cards. In Hold 'Em, if there are four hearts on the board and you have an Ace of hearts in the hole, you've got the nut flush.

Off suit: When two or more cards are of varying suits. If all four suits are visible, it is called a *rainbow*.

On the bubble: When a player in a tournament is a place or two behind the point where cash prizes are given out. Let's say that a tournament pays the top 30 finishers, but there are 32 left and you're number 32: You might say, "I'm on the bubble, but it won't affect my strategy. I'm still playing to win."

On tilt: The emotional state of a player who blows a couple of big hands, loses his composure, and starts making bad plays (usually being too aggressive, or playing like a maniac). "A few bad beats and Stu Ungar would go on tilt." Also known as *steaming*.

Open: To make the first bet.

Open-end straight draw: The opposite of a gut-shot or belly-buster, it's when you are one card away from hitting a straight from the top or bottom. If you hold 4-5-6-7, you are on an open ended straight draw, as it'll be made with either a 3 or an 8.

Outs: Number of unexposed cards that can turn your drawing hand into a made hand. If you hold an Ace and need another to win the hand, you have three outs if no other Aces are exposed at the table.

Overcard: Any card higher than the highest card on the board.

Pot odds: The size of the pot divided by the cost of calling a bet. If it costs only $5 to possibly win a $100 pot, you are getting 20-to-1 odds.

Quads: Four of a kind.

Quarter: A $25 chip or bet.

Rag: A small card that doesn't help your hand.

Railbird: A spectator at a poker event. The name comes from the term *rail*, which is used to describe the waist-high divider that separates the players from the fans. When a player busts out of a tournament, he goes to *sit on the rail*.

Raise: To match an opponent's bet and then add at least 100 percent more to it.

Read: To evaluate another player based on body language and betting patterns in order to make your best guess about the strength of his hand.

Rebuy: To purchase another set of chips for use in a tournament. A select few events at the World Series permit rebuys in the first few hours of competition. In 2004, Daniel Negreanu set a record by rebuying 27 times in a $1,000 no-limit Hold 'Em event.

River: The last card dealt in a poker hand. In Seven-Card Stud, the river is dealt to each player face-down. In Texas Hold 'Em, it's the final community card and is also known as *Fifth Street*.

Rounder: A professional gambler who plays for high stakes and frequently travels the country to find the best games.

Scoop: When you are playing Hi/Lo and you win with the high as well as with the low. "Cyndy Violette scooped the pot with a 6-low and a flush."

Semi bluffing: Betting high with an unmade hand that has a reasonable chance to improving.

Set: Three of a kind.

Short-handed: A poker game with fewer than five players.

Sixth Street: The sixth card.

Slow play: To have a strong hand and not bet it in order to induce other players to stay in and bet. The danger, of course, is that a weak hand can become a strong one because you're allowing people to stay in cheaply and see additional cards.

Steal: A player is said to *steal* when he wins a pot by bluffing. Often referred to in conjunction with blinds—when a player with low cards bets high before the flop and steals blinds.

Steaming: See *on tilt.*

Stragglers: Early-position players who go in for the minimum bet. Also known as *limpers.*

Stuck: To be losing. "I can't go to sleep now, not when I'm stuck $20,000."

Table image: The way other players at the table see you, whether it's created by your play or your overall persona. David "Devilfish" Ulliott built an intimidating table image with sunglasses and a pair of brass knuckle-dusting rings.

Tell: A nervous or involuntary habit or tic that allows an opponent to read the strength of your hand. Amarillo Slim is a master of using casual conversation to elicit tells from his opponents.

Tight: A style in which you are extremely selective in choosing which hands to play. Phil Hellmuth is known for playing extremely tight.

Turn: The fourth community card in Texas Hold 'Em or Omaha. Also known as *Fourth Street.*

Under the gun: First player to bet or fold.

Up cards: The cards that have been turned up and exposed to all players at the table.

Value bet: A bet in which your primary objective is to increase the size of the pot and not to make your opponents fold.

Wheel: Ace through 5, which, in some Hi/Lo games can be played as the highest and lowest hand (a straight to the 5, and a perfect low).

Wired: Adjective used to describe the first two cards when they're a pair. "I started with wired Aces, but I couldn't catch a set."

Acknowledgments

ALTHOUGH THERE ARE ONLY TWO names on the cover, this book was a collaboration among three people: Our editor, Tom Foster, was the indispensable third partner. His talent and dedication improved this book immeasurably. Copy editor Robert Firpo-Cappiello smoothed out the finished manuscript, and everyone else at Wenner Books, including Jann Wenner, Bob Wallace, and Kate Rockland, has been helpful and dedicated to the project. Kim Witherspoon, David Forrer, and the staff at InkWell-Management shepherded the idea from concept to reality and handled loads of details in between. The Las Vegas Club, across the street from Binion's Horseshoe, provided our base camp for most of the reporting. Staff and accommodations there were aces. And thanks to Robert Varkonyi, who allowed us to photograph his World Series bracelet for the cover.

The subjects of these chapters each gave us hours of their time, both in person and over the telephone, and we are enormously grateful to them. Additional thanks goes out to those in the poker world who provided illuminating insights and/or helped pave the way for access to some interview subjects: Eric Drache, Nolan Dalla, Billy Baxter, Jack Binion, Howard Schwartz and the Gambler's Book Club, Larry Grossman, the late Andy Glazer, Larry Flynt, superhost Steve Cyr, Golden Nugget owners Tim Poster and Tom Breitling, Steve Pearson, Melissa Hayden, Wendeen Eolis, Russ Hamilton, Adam Schoenfeld, Alan Boston, Mickey Appleman, and Diego Cordovez. Authors from whom we drew inspiration include James McManus (*Positively Fifth Street*), Jon Bradshaw (*Fast Company*), Richard Munchkin (*Gambling Wizards*) and A. Alvarez (*The Biggest Game In Town*).

Finally, we'd like to thank Henry Orenstein. He invented the technology that allows viewers at home to see players' hole cards during televised poker events. His innovation spawned the *World Poker Tour*, kick-started ESPN's coverage of the World Series of Poker, and pushed our favorite game into the mainstream. Without Henry, we almost certainly would not have had the opportunity to write this book about these marvelous characters.

—MICHAEL KAPLAN AND BRAD REAGAN

A few of the chapters in this book had their genesis as magazine articles, and most of them were written prior to poker's big boom. Smart editors with the vision to recognize compelling stories about a great game include Marvin Shanken, Gordon Mott, and Shandana Duranni at *Cigar Aficionado*; Chris Anderson, Bob Cohn, and Susan Murcko at *Wired*; Laurie Ochoa, Kateri Butler, Joe Donnelly, and Marc Cooper at *L.A. Weekly*; and Robin Dolch at *Icon*.

Thanks to my dad, Stanley, who first taught me how to play poker, and my brother Ron, who endlessly regales me with his card-room exploits. Appreciation also goes to my mother, Gladys, and sister, Randi—nonplayers who've had to endure endless bad-beat stories around the dinner table. Mucho gracias to Leonor Pena for keeping things running smoothly at home. And, finally, no-limit gratitude and love to Melodie, Lola, and Chloe, three queens who are always there for me and never less than inspirational.

—MICHAEL KAPLAN

My involvement in this project started with an article in *Men's Journal* edited by Peter J. Frank, so thanks to Peter for making it memorable to the right people. Bill and Jennifer Smith provided much-needed down-home hospitality in Las Vegas, and Dave and Nancy Roy shared their lovely home with me in Manhattan Beach. My brother, Rob, took me to my first poker tournament. And my wonderful stable of friends, including Alison Mitchell, John Hall, Chip Evans, Charlie and Becky Hanger, Geoff and Stefania Van Dyke, Geraldine Sealey, Mike Bruno, Liz Zack, and Samantha Schabel, were sources of support and laughter when I needed them most.

—BRAD REAGAN